Just Missed the Sixties

by

Robert Henry Keith

Text Copyright ©2013 Robert H Keith

2024 Edit by Robert H Keith

All Rights Reserved

Cover Design by Robert H Keith
Back cover photo by Sandra Keith
Bronze Fonz photo from visitmilwaukee.org
Joni Mitchell Clouds cover art by Joni Mitchell
Mark Spitz photo from wordpress.com
Napoleon on Elba image from wordpress.com
Back of quarter photo from piedmontrarecoins.com
Emperor Napoleon in his Study at the Tuileries by Jaques-Louis David 1812
Chart depicting the loss of French Soldiers during the Russian Campaign by Charles Minard 1869

This book is dedicated to every dormitory director at every college campus worldwide.
Many of the events in this book actually happened.

Other Works by Robert Henry Keith
Available at Amazon.com

- *Irreverent Shorts*
- *Fireworks Wars: Battle of the Cul-de-Sac*

Just Missed the Sixties

Hyer Hall

Robert Henry Keith

JUST MISSED THE SIXTIES

Prologue

I arrived at the city courthouse at the exact time indicated on my summons. I had no idea what was about to go down. At the entrance to Courtroom #2, I handed the summons to an officer at the door.

He pointed and said, "Sit on the defendant's bench, over there, and wait until they call your name."

I took a seat. There were thirty to forty other defendants of various ages, male and female, casually dressed and looking grim. I sat as far from them as possible.

Oh my God, I don't want to look at these people. They all look so... guilty!

Instead, I looked around the room. It was a typical small-town courtroom. There were rows of wooden benches resembling pews. The Judge sat behind an elevated, cherry-finished wooden bench. To his right hung the American flag, and to his left hung the Wisconsin state flag. A bailiff and a court reporter were seated below. A couple of cops loitered against the wall. The Judge pounded his gavel, and another day of court began.

The cases before mine passed in a blur. Names were called, defendants approached the bench, charges were read, and pleas were requested. The folks who pled guilty were sentenced, and those with a not-guilty plea were instructed to schedule a follow-up court date with the clerk at the back of the room. It was quick and efficient, an assembly line of justice. My mind was racing.

JUST MISSED THE SIXTIES

What a fry! How did I get into this mess? I bet that cop lied to me! What are they going to do to me? What if my folks find out? What if Al finds out? He'll kill me for sure! He can never find out! If I'm lucky, the cops will never catch him. Maybe I can think of something clever to say to the Judge.

"Joseph Roman, please rise and approach the bench."

JUST MISSED THE SIXTIES

The miracle is not to fly in the air or to walk on the water but to walk on the earth.
Chinese Proverb

Peace, Love, and Rock & Roll
(Seven months earlier)

After three hours of picking my way through the sleeping crowd, I finally reached the front. Massive speaker towers rose to the clouds on both my left and right. Before me lay an eclectic collection of musical instruments and electrical cables, although no one was onstage yet. Looking back to the terrain I had just traversed was a scene of tents, sleeping bags, blankets, homemade banners, trash, and mud as far as the eye could see.

Oh my God! There must be over a million people here! So, where can I find the peace, love, and rock and roll?

I heard a screeching noise behind me, feedback from an amplifier. I spun around to see a tall, lone figure striding toward center stage. He was holding a cream-white Fender Stratocaster, dressed in jeans, boots, and a white leather top. Hanging from the sleeves and bottom of his top were the longest beaded fringes I'd ever seen. A wide, red bandana was tied around his bushy, black afro.

It's Jimi Hendrix! He looks so cool!

I was thrilled. *He's only the best god-damned guitar player in rock and roll history, and I'm right in front of the stage!* Then, I swear he looked at me and flashed a peace sign! I flashed him back. He smiled and stepped up to the microphone.

JUST MISSED THE SIXTIES

"Good morning, Woodstock! Time to wake up! Right now, I'm gonna play you a little something that should make everyone get up and stand at attention!"

He started playing the "Star Spangled Banner". It was just Jimi: no bass, keyboard, or drums. He took that tune and soared away, making it his - forever. I turned to see the reaction of the crowd. Everywhere I looked, life was returning to the festival. They were coming out of their tents, sleeping bags, and under their blankets. They were mostly young; some were hippies, and others were not. Everyone was a fellow traveler. Campfires were started, and joints were passed.

Ah… the first toke of the day!

Jimi swooped from the banner into *Purple Haze,* and the festival grounds started rocking. A covey of nubile hippie girls rushed the stage, surrounding me, swaying and grinding their hips into my sides. The one on my left was young and cute, with flowers in her hair. She turned to me and smiled. I smiled back. She reached for me, and I went for her. We hugged, and I felt her breasts pressing against my chest. She put her lips to mine, and I kissed back, at first lightly and then passionately. Thirty seconds later, she let go, stepped back, and pointed to a tent pitched in the woods off to one side. She raised an eyebrow in question. I nodded my head to say, "Yes." She took my hand, and we walked towards the tent.

I think I found the love!

She entered first. I stood in the entranceway, my eyes adjusting to the reduced light. I could see her silhouette against the rear wall of the tent. She was removing her clothes; first came the top over her head; next, she pushed her jeans down her legs. Finally, off came the panties, which she tossed at my face.

Behind me, the music had stopped. Someone was making announcements.

"Attention! Attention, everyone! For your safety, do not take the brown acid! I repeat, do not take the brown acid! Oh, and one more thing, Joseph Roman, please wake up!"

JUST MISSED THE SIXTIES

I spun around to look and fell out of bed right onto my bedroom floor.

"Ouch!"

My mother yelled again, "Joseph! What was that noise? Are you alright? It's time to get up now! Your father will be home soon! It's time to drive you back to school!"

Holy shit, I was having that Woodstock dream again! God, I so wish I could have been there!

"Joseph, get up now! Don't make me go up the stairs to get you out of bed!"

"Okay! Okay! I'm already out of bed! I'll be right down after I wash up and get dressed!"

I shuffled into the bathroom and leaned on the sink. Looking into the mirror, I saw my shoulder-length, curly blonde hair. It had taken quite a long time to grow, and I was very proud. I smiled.

Too bad Father hates my long hair!

Recently, I began saying a morning mantra to the mirror: "I'm nineteen years old, I've always been nineteen, and I'll always be nineteen." Somehow, it helped me stay in the present.

After washing and dressing, I went to the kitchen for breakfast. Grabbing a bowl of cereal, I sat beside my mother at the kitchen table. She was busy reading the Milwaukee Sentinel morning newspaper while enjoying coffee and an L&M cigarette.

She said, "I just read an article about those boys they caught for burning down the new West High School. They think they were under the influence of drugs. I bet it was that maroin and that herijuana! I hope you never come across that stuff."

"Mom, they're called heroin and marijuana, not maroin and herijuana."

"How do you know that?"

"Everyone does; they teach us about that stuff at school nowadays."

"Why would they want to teach you about those things?"

"You know, they teach us that they're - dangerous and stuff like that."

JUST MISSED THE SIXTIES

"Oh, well, anyway," she said, looking out the kitchen window at the driveway, "Your father's back from golfing now. Finish your breakfast so you can get your things to load in the car."

After breakfast, the first thing I did was carry out my suitcases. Then came all the cool stuff I'd acquired during the summer to decorate my sophomore dorm room, including psychedelic posters, tie-dye sheets, and velvet paintings of forest scenes. Lastly, I brought down my most precious possessions – the record collection and new sound system. The record collection was a pretty typical compilation for the times, consisting of Beatles, Stones, Doors, Zeppelin, Tull, CSN&Y, and others. I especially loved the San Francisco Sound, including bands like the Jefferson Airplane, Quicksilver or the Dead. To play these LPs at college, I acquired during this past summer, piece-by-piece as I'd earned the bread, a brand-new sound system consisting of a Pioneer amplifier, a Dual direct drive turn-table, and a pair of dark walnut-paneled Sansui speakers containing ten-inch woofers and three-inch tweeters. The new sound system was my pride and joy.

On one trip through the house, I glanced into the small room we called the Den. It was our TV room. Set before a wall of knotty pine was the bulky, large-screen television on which I'd watched the country undergo incredible changes in the last ten years. The oldest events I could recall were those of the civil rights movement. Black Americans were demanding equal opportunities in education, jobs, and housing, as well as an end to the repressive apartheid defined by the Jim Crow laws of the Deep South. I wished I could have ridden with the Freedom Riders, but I was still in grade school.

I saw the emergence of the Beatniks followed by the Hippie lifestyle, which arose in response to the growing fears of nuclear annihilation and the stifling conformist culture of the Fifties. Later, young people on college campuses began protesting the War in Vietnam. I wanted to be there with them, chanting, throwing back tear gas canisters, and putting flowers into the rifle barrels of national guardsmen, but I was only in middle school.

I watched the TV news reports about the Summer of Love and the Woodstock Festival. I wanted to be there, too, dancing with the scantily clad hippie chicks and getting my share of the free love, but I was just a freshman in high school and couldn't even drive a car.

Maybe this year, in college, will be my time!

I continued making trips up to my room and down to the back of the house, piling my stuff on the driveway behind Dad's white Lincoln Town Car. My father, Joseph Roman Sr., was sitting on the patio in a deck chair - busily scraping the dirt of the country club from the cleats of his golf shoes.

Golf! Man, he is so square!

"Joseph, here's the key to open the trunk. Please remove my clubs and put them in the garage before you start putting in your things. Okay?"

"Sure, Pops."

"Thanks."

I looked at my dad as he was about to toss the keys. I had to admit that for an "establishment type," the ladies would probably say he was handsome. He was always well-dressed. With his cushy V.P. job at a downtown bank, he could afford to. I wasn't sure what he did there, but it paid him enough for our well-furnished, two-story brick suburban home, his luxury car, well-tailored suits, dry-cleaner service, milk delivery, and country club membership. The bank, The First Wisconsin, was located in the tallest building in downtown Milwaukee (a modest 42 floors) known as the First Wisconsin Building.

It was a quick, twenty-minute drive from our suburban home in Wauwatosa to Dad's bank. My mother once told me that the name Wauwatosa came from the language of the Menomonie Indians and meant Land of the Fireflies. My mother said many things; I took everything she said with a grain of salt, and that is when I was actually listening to my mother.

A couple of blocks from my father's bank, Milwaukee would someday erect an 8-foot bronze statue of Henry Winkler, in character as The Fonz from the TV Show Happy Days. That's quite an honor for the city, a 'thumbs up' forever.

JUST MISSED THE SIXTIES

The Bronze Fonz giving thumbs-up by the banks of the Milwaukee River

I always thought the Fonz was super-cool. He could start a jukebox with a crack of his knuckles or get hot babes with a snap of his fingers. Many times, I'd wished for that finger-snapping power!

After I'd loaded the last of my stuff into the trunk of Dad's car, tenderly wrapping blankets around my precious new sound system, I turned to find Father standing uncomfortably close to me. I sensed that he wanted to say something.

"Um. Hey, Dad. What's on your mind?"

"Joseph, here's a little piece of advice: Be careful who you choose for friends because your friends can get you into trouble."

There was an awkward moment of silence as I digested what was happening.

Wow, the Old Man is giving me some words of wisdom! I was probably ten years old the last time he did that, and he told me not to stick my fork in the toaster!

I think there was an awkward moment of silence that time, too.

Finally, he said, "Understand what I mean, son?"

"Yeah. Sure, Dad." And then I was saved by mother, calling from the back door.

"Joseph, you've got a phone call from Casey! Tell him you can't talk too long because we have to get going! I have Bridge Club tonight, you know!"

JUST MISSED THE SIXTIES

Life for Mother is just one club after another! Bridge Club, Garden Club, Church Club, Boring Housewives Club, blah, blah.

"Hey, Dad, speaking of friends, I've got to go and talk to one now. I'll be right back!" I went inside the den to take the call.

"Hi, Casey. I can't talk too long because I'm all packed up, and we're about ready to truck out of here."

"That's cool. I just wanted to make sure you brought all the new stuff for your room, like your posters and shit. Oh, and by the way, do you remember where we hid those birch logs we found in the North Campus Woods last spring?"

"Oh yeah, I know just where to find them."

"Cool! We're going to have the most far-out dorm rooms ever! You will be so thankful that we moved from that all-guys dorm to one of those new co-ed dorms! Just imagine all that pussy on the floors above us walking around right over our heads! Oh, man! I'm drooling here just thinking about it!"

"Yeah, that'll be great."

"And I know this will be the year Joseph Roman finally gets his rocks off! I guarantee it!"

"One can only hope..."

"Take it from me. With your new single room, great décor, and grooving sound system, Joseph Roman is going all the way!"

"Listen, Casey, I'd be happy just to get to first base!"

"Hey, Joe, I'll be your base coach, man! I'll tell you when to steal second, try for third and take home! Just watch me for the signs! You know I've had plenty of experience!"

Yeah, I do. And you've always been much too happy to share your exploits with me.

I'd known Casey since third grade. I'd always thought I was more intelligent and better looking than Casey, but still, he'd get the babes, and I'd get nothing. How was that possible? Casey was short and squat; by third grade, he already had a receding hairline! Casey's hair was dark black, and he sported some stylish 'pork-chop' sideburns. I swear he must have been shaving since third grade. That's the **only** feature I could imagine that he had, and I didn't have that I knew could possibly draw the babes – facial hair. Me, I couldn't even muster a crop of peach fuzz.

And, oh my God, how he liked to brag about his feats! It all started when we were in grade school. One day during recess, I was hanging out on the playground when Casey ran up to me, gasping for air.

"Joe! Listen to this! Wendy and I were sitting together on the teeter-totter, and she let me grab her booby!"

"What?"

"Yeah, Jill and Alex were on the other side, and when they sat down, we flew up in the air. I was trying to keep from falling off, and I accidentally grabbed one!"

"Really? Did she get mad?"

"I said I was sorry, but she just turned around and smiled! Then she said, 'That's okay, hang on tighter next time!' And I did!"

"Wow! What did it feel like?"

"Oh, they're kind of soft and squishy. You'll have to try it sometime!"

"Yeah, gosh, I wish I could!"

As we aged, the stories improved and always included some odd but fascinating details.

"Listen to this! I was with Jenny, at her house after school, the other day and we went to her room, and she said she had to change her top and she did it, right in front of me! She was wearing a bra, but she let me peek behind one of the cups and showed me the size – she was so proud of it. It was a size C! And, by the way, did you know she has little black hair growing right around her nipples?"

"Wow! I would never have guessed!"

Casey continued to set the bar, always higher, with every story. I'd get tripped up before even getting close to the jump. I had many dates, but all I had to show for them was a peck and a "good night." Was it because I was boring, or was it because I reeked of desperation? The closest I ever got to scoring was with Sue. We were kissing pretty heavily at the drive-in movie. The windows were steaming up. I thought, "This is my time", but when I tried to cop a feel, she said, "I'm sorry, Joe, but I'm not ready for that yet."

What does that mean, "not ready, yet"?

When I called her house the next day, her mother told me Sue didn't want to talk to me. Oh no, I was mother-dumped!

One week later, Casey had another exploit to share, and guess what? It was with the same Sue who'd mother-dumped me.

"You won't believe it, Joe! I was in Sue's neighborhood, you know, just walking by her house, minding my own business, and I saw Sue sitting on her front porch. She says, 'Hey, Casey, listen to my latest piece on the flute.' We're both in the band, you know. I said, 'Okay,' and the next thing you know, we're down in her basement, necking on the couch. I put my hand down her pants, and she let me finger the hell out of her! Can you believe it?"

Now she's ready? Did I miss my chance by one week?

"Oh, and you want to hear something weird? She's got this little bump in her pussy; I don't know what it is, a pubic bone or something? I bet that little bump's gonna make some guy happy someday!"

Oh my God, Casey is really starting to piss me off.

Pissed off or not, I double-dated with Casey to the senior prom. I took a nice girl who lived on my block, someone else I'd known since third grade. At the night's end, I received the usual peck on the cheek. Overall, it was a fairly uneventful evening, at least for me. Casey, on the other hand, was the lucky recipient of multiple blow jobs in the back seat of my Father's Lincoln Town Car (which Dad had let me borrow for the big event). The night began when I picked up everyone at their homes. Driving to the dance, I heard a rear power window go down. I was surprised that anyone would open a window because it was freezing outside.

"What's going on back there?"

"Nothing, Joe, just keep on driving." I looked in the rearview mirror just in time to see Casey's date spitting out the window.

"All righty then..." My date was oblivious.

JUST MISSED THE SIXTIES

And that was just the drive to the dance. Then, there was the drive to the restaurant, the drive to the bowling alley, and the drive to the coffee shop.

I said, "Casey, don't wear out the window!"

Casey said, "That's not the only thing getting worn out!"

Yep, Casey's always been the lucky one, but this year will be different. There will be no roommate to slow me down. There will be girls nearby, right in the same dorm. And best of all, my room will be a super cool, irresistible love-shack.

I said, "Goodbye." and "See you this afternoon." to Casey and hung up. Soon, I was sitting in the back seat of my father's car rolling down Highway 41.

There are only two kinds of stories: a child leaves home, and a stranger comes to town.
Faulkner

Once, a child left home and got strange.
Joseph Roman

On the Road Again

Looking out Dad's Town Car window, I scanned the pastoral Wisconsin countryside. Dotting the landscape were the typical dairy farms, corn fields, and cow pastures surrounding a center compound containing the family home, some barns, and feed silos.

My mother said, "Did you know that if the cows are lying in the field, it will rain?"

"No, Mom, and I didn't know it the first time you said it about ten years ago."

Mother responded by lighting a cigarette.

Father said, "Doris, if you're going to do that, could you please open a window?"

"Hey, Mom, could you turn on the radio please?"

Mother opened a window and turned on the radio. I first heard the laid-back sound of Bing Crosby crooning "Pennies from Heaven."

"No! No, Mom! Hit the second button. That's my station!"

Mom hit the third button, and "the girl next door," Doris Day, was sweetly singing "Que Sera Sera."

Oh, Man! "Whatever Will Be Will Be" will not be pretty if I hear that song again!

JUST MISSED THE SIXTIES

"No, Mom! It's the second button from the left, not the second button from the right!"

"But I like that song."

"Please, Mom, you can listen to your station on your way back, and anytime you want now that I'm going to college again!"

"Well, it will be nice to have a little peace and quiet around the house."

With all the kids gone, she'll definitely have some peace and quiet. My older sister and brother moved out years ago. My sister was married and living in Florida, and my brother joined the army and is currently stationed in Germany.

This time, Mom hit the correct second button, and I was rewarded with my favorite song of all time, "Incense and Peppermints," by the Strawberry Alarm Clock. I closed my eyes and felt the Sixties coursing through my veins and into my brain.

"You call this music?"

Ah, Dad speaks again.

He continued, "This song makes me think of those dirty hippies that took over San Diego!"

"No, Dad, they were in San Francisco, not San Diego, and they didn't 'take over'. They just lived in one little area in the city and tried to show the world that people didn't have to live their lives the way they did back in the Fifties. You know, people don't have to work themselves to death to try to 'keep up with the Jones.' Anyway, they've moved to the country now, into communes. They grow their own food organically; it's healthier that way."

"Yeah, well, good luck with that."

Mom changed the subject, "So you're a biology major now? What happened to being a forest ranger? After all, that's why you chose this college."

"I told you already, I had trouble memorizing the names of all the trees, and I found biology much more interesting."

Yeah, and I learned that being a forest ranger is more than just smoking pot in the woods.

"Mom, did you know that every living thing is made up of the same four essential components? Can you name them?"

Mother laughed and said, "How about sugar and spice and everything nice?"

Father said, "Why, Doris, I'm surprised you didn't mention tobacco."

"Oh, yeah? And maybe I should have mentioned scotch and gin, too!"

I'm getting away just in time.

"Well, all righty then, Mom, you did name one of the four things - sugar! Anyway, here's the answer: The four components of all living things are sugar, fat, protein, and nucleic acids. It's just how they're put together that can give you different species!"

"Well, maybe you'll find some of the female species in your new co-ed dorm this year!"

"Mom, females aren't a different species!"

Dad piped in, "I hope a co-ed dorm won't be a distraction."

Mom asked, "So, why didn't you want a roommate this year?"

"Mom, I already told you how my roommates didn't work out last year. They were too much of a… a distraction!"

Thanks, Dad, for the right word at the right time.

'Distraction' was a pretty good word to describe last year's roommates. My first-semester roommate, Ned, was from a small town in Indiana.

When we first met, he saw my long hair, and as we shook hands, he said, "Far fucking out, I was hoping I'd room with a fucking long hair!"

What a weird thing to say! Does he expect me to provide him with his fantasy college hippie experience? Man, I can't handle the responsibility!

As it turned out, I didn't have to worry. Within a week, he found some skanky girlfriend and immediately developed a signaling technique to indicate if she was in the room with him.

JUST MISSED THE SIXTIES

He said, "Hey, Joe, I just want you to know, if you see a necktie hanging on the doorknob, that means 'do not disturb.' Can you dig that?"

Who the hell brings a necktie to college?

After seeing Ned's necktie on the doorknob one too many times, I decided to find a new roommate for the second semester. Oh, and there was another problem with Ned: his favorite "rock" song was the theme for the movie *The Good, the Bad, and the Ugly*.

That's not rock! That's a movie soundtrack, for God's sake! The next thing he'll be playing is "Supercalifragilisticexpealidoscious"!

I had higher hopes for my second-semester roommate, John. Casey met him in a class and invited him to have a toke with us in the Campus North Woods. He was from Milwaukee, so I knew he wasn't some country red-neck. After we toked together, I thought he would work out okay as a roommate, especially since he didn't have a girlfriend like Ned. Unfortunately, John had a special relationship with one of Milwaukee's most famous products, beer. He was sloppy, too; I'd always find beer cans (and toe-nail clippings-yech!) strewn about the room. The last straw occurred when he shared a beer with my pet, Goldfish, Cannabis. Soon, Cannabis was floating upside-down at the top of the tank. I was standing there in shock when John grabbed the poor fish and chucked its corpse out the window, striking an equally shocked co-ed in the face down below on the sidewalk. John thought it was hilarious.

Man! That dude has no respect for my stuff!

Oh, and another problem with John was his choice of music. Once again, my roommate's musical taste was not a good match to mine. I remember thinking:

If I hear "Thirty Days in the Hole" one more time, I'm going to shoot myself!

I tried to impress him with Pink Floyd's latest album, *Dark Side of the Moon*, but he wasn't moved in the slightest.

He said, "Oh my God, those cash register and clock sound effects are so cheesy, and that screaming woman, someone, please put her out of her misery! Mark my words; they won't sell many of those records!"

He was definitely not prophetic, as that LP went on to be one of the best sellers of all time. Anyway, John quit school a month before the end of the semester to become a fireman back in Milwaukee.

I wonder if he can put out a fire with a beer?

After John left, I got a taste of life without a roommate for one glorious month. It was great. I could come and go as I pleased, listen to any music I wanted, and only have my mess to clean.

So, when Casey said that next year we should move to the co-ed dorm, Hyer Hall, I said, "Yes, and I'm getting a single room." Casey had been sharing a room with another high-school friend, Don. They decided to continue as roommates in Hyer Hall.

Outside Dad's car, the landscape transitioned from dairy farms to forests as we approached Stevens Point, Wisconsin, a town on the edge of "The Great North Woods."

JUST MISSED THE SIXTIES

Stevens Point & the Great North Woods

The city of Stevens Point (aka Point) is located almost precisely in the center of Wisconsin. To the north is the beginning of the regrowth of The Great North Woods. The original Great North Woods, of Paul Bunyan fame, was decimated by 19th-century loggers. Giant trees were felled, floated down the Wisconsin River to Stevens Point sawmills, cut into boards, and shipped by rail across the Midwest. Wisconsin lumber built Chicago in the 1860s and was burned in the Great Chicago Fire of 1871. After the forests were gone, the sawmills were replaced by insurance companies, furniture makers, a brewery (Point Beer), vegetable canneries, and, of course, the University of Wisconsin extension school, UWSP, noted for its elementary education and natural resources departments.

We'll be ready with the forest rangers when the North Woods grow back!

Currently, Stevens Point boasts of its downtown area, the Wisconsin Main Street Community, an enclosed shopping mall offering specialty shops, restaurants, and offices. Back in the day, this same area was called "The Square," and it was packed with bars and nothing else, just two solid blocks of bars. In 1972, the Wisconsin Legislature lowered the minimum drinking age from twenty-one to eighteen. There was (legal) alcohol money to be made from college students. The Square was there to reap the profits.

When Father drove the Lincoln through Point, we didn't pass through The Square; instead, we headed directly to the UWSP campus on the north side of town. And, boy, did the school look fantastic! Broad elms and oaks on the campus grounds were lush with a whole summer's growth. The day was perfect, sunny, and mild, with just a hint of fall in the north breeze. Old Main was grand, with ivy covering the sides of its one-hundred-year-old brick walls. There was a hustle and bustle atmosphere with all the newly arriving students. Everywhere I looked, I saw happy, smiling faces. So much promise in the air! New things to learn! It was much too early to think about homework, exams, and grades. I'd done pretty well last year as a freshman (3.6 GPA), but this year, I hoped to do much more than get good grades.

We passed the sleek, new Performing Arts building and the old Gymnasium with its surrounding fields before reaching the dormitories. Before the road entered the campus's north woods, the last dormitory was to be my new home, Hyer Hall.

A banner hanging on the front of the building said, "Welcome Students of 1973 – You're Out of Sight!"

Mother read the sign aloud and said, "I wonder what that means. Why are the students not in sight? Are they hiding? That's so silly; they're just not here yet! Tomorrow, they will all be within sight, of course."

"No, Mom, that's just an expression, like cool, you know, like if you say something is 'cool,' it doesn't really mean that it's cold."

Dad couldn't resist: "No, dear. It could mean that the Director of Hyer Hall is visually challenged and cannot see the students."

Mom laughed.

Thank God we're here!

Hyer Hall

    Dad parked the car in the gravel lot situated on the north side of Hyer Hall, right between the red brick box-shaped dormitory and the Campus North Woods. Looking at the building, one could see that it was smaller than last year's dorm. Both dormitories had four floors, but Hyer Hall had just two, an East and a West, instead of three wings per floor. The lobby, front desk, dorm director's office, mailroom, and the center stairwell were between the two wings on the first floor. The dorm director lived in a small one-story flat extending southwards from the center lobby.

    The first and second floors were for the male co-eds, while the females resided in the top two. My room was on the second floor.

    Mom said, "Well, at least we don't have to take your things up to the fourth floor like we did last year."

    "Yeah! This dorm is so much better, and look - the woods are right next door! That's great, in case I need to take a walk and get another hit... I mean, get a breath of fresh air."

    Right - Have another hit... of fresh air. That was close!

    I said, "Before we start taking stuff up to my room, I've got to get a key from the front desk."

    Dad said, "Okay, but we can grab a suitcase or two this trip, so when you get the key, we can go right up to your room without having to go back out to the car."

    "Sure."

    We walked into the lobby and headed for the front desk. I was standing in a corner, suitcase in my hand, when suddenly, my new dorm director, Gertrude Kaiser, came forward to greet us. She had sternly cut blonde hair and a business-like demeanor. Despite her height of about five feet three inches, she projected a personality of strength.

Oh my God, she's a little stormtrooper!

She reached out a hand to Father, "Welcome (Velcome) to Hyer Hall. My name is Gertrude Kaiser. I am the Dormitory Director."

Did she just say velcome?

Father introduced Mother to Gertrude. Mother said, "Hello, Gertrude, we just made a joke in the car about you. Mr. Roman said that you might be blind! Now, isn't that silly? Why, you can see perfectly well, can't you?"

Gertrude paused briefly before responding, "Yes, I can, Mrs. Roman, and you can trust that I will be keeping an eye on your son, Joseph."

She knows my name, but Father hasn't introduced me yet!

I shook my head in disbelief, and then it was my turn at the front desk to get my room key. Soon, my folks and I were making regular trips back and forth from the car to my room. With the three of us working, the unloading process went much quicker than the loading process this morning when I was the only one doing the work. Soon, we were finished, standing in my room and looking at the unpacking and putting away work that loomed in my future. I started putting up some of the wall decorations.

Dad said, "What is that stuff? Is this place going to look like some kind of opium den?"

You have no idea!

My mother picked up my 3-foot square window fan and asked, "What do you need this big fan for? It's freezing cold up here most of the time!"

I was ready with an answer, "Well, you see, Mom, a lot of college kids smoke cigarettes, and the fan is perfect for getting the cigarette smoke out of the room; I'm sure Dad can understand that."

Dad spoke up, as if on cue, "Makes sense to me."

Yeah, that's right, I'll be getting rid of the smoke, alright, but it might not be tobacco smoke.

Just then, Casey and Don appeared. Casey spoke first, doing his finest Eddie Haskell impression. "Well, hello, it's so good to see you again, Mr. and Mrs. Roman. Do you remember our mutual friend, Don? Hello, Joseph. Welcome to Hyer Hall."

My folks and I said hello to Casey and Don. Then Mother said, "It's nice to see you too, Casey and Don. Do you boys have all your things in your rooms already?"

"Almost, Mrs. Roman. You see, Don and I are sharing a room. Don's got his stuff in there, but my stuff is still in the hallway. That's because I'm not allowed to move my stuff into the room until Mother has wiped down every square inch with Lysol."

That's right, I remember his mother is neurotic.

Mother said, "You boys were all together at Knutzen Hall last year, right?"

"Yes, we were, Mrs. Roman."

"And now, you've all come over here to meet some girls! That is so sweet. Well, Casey, I wish you luck!"

Like he needs any!

Mother said, "I'm going to go down to your room, Casey, to say hello to your mother."

Casey said, "I'll go with you, Mrs. Roman. Maybe she's done by now."

As they walked away, Casey said, "Too bad about those Cubs, Mrs. Roman, they were so close this year!"

"Oh well, you know what they always say, 'Maybe next year!'"

Man, I hope this is my "next year".

Meanwhile, Don looked around my room at the decorations I'd put up.

"Hey, Joe, looks like you're gonna have a pretty far-out pad this year!"

Father asked, "So, Don, where's your family?"

Don said, "Oh, they took off already; we got here pretty early this morning."

JUST MISSED THE SIXTIES

"Doesn't your family own a cottage on Elkhart Lake? I think Joseph mentioned more than once about going there for ice-fishing trips."

It's more like we were getting blasted with a keg of beer. Ah yes, those were some good times - going to Don's summer cottage on a winter weekend. With nothing but a deck of cards and a quarter barrel of Pabst Blue Ribbon. We'd drink till we couldn't see the cards anymore, stumble outside singing "Chantilly Lace" at the top of our lungs, and climax the evening with a puke-fest in the woods. Yep, there's nothing like getting back to nature.

Don stroked his wispy little goatee and pondered, "Yeah, unfortunately, we had to sell the cottage. Since my father lost his job, the folks are getting a little tight with the bread."

"I'm sorry to hear that, Don."

"Oh, we'll survive. I'm going to try to get a job here to help with tuition and pay for some of the necessities."

Like weed?

I felt bad for Don. We had a special connection. We were together when we heard "Stairway to Heaven" for the first time. It was a memorable moment, like the JFK assassination, the moon landing, or the Beatle's first appearance on the Ed Sullivan Show.

"I've put in a job application for the night shift at the local UPS. That way, it won't interfere with my classes during the day."

Father said, "My goodness, Don, when will you sleep?"

In class?

"Oh, I'll catch an hour here and there."

"Well, I hope that works out for you. I see that Joseph's mother is returning. Right now, we're going to grab some lunch at the Country Kitchen. Would you like to join us, Don?"

"No, thank you, Mr. Roman. I already had some grub. I think I'll take a walk out in the North Campus Woods – it's a beautiful day!"

Yeah, a "walk in the woods"; he's probably going to toke a joint in The Clearing!

Last year, Casey, Don, and I discovered The Clearing one Saturday afternoon while hiking through the woods, looking for a good place to smoke some reefer. Following a narrow deer path through some dense undergrowth, we emerged, blinking, into a large grassy field. Three small pine trees formed an equilateral triangle in the middle of the clearing. Inside the triangle, we stumbled upon a crude lean-to consisting of a long tree trunk supported by a low branch. It was about five feet above the ground with a covering of pine boughs to form a roof. At the apex was a small opening, and wisps of smoke were curling out of the hole.

That's interesting. There's a fire inside. There must be people in there!

We got down on our hands and knees and peeked into the entrance of the lean-to. We saw four hippies, three guys and one girl, who looked as if they just stepped from the pages of Hippie Commune Living. They wore fringed leather tops, denim pants, bandanas, and sandals. A homemade clay pipe was being passed. The pipe was decorated with colorful feathers hanging by leather straps.

They're Woodsy Commune Hippies!

One of them said, "Well, my, my, it looks like we have company! Come in and join us! My name is Gary."

We crawled inside, sat on the carpet of pine needles, and introduced ourselves. I looked around at some of their accessories. There were top-of-the-line Eddie Bauer backpacks secured to lightweight aluminum frames. Also strapped onto the frames were costly goose-down sleeping bags, probably good for 40 degrees below zero. Lying beside the backpacks, I spied pricey down jackets, vests, and mountain-grade hiking boots with seriously waffled soles. It looked like they planned on hiking into the woods and camping overnight or maybe climbing Mt. Kilimanjaro!

These aren't Woodsy Commune Hippies! No! They're Rich Urban Camping Hippies!

Casey said, "Say, Gary, why are you guys camping out here? It's going to be freezing cold tonight!"

Gary said, "We're out here to see the mating ritual of the American Woodcock!

"No shit!"

JUST MISSED THE SIXTIES

"Yes, shit! It's something to behold! Picture this: at dusk, the males flap high into the sky. Then they start swooping and circling - all in a show for the ladies! Next, when a male spies the female he wants, he zooms down, zig-zagging all the way down to the ground, and lands right in front of her. Standing there, he swells up his chest and struts around, trying to entice her. If he's lucky, she'll think, 'Oh, what a manly Woodcock you are! I sure would like a piece of that wood–cock!' Ha!"

Hmm, I wonder if that's one of Casey's tricks.
Casey said, "Wow! That does sound pretty far-out."

So, we smoked and talked some more. Later, when it started getting colder, we thanked Gary for the tokes and wished him good luck with the Woodcocks. Gary invited us to visit his room in Hyer Hall sometime. We agreed and planned a visit for the following evening.

We were glad he'd invited us because Gary's room was incredible. It was a vision of the Great North Woods in its former glory. Shrubs and branches decorated every nook and cranny. Above us, two white birch logs rested on and between the wall-mounted light fixtures just under the ceiling. Hanging between the birch logs was a black fabric sky decorated with hundreds of shining stars that formed glowing constellations. A stuffed owl was perched on a tree trunk in the middle of the room. Gary was taking lessons in taxidermy, and his homework assignments decorated the room. Looking around, I spotted a rabbit and a raccoon.

Gary said, "I like to pose the animals in natural positions."

On the dresser, I spotted a pair of squirrels posed with tiny tennis rackets and a net.

Hmm, do squirrels play tennis?

Gary introduced us to some of his friends. We found all of Gary's friends to be handsome and witty.

I wonder. How does it feel to be one of the beautiful people?

Casey said, "Thank you, Gary, for letting us see your room. It's really cool!"

I said, "It's like the Garden of Eden, man!"

And Don said, "More like the Garden of Far-Out, man!"

JUST MISSED THE SIXTIES

"Thank you, Casey, Don, and Joe. What do you say - how about I fire up the water pipe?" And then, he pulled a giant hookah out from behind his desk.

I said, "Wait! What about the smell? We'll get in trouble!"

"No need to worry! Let me show you why."

Gary parted a bead curtain at the back of the room so we could see a large fan mounted on the back window sill.

"This baby sucks all the air right out of the room, so no smoke goes into the hall! We'll also throw a few towels down by the threshold just to be safe."

"No Shit!"

Gary said, "Let's smoke!" And we did.

Ten minutes and several puffs later, I was, once again, admiring the stuffed owl in the center of the room. And that's when I saw it.

"The owl! I swear! It just winked at me!"

Gary said, "Sooner or later, the owl winks at everyone."

After that evening at Gary's, I was inspired to go all out next year, decorating my new room in Hyer Hall. Casey and I decided we needed birch logs in our rooms, just like Gary's. During the last week of the semester, we scoured the woods until we found some good-sized trunks lying on the ground. After sawing them to fit into a dorm room, we hid them in a bushy area close to the Hyer Hall parking lot.

Now, Casey and I just needed to retrieve the trunks so we could finish decorating our rooms.

After lunch at the Country Kitchen, Mom and Dad dropped me off at the dorm entrance. Just before they drove away, Dad warned me again, "Be careful who you choose for friends because they can get you into trouble!"

As it turned out, I should have listened to my old man.

Second East Sophomores

Casey had already grabbed a burger with his folks at the Student Union and was waiting for my return. He was anxious to get his room into shape.

"God, I thought my mom would never finish with her cleaning!"

"Well, at least you know it's been sanitized for your protection!"

"Yeah, that's right. Let's go get those logs."

We quickly found the logs and carried them up the east-side stairway to our rooms. I propped the first one up onto the light fixtures above the desks by the window and the second one onto the light fixtures over the dressers in the front of the room. Next, I hung my 'sky' between the logs. It was a tie-dye sheet decorated with fluorescent orange stars. Lastly, I installed my precious new sound system on one of the desks, mounting the stereo speakers onto the birch logs by the ceiling.

These acoustics are going to be a dynamite trip, man!

Don poked his head in the room, "Wow! That ceiling is blowing my mind!"

Looking at Don, I saw that his eyes were bloodshot-red slits. "Oh my God, Don, are you stoned already? Did you toke in the Clearing?"

"No. I didn't toke in the Clearing. But hey, wait. Speaking of the Clearing, man, dig this! Remember Gary's little lean-to hut-thingy? Well, it's gone now. There's no sign it was ever there! All that's left, man, is a few ashes and rocks where the fire pit used to be. That's all! That's pretty freaky, eh?"

JUST MISSED THE SIXTIES

Then Casey walked into the room, looked at the ceiling, looked at Don, and said, "Nice job, Joe. It looks good. Don, where did you cop a buzz already?"

I said, "Don told me he didn't smoke at the Clearing, although he was there and noticed that Gary's lean-to was gone. The mystery remains: where did Don partake in the illegal weed? Don?"

"Where did I partake in the… oh yeah, listen to this. I was walking back from the Clearing, and right before I got back onto the campus grounds, there was this mob of 30 or 40 students, all passing joints, man! It was insane! Of course, I had to join them and get a little taste of it, you know what I mean. Look out your window! Look! You can see them! Wow, man, they're still out there!"

Cool. Looks like the students of 1973 will be "out of sight"!

There was a knock on the door frame. Two unknown students entered the room through the open door.

One said, "Whoa, get a load of this room! It's fucking far-out, man!"

The other said, "Oh yeah, it's truly a mind-altering experience!"

Are they being facetious?

Casey spoke first. He put a hand on my shoulder and said, "Welcome to the room where my friend, Joseph Roman, will have his first score with some foxy lady. I guarantee it!"

Don chimed in, "Or any lady at all!"

"Hah! Good luck! My name's Jim, although everyone calls me QP, and this is my roommate, Chuck. We're your new next-door neighbors, Joseph, right?"

"Joe is fine. These are my friends, I think, Casey and Don. They're roommates, too, although their room is at the far end of the wing, and if we're lucky, they'll stay down there. Me, I don't have a roommate. I'm flying solo this year. Oh yeah!"

"This year? Does that mean you guys are sophomores?"

"Yeah, that's right. Last year, we were in Knutzen Hall, an all-guys dorm, you know. So, this year, we thought we'd try a co-ed dorm to see what it's like. Hey, were you guys here last year? Maybe you can fill us in on what it's like in a co-ed dorm?"

"Yeah, we were here last year. We had some good times."

Casey said, "Hey, what do you say we go to the Student Union and get ourselves a cup of hot joe, and you can tell us all about it?

QP and Chuck agreed to go, and I said, "Right on!" as I pumped my fist.

Don said, "Far out!"

QP said, "Right arm!" and pumped his fist.

Chuck said, "Farm out!"

Is that what it's come to in the seventies? Now, we mock the sayings of our sixty's brethren?

As we walked to the Union, I checked out our new wingmates. QP was tall and lean with a curly Harpo Marx mop of blonde hair.

That must have been the inspiration for his nickname.

He was wearing a t-shirt with a picture of Buddy Holly. Underneath the picture, it read, "Feb. 3, 1959: The Day the Music Died."

Chuck was average height with shaggy black hair curled up at the ends.

Chuck, pushing his chunky black glasses up to the bridge of his nose, said, "QP's from Racine, and I'm from Plover, actually a farm just outside of Plover, but don't hold that against me. I'm cool."

QP said, "Yeah, they don't just grow cows and potatoes at Chuck's farm if you know what I'm talking about!"

Chuck laughed and said, "Yeah, right! Shut up, QP."

We entered the Union, bought some coffee, and went to a table on the patio.

Don said, "I hope this coffee helps me get my head back together after toking with that mob by the woods!"

Chuck said, "I know, we saw them too! What a way to start the semester!"

Don said, "And I've got to be ready for an interview in an hour."

QP said, "What interview?"

"Well, I've got to get a job to help the folks pay my college bills. You know, 'cause it's rough times and all that. Hopefully, I can land a gig at the local UPS in delivery. It's a night job – so if I get the job, I guess you won't see much of me this semester."

QP said, "Well, that sucks. It would be nice to have a good wing this year, you know, where everybody is cool, and it's not a bunch of red-necks like we had last year."

Casey said, "Tell me about it! Knutzen Hall was full of red-necks!"

I said, "Oh, and get this. At Knutzen, the rednecks loved to play ice hockey, except it was in the hallway! You couldn't step outside your room without the constant danger of some puck getting slap-shot into your face!"

QP said, "Well, that pucks!"

Don said, "Oh yeah! And everyone had a gun, and all they ever talked about was hunting!"

QP said, "Yeah, yeah! We had some of those guys. Apparently, the only clothes they own are camouflage!"

I said, "So, besides you guys, is anyone else returning to Second East this year?"

QP said, "No, thank God! All those guys either dropped out or moved off-campus. I'd move off campus, too, except for that stupid rule that we have to live in the dorms for our freshman and sophomore years. Isn't that fucked-up?"

I guess so. But it's kind of nice here, having my food taken care of and getting clean sheets every week.

I said, "How can that even be legal?"

Casey asked, "Did you know a guy named Gary who lived in Hyer Hall last year? We met him in the woods, and he invited us to his room, which was full of stuffed animals."

QP said, "Oh yeah, Gary. I never hung out with the dude. He was on First West. I heard about his room, though. It sounded pretty cool."

I said, "He inspired us to put more effort into our room decorations, and, most importantly, he taught us about **the fan**."

"The fan?"

"Yeah. I'll have to invite you guys to my room really soon to see the fan in action!"

QP said, "Cool. Anyway, I heard that Gary wasn't coming back this year. I think he transferred to someplace out West, like Wyoming or Alaska."

Don said, "I bet he's trying to stuff a Grizzly!"

I said, "Either that or, like the Woodcock, he wants to watch their mating ritual."

QP said, "So anyway, fellows. Do you realize what this means?"

"Huh? What's that?"

"It means that every sophomore in Second East is sitting at this table! All the rest are little newbie freshmen!"

Chuck said, "Oh yeah! We get to rule the roost!"

I said, "Far fuckin'-out!"

QP said, "Let's blow their tiny, little freshmen minds!"

I said, "Hey guys, what do you say we form a little Welcoming Committee? Let's go back to the dorm and greet our new wingmates!"

The Rest of Second East

We started at the east end, across from Casey's and Don's room, and worked west, towards the middle of the building. The Welcoming Committee consisted of Casey, Chuck, QP, and me. Don had to leave for his interview at UPS. The wing was abuzz with new students carrying up their gear, unpacking, and decorating their rooms.

First, we met roommates Jay and William. Looking at Jay, I thought *suave*. His shoulder-length black hair was perfectly cut, and his mustache was impeccably trimmed.

After introducing ourselves as the Welcome Committee, Jay said, with a voice like silk, "Nice to meet you, gentlemen. This is far out. I hope everybody is cool here. It'd be nice if we had a wing full of heads. Hey, listen. If you gentlemen ever need… anything, don't hesitate to ask. I'm your man."

Oh my God! He's a pusher!

As if reading my mind, he said, "I'm not a pusher, man. I'm a dealer. There's a difference. You know what I'm talking about?"

Yeah, God damn the pusherman!

"So, listen, gentlemen. Acapulco Gold or Panama Red, whatever your pleasure, I've got it. Oh, and by the way, do any of you fellows know of a student activist group on campus? I'd like to do something good for… mankind."

Wow! He wants to be a student activist, just like me! Or maybe he's just looking for potential customers?

I said, "Nothing I know of, Jay, but let's keep our eyes open 'because I'd like to get involved in a good cause, too."

"Right on. That's heavy, man."

JUST MISSED THE SIXTIES

Jay's roommate, William, entered the room carrying a stack of boxes. I swear to God, he looked just like the Marlboro man from the TV commercials. He wore a large Stetson hat, leather vest, chaps, and cowboy boots.

We introduced ourselves. He said nothing. Instead, he set down the boxes, grabbed a cigarette from behind his ear, and placed it between his lips. Next, he pulled out a large, silver Zippo lighter from his jacket pocket and swiped it across his thigh, first one way to open it. CLICK! Then back to strike the flint. CLICK! WHOOSH! A three-inch-tall orange flame burst forth from the lighter. He tilted his head to a 45-degree angle and slowly sucked the flame toward the cigarette. The light from the flame dramatically enhanced his facial features and the brim of his hat.

What a performance!

After puffing out some smoke, he closed the lighter with a flick. CLICK!

"Howdy, boys. I'm William. Let me tell you a few things about myself. I like cigarettes, booze, and skinny women, especially when the skinny women are strategically covered with whipped cream. And listen to this: I won't abide anyone making fun of the way I look. Can you dig that?"

QP said, "With a shovel, man!"

He's not that big of a guy. What makes him so tough?

I said, "Jay and William, I'm inviting everyone on the wing to my room tomorrow, after supper, for a taste of the local brew and a chance to meet everyone else on the wing. I hope to see you there. I'm in room 206." They said they would be there.

We moved up the hall and knocked on the next door.

A voice inside the room said, "Come in!" and said, "Oh my God, I can't believe I'm in college!

Oh my God, it's the first day, and this guy's already freaking out?

We opened the door, and QP started the introduction, "Hi, we're the Sophomore Welcome Committee, and we're here to say welcome to Hyer Hall and the University of Stevens Point."

"I mean, where do I get my books? How do I find my classes? Shit, there's so much to learn!"

I looked at the guy and immediately thought he didn't look like the type to be freaked out.

What the... This guy is handsome and physically fit! Hmmm... I like that three-day stubble look.

I said, "Don't worry. Stay calm. We're all here to help you. Ah, what's your name?"

"Tim."

Casey said, "Tim, where are you from?"

"St. Germain."

Ah, small town, that explains things.

"Our family runs a tourist lodge on the lake."

"And what do you do there?"

"I perform stunts in a water ski show."

I said, "Tim, what's your major?"

"Premed."

"Premed means you need to take many science classes, right? So, besides being good at water skis, you're probably a pretty smart guy, too. Don't worry; you'll figure out how to get around this place in no time, and then it will seem as easy as skiing on one ski."

"You think? Hey, I can ski barefoot!"

"I bet you can, Tim. It won't take long for you to get up to speed."

Suddenly, Jay poked his head in the door and said, "Yeah, then you can spend your time getting wasted with us!"

Tim freaked again, "Oh my God! Who was that? What a fry!"

"Tim?"

"Yeah?"

"You'll be fine. Be at my room tomorrow after supper, and then you can meet everyone else on the wing. Okay?"

"Okay."

We moved to the next door. Just before I could knock, the door opened, and there stood the spitting image of Mark Spitz.

Or should I say the spitzing image?

JUST MISSED THE SIXTIES

Mark Spitz and his Olympic Swimming Medals

QP said, "Excuse me, young man. Could you please take off your shirt? We'd like to see your medals!"

Chuck said, "Don't listen to him. Hi. We're the Sophomore Welcoming Committee. We just came by to say, 'Hello,' and welcome you to our pool, I mean school."

"Okay, this is nothing I haven't heard before. My name is Tom, but you can call me Spitz. Everyone else does."

We introduced ourselves, and I invited him to my get-together. Soon, we were on our way to the next room.

Several doors and introductions later, we realized we hadn't found a single red-neck in the bunch.

QP said, "This wing is starting to look pretty good!"

"I'm stoked!"

One of our new wingmates said his friends called him 'The Professor.'

I said, "That's cool; just don't give us any tests." Looking behind The Professor, I saw, lying about in his room, several boxes with intriguing contents, some electrical and some chemical.

I wonder what he's up to.

The third-to-last door in the wing was slightly ajar, so we peeked inside. Sitting on the floor, cross-legged, was a large, pudgy dude. His long hair was almost Johnny Winters white, that is, what was left of his hair. His hairline was badly receded, and he had a giant shining dome of baldness on the back of his head. A few wrinkles were next to his eyes, and he had no discernible facial hair. He was wearing a massive set of "double-bagel" headphones and sitting perfectly still, staring forward with a vacant look. We shuffled inside and began waving our hands in his field of vision so he could see us. Suddenly, he tore off his headphones.

"What the fuck do you losers want? Do you know what you're doing? You're interrupting my quiet time! Doc said I must have some quiet time every day; otherwise, I get too worked up! And you don't want to see me get worked up! Do you?"

QP said, "Hi, we're here to welcome the new freshmen to Hyer Hall. So, ah, welcome and see you around!"

"So...you're the Welcoming Committee, are you? Well then, where's my fucking fruit basket?"

"Well, ah..."

He laughed, "No, shit! I'm just joking around. Hey, thanks for coming by, dudes. Say, what's this wing looking like?"

I said, "It looks like we have a fantastic freak-to-red-neck ratio, which is all freak and no red-necks!"

"Well, that's way cool, nifty, neato. Oh, you gotta meet my friend from Tomah, Steve. Hey, Steve, get your ass outta bed and meet my new college friends. Steve isn't signed up for college, but he will probably visit me a lot. You see, he doesn't have any other life. Right, Steve?"

JUST MISSED THE SIXTIES

We looked around and didn't see anyone else in the room. Suddenly, there was a loud yell, "Booyah!" followed by a long, blonde-haired, half-naked body bursting forth from the sheets of one of the beds.

"Howdy, boys! I'm Al's party buddy, Steve!" Steve was wearing nothing but a pair of tightey-whiteys and a huge boyish grin. In contrast to Al, Steve's physique was well-toned. His long, wavy blonde hair reminded me of Led Zeppelin's Robert Plant, and I noticed that his eyes had a slight tilt, perhaps an indication of East Asia in his ancestry.

I invited them to my get-together.

Al said, "Steve won't be here tomorrow, but I'll be there, and I plan on getting wired!"

We left Al's room and paused in the hallway. I could feel the excitement building.

Finally, QP said what we were all thinking, "This wing is freakin' unbelievable!"

"I know, I know! Wow!"

We knocked on the next door and were surprised to see an African American (70's speak) open it.

Hmmm, it's one of those brown-skinned human beings. I've heard about them.

Believe it or not, I'd never spoken to a black person in my entire life. They didn't call Wauwatosa lily-white for nothing. My parents had been quiet on the subject of race; all I knew was from TV. I'd seen the marches and protests. When Martin Luther King was assassinated, I saw the pain and anger. How could people treat each other so badly? Why do people hate each other?

I remembered encountering the hate one day about five years ago when all I wanted was a haircut. I was waiting my turn in the Patriot Barbershop on 88th and North Avenue. Only three of us were in the shop: the barber and the customer ahead of me seated on the barber chair. Looking around the place, I saw the decorations matched the shop's name. Besides, American flags of all sizes were stuck everywhere; on the walls were framed replicas of the Constitution, the Bill of Rights, and the Declaration of Independence. Even the

JUST MISSED THE SIXTIES

wallpaper had images of Revolutionary War soldiers with muskets and cannons. Bored, I began listening to the barber's conversation with the customer.

"Yeah, I see now they've moved up to 43rd Street."

"I know. I told my brother to move out of there fast before it's too late!"

"The next thing, you know, they'll be on 50th street, and then the next thing, you know, they'll be in 'Tosa! God forbid!"

"And, the worst thing is, there ain't nothing we can do about it! With these new housing laws, pretty much anyone can live anywhere they please, and nobody can stop 'em!"

"I know. It's a damn shame. And after they move in, the neighborhoods are never the same."

"You got that right! Maybe we should start wearing white sheets and burning crosses like down south."

The barber finished the job, and the customer paid for his haircut and left. It was my turn. The barber waved me over to the seat. I didn't know what possessed me when I approached the barber's chair, but I decided to call him out.

"I heard what you said to the man before me. Are you a bigot?"

The barber quickly responded, "Let me ask you something, son. Did you know that even the Lord, God, himself, has a favorite kind of people? He calls them his chosen people. You can check it out; it says so in the Bible. It says that the Jews are God's chosen people. If God can have a favorite people, it's all right for me, too. And I choose the white people as my favorite people."

I didn't reply. I'd just met hate and learned that hate has its own logic that I'll never understand. If he genuinely wanted to follow the word of God, well, instead of hating people, shouldn't he be giving special deals to Jewish people?

I can see the sign in the window now: Half-off for Hebrews.

Back at the door, QP began the welcome spiel. "Hello! Welcome to Hyer Hall-Second East. We're the Sophomore Welcoming Committee. I'm QP. This is Chuck, Casey, and Joe."

JUST MISSED THE SIXTIES

"Hi! My name is Lewis. Thank you for the welcome. I'd love to chat with you, but I am just leaving for a meeting with my orientation group. Anyway, I'll be seeing you around. Keep cool."

Lewis stepped into the hallway, locked the door behind him, and walked away.

QP said to his back, "Don't be afraid to ask us a question if you need any help!"

"Right on, brother!"

Darn, I didn't get to ask him to my get-together.

And finally, there was one room left. We'd purposefully saved it for last because we knew it was the room of the Wing Director. Let me explain: The Wing Director is a student who actually gets paid to live in the dorm. He has two functions, one good and the other not so good. The good function first: He can help the new freshmen with all their questions about college. The not-so-good: Don and I found out the hard way last year about that one.

One week into the first semester, Don came to my room with a bottle of tequila.

He said, "Hey, Joe! Let's do a shot!"

And we did. Followed by another one. But then, Don had this great idea. He said, "I've got to take a shot to Casey's room!" So, he poured a shot, picked it up, and before I could say, "Careful!" he walked out the door and *bam!* Right into the Wing Director. Now, this Wing Director was a pretty nice guy, but there was no way he would ignore a shot of tequila splashed all over his shirt.

"Sorry, guys, but I must report this to the Dorm Director."

The next day, Don and I talked with the Dorm Director. He explained the school's alcohol policy (only beer and only in the common room) and then told us we each had one strike.

"Remember, boys, we have a two-strike system. After your first one, you get a warning. After the second one, let's say things get a lot more serious. Okay?"

We promised to be good and follow the rules. The incident mostly faded from my memory until now: on my way to meet my new Wing Director.

JUST MISSED THE SIXTIES

Hey, I'm in a new dorm. Maybe I get a clean slate?

QP knocked, and the door was opened by a tall, skinny, well-tanned dude with a big toothy grin and a porn-star mustache.

He spoke with an aw-shucks voice, "Well, howdy there, guys. I was just about to go around and introduce myself to everyone. Why don't you fellows step inside for a minute, take a seat and let me introduce myself. My name is Kerry. I'm a junior. I'm a psychology major, which is short for psychology, and I'm going to be your Wing Director. Are you familiar with the role of the Wing Director? Before you answer that, why don't you guys tell me who you are? Okay?"

We sat a moment, absorbing the new information. I looked around the room.

It looks like he has a single room, too. Not many decorations, only a few photos, and it's kind of Spartan.

On his dresser top, I noticed a wooden chess board with onyx-carved playing pieces, like the kind sold to tourists in Mexico. Sitting next to the chessboard was a red cardboard box decorated with the familiar Trojan icon. The box read, "Lubricated Condoms—24 pack."

What kind of message is that supposed to send to the wing?

QP broke the silence, pointing to us as he spoke, "Hi, I'm QP. This is Chuck, Casey, and Joe. We represent almost all of the sophomores of Second East. We just went through the entire wing, introducing ourselves to the incoming freshmen."

Chuck said, "Yeah, and we said they could see us if they had any questions. We'd be happy to help.

"You did? What a groovy idea!"

Did he say groovy?

Kerry continued, "Tell you what, guys, since you all just went around the wing and welcomed everyone, I don't have to! I'll go around later, like tonight or maybe tomorrow morning." He stood up, pulled a condom from the box, and shoved it in his pocket.

"I'm going over to Whitney Hall now. I've got to see how my girlfriend is doing with her moving in and all that. Yeah, she might need some help moving in.

He likely wants to help her with some moving in and out.

JUST MISSED THE SIXTIES

Well, it was nice meeting you guys. It was really groovy!"
Wow, he just said groovy again!
He shook our hands. We filed out the door.

Come Together

    Most of Hyer Hall, Second East, came to my room the next night for our little wing party, the "meet your new wingmates" festivity. I was looking forward to showing off my room. QP, Chuck, Casey, and I ate dinner together and went directly to my room from the dining hall. Soon, there was knocking on the door, and the new wingmates began arriving in a steady stream. Quickly, there were 12 of us crammed onto the two beds, desk chairs, or seated on the floor. Most everyone offered compliments on either the room décor or the sound system, which at the moment was playing *Abbey Road*.

    Yes! This is why I put in all that effort!

    Al said, "Nice stereo, how many watts?"

    "50."

    "Cool – mine's 100."

    I looked at QP. He cleared his throat and began addressing the group. "Thanks, everybody, for coming to our little get-together. I hope you had a good first day, finding your classes and all that fun stuff." He paused as if he'd just run out of things to say, then continued, "Oh yeah, by the way, in case you forgot, I'm QP. Even though we met you all yesterday, why don't we just go around the room and everyone say their names for everyone else to hear? Okay? You start it out, Jay."

    "Hi, I'm Jay. I'm in room 201. Come by and say 'Hi' anytime you want, you know what I mean. Also, most importantly, if you need something special, you know what I mean; I can probably help you out. And, oh yeah, my roommate, William, couldn't make it tonight. He had to go home and visit his girlfriend one more time if you know what I mean."

JUST MISSED THE SIXTIES

Alright, we know what you mean already!

The last to say his name was Casey. Immediately after Casey introduced himself, Al said, "Quick! Someone alert Hollywood! One of the munchkins has escaped! Heh, heh, heh!"

Oh no! He's making fun of Casey's height!

There was a moment of silence, and then Tim said, "What a fry!"

Casey looks upset! I must think of a distraction! Quickly!

I said, "Hey! I promised you guys a taste of the local brew! Well, Spitz, could you do us all a favor and open up my little mini-fridge in the closet and start passing around the Point Beers? This brew has an interesting flavor, slightly different from your Miller or your Pabst. There's more flavor to it if you know what I mean."

Oh brother, now I'm talking like Jay!

Everyone was excited to try a can of Point Beer. It was fun to see their reactions. I felt like a good host.

Al said, "I hear we got a wing full of far-out hippie freaks!"

QP said, "Yeah! We're all cool."

Al said, "Well, that's just great. I came to college to learn stuff and get educated, and they go and put me in a wing with a bunch of brain-dead, stoner fuck-ups. That's just fucking great... well actually... I love it!"

Casey said, "Speak for yourself, Al."

Al said, "Oh yeah? Well fuck you too. Heh, heh, heh!'

Shit! I've got to think quickly again. Oh yeah! The fan!

I said, "Hey, Guys! I've got just the thing to go with that Point Beer, " and pulled out a joint.

Tim said, "Hey, you can't smoke that in here! You'll get us all into trouble!"

"No worries! I've got a fan!" I walked to the window, opened the curtain, and did my best, Vanna White. Taa-daa!

"I will now turn on this fan and light a marijuana cigarette. Say, Jay, could you push that towel over by the bottom of the door so it blocks the crack?"

JUST MISSED THE SIXTIES

I lit the joint and took a puff. I blew out smoke in front of the fan, so everyone could see it get sucked away and quickly exit out the window.

Spitz said, "That's fantastic! I've got to get one of those!"

I turned around just in time to see ten joints being lit simultaneously.

Holy shit! Good crowd!

Tim said, "What a fry!"

After that, it got intense, puffing and passing all those joints. It started quickly: puff, pass, puff, pass, puff, pass. Then time seemed to slow: puff..., pass..., puff..., pass... People got confused and started to giggle.

I forgot – am I supposed to puff now or pass?

I looked around the room—everyone was smiling. I said, "Hey, everyone! Yesterday, our new Wing Director, Kerry, said our wing is really... dig this. He said our wing is really... groovy! Hee! Hee! Hee!"

Al said, "Wow! Look at me! I'm groovy!"

I started laughing and couldn't stop. Soon, everyone was laughing nonstop.

Fifteen minutes later, QP said, "Whew! Man, I'm starving. Joe, do you have any food?"

Oh damn! I forgot about the munchies!

I said, "Hey, I got an idea! Why don't we truck to the K-Mart a block away and pick up something to eat? Personally, I could use a bowl of Sugar Pops right now!"

Spitz said, "Mmmmm, Sugar Pops! That sounds soooo good!"

Chuck said, "Oh yeah, and while we're there, we can pick up a fan for our room, right QP?"

"That's cool."

Spitz said, "Field trip!"

Ten minutes later, we were standing in the cereal aisle at K-mart.

Spitz said, "Ah, Fruit Loops, I love those!"

JUST MISSED THE SIXTIES

"Just pick out your favorite, guys. I'll get some plastic bowls and spoons. Meet me by the fans."

I wondered what the lady at the check-out thought when she rang up twelve of us in a row, each holding a box of cereal and a window fan. I was last in line with a large jug of milk, a box of Sugar Pops, and some bowls and spoons.

Looking at the weary, middle-aged cashier, I said, "Pretty unusual sight, eh?"

She looked up, straight into my bloodshot eyes, and said, "Ain't nothing I ain't never seen before."

I'm impressed! That had to be a quadruple negative!

We returned to my room and enjoyed our feast. Nothing could have tasted better. After everyone had their fill, my new wingmates said good night and left for their rooms, fans in their hands.

The next day, leaving for my morning classes, I glanced back at the dorm and the windows of Second East. Every one of them, but two, contained a large fan.

Wow! That's a lot of suction!

It was said that when all the fans of Second East were spinning, the breeze would blow all the papers off the desk in the lobby, and the updraft in the stairwell could knock your hat off!

JUST MISSED THE SIXTIES

The Co-ed Wing Party

The next day, after our last afternoon classes, Casey and I met at the Student Union for a few games of pinball. As usual, Casey dominated the game with his crazy flipper fingers. In contrast, my greatest skill was always the tilt.

Walking back into Second East, we noticed a new posting on the wing bulletin board. It read like an invitation:

> What: Co-Ed Wing Party
> Who: Second East and Third East, Hyer Hall
> When: This Friday at 7:00 PM
> Where: Second Floor Common Room
> Why: Make new friends and have fun!
> Beverages will be provided.

Great! This is my chance to meet some of the girls in the dorm!
As if reading my mind, Casey said, "Hey, Joe, looks like this will be your opportunity to get some female action!"

I said, "What about you, Casey? You're not going to spend Friday night staring at the wall, are you?"

"No sirree, Joe, you don't have to worry about me; I'll be getting my share!" he started singing, "They got a crazy way of loving there, and I'm gonna get me some."

Soon, it was Friday, and Casey came by to walk with me to the party.

I said, "Hey, Casey, where's Don? Doesn't he want to come?"

"Oh, he's probably at the UPS. Since he got that job, I hardly see him anymore."

I started thinking of a game plan for the party.

Okay, once the introductions are done, when there's a good time, I'll ask a girl if she'd like to come to my room to check out the decorations, have some wine, and listen to music. That's it. That's the plan. Now focus!

With a strategy in mind, I entered the Common Room. On the center table was a shiny aluminum barrel of brew, surrounded by stacks of red plastic cups. On opposite sides of the table were two circles of chairs. Sitting in the front circle, Kerry spotted Casey and me and waved us over.

"Come over here, fellas! I'm so glad you could join us! Patti, the Wing Director of the third floor, has already filled up her group. So, I guess you're stuck with me. Don't worry, I don't bite! Har! Har! Grab a beer and set yourself down. It's time to start this groovy little hootenanny."

What the hell's a hootenanny? Anyway, it looks like they got something planned.

We got some beer and sat down in Kerry's circle. Kerry told us to sit alternating boys and girls.

Okay! That gives me two girls to hit on, for starters!

I nodded to my new wingmates in the circle.

Kerry started the party. "Well, howdy, everyone!" He displayed his big, toothy grin. "Welcome to our first Hyer Hall co-ed party of the year. My name is Kerry, and I'm the Wing Director of Second East. On the other side of the table is Patti, the Wing Director of Third East. I'd like to start the evening with a little ice-breaker called the Name Game. It's really simple. Here's how to play. I'm going to point at someone, and that person has to say their name followed by something they like; it could be anything, but it has to start with the same first letter as your name. For example, let's say I'm starting. I could say my name is Kerry, and I like koala bears. See? It's no big deal. Then, I will point to the next person who has to say their name, followed by what I said I like and THEN what they like. So, let's say I point to some guy named Bob

JUST MISSED THE SIXTIES

(I know there's no Bob here); Bob has to say, my name is Bob, and I like koala bears and balloons. And then, Bob points to the next person. Get it? You see, it starts to build up, and it gets harder. The third guy has to say three likes – koala Bears, balloons, and what they like. Etc. Etc. If you goof, you have to chug your beer and start it going again. Eventually, by golly, you'll learn everybody's names!

"Okay, I'll start. My name is Kerry, and I like koala bears." Then he pointed at Jay.

Really? Koala bears? He couldn't think of anything new?

"Okay, my name is Jay, and I like koala bears and..."

I wonder if he's thinking of joints.

"Jelly toast!" Then he pointed at Casey.

"My name is Casey, and I like koala bears and jelly toast and..."

I bet Casey is thinking cunts.

"Cameras!" Then he pointed at a girl directly across from him.

Al said, "Gosh, Casey, I thought you would say 'caves.'"

Casey said, "Now, why would I say caves, Al?"

Al said, "Because Hobbits live in caves. Heh, heh, heh!"

Casey replied, deadpan, "Ha, Ha, very funny, Al."

The girl across from Casey decided she'd better continue the game and said, "Uh, hi. My name is Rita, and I like koala bears, jelly toast, cameras, and, uh... rutabagas!" Everyone laughed. She pointed at Al.

What the hell is he going to say?

Al said, "Well, let's see. My name is Al, and I like koala bears, jelly toast, cameras, rutabagas and, and, I don't know... ass?"

That elicited some gasps from the group; one girl looked at Kerry to see his reaction.

Casey said quietly, "It takes one to know one."

Kerry smiled his big toothy grin and said, "Oh, that's fine. Now everyone has to say they like ass too!"

This is going to be fun!

The game continued. In the beginning, most of us goofed up at about 9 or 10 items (except for the Professor, who displayed an incredible memory), so plenty of beer was consumed. As time went by, just remembering three items became difficult. But eventually (by golly), we knew the names of everyone in our group. There was a lull, and I turned to the girl on my left, a dark-haired Annette Funicello-type with an unusually loud laugh.

"Hi there, Alice, who likes apples. Would you like to see my room? It's decorated really cool."

Alice laughed loudly, looked into my eyes, and said, "I better not."

What does that mean, "I better not?" That sounds like a chocolate bar: delicious but fattening.

I turned to the red-haired, freckle-faced girl on my right and worked the same pitch: "Hello, Sarah, who likes snowflakes, would…"

"No! Thank you."

Man! I was shot down before I could even deliver the pitch! I need another beer.

As I approached the keg, I saw a blonde blur out of the corner of my eye. I turned to apologize for possibly skipping in line. I couldn't believe my eyes.

Is Joni Mitchell at our party?

Joni Mitchell on the *Clouds* LP

JUST MISSED THE SIXTIES

Without realizing it, I said aloud, "Joni Mitchell!"

She looked at me with cobalt blue eyes and said, "I'm sorry, did you say something?"

"Oh! I'm sorry! I was thinking to myself how nice it would be to hear some Joni Mitchell right now."

"Oh really? I have all her albums!"

"That's cool! Say, ah, can I fill a glass of beer for you?"

"I don't know. I was debating with myself about getting another glass. You see, I'm not a big fan of beer. I know that sounds weird, living in Milwaukee and all that."

"You live in Milwaukee?"

"Well, I used to; now, I live about 20 miles outside Milwaukee, in Germantown. But I grew up on 91st Street."

"Oh my God, I live on 91st Street! But it's actually in Wauwatosa, not Milwaukee."

"Oooh… Wauwatosa… that must be nice!"

"Yeah, I guess. Hey, I've got an idea. I've got some wine in my room. Why don't you grab a couple of your Joni Mitchell albums? We can listen to them on my new stereo system and drink some wine!"

"That sounds like fun! I've got some chocolate chip cookies – I'll bring those too!"

Hmmm, do chocolate chip cookies really go with Strawberry Hill?

"Yeah, that'll be great. I'm in room 206. Oh yeah, I'm Joe, and you are?"

"Rachel. I'll see you soon!"

Minutes later, we were sitting cross-legged on my bed, facing each other. Between us lay a plate of cookies and two plastic glasses full of bright red artificially colored and flavored wine. Joni Mitchell's "Chelsea Morning" was playing on the sound system. It sounded great.

I said, "Man, I love this song. It is so upbeat!"

"I love it too!"

"After this, I'll have to play some of my Bob Dylan collection for you."

JUST MISSED THE SIXTIES

"Oh yeah, that would be far out. I love some of his early stuff like "Blowing in the Wind" and "A Hard Rain's Gonna Fall." That's when he was writing songs to try and change the world."

"I know what you mean! Once, there was a time when people wrote songs that really meant something, you know? Say, what are you here at Stevens Point for? You don't want to be a forest ranger, do you?"

She laughed, "Oh, no, I don't want to be a forest ranger, although I love the woods. You do realize that besides forestry, Point has a great Elementary Education Department? Anyway, I want to be a teacher. Maybe I'll teach on one of those Indian reservations up north. They can use the help."

"What a nice idea."

Wow, this is going great!

Then, the mood was broken by a knock on the door.

Oh damn! Who could that be? That's why I got a single room - so I wouldn't be disturbed!

It was Casey, and he wasn't alone. Standing very close to Casey, so close that a single molecule of air couldn't have blown between them, was a short, perky honey-blonde with a pixie cut.

Wow! He found someone shorter than he is!

"Hey, Joe, I was hoping we'd find you here. Can we join you? You know, it's kind of nice to get away from that party. And that Al is starting to get on my nerves!"

Hmmm. Maybe I should have put a necktie on my doorknob. Oh, that's right... I don't have a necktie!

They walked in before I could answer and made themselves comfortable on the other bed. I introduced Rachel to Casey and Cricket, and Casey introduced us to Cricket.

Is she going to start chirping or hop right into the sack?

Soon, I discovered that Cricket's favorite word was "yes."

I said, "Would you like some wine?"

"Yes."

Rachel said, "Would you like a cookie?"

"Yes."

Casey said, "Would you like to make out?"

"Yes!"

It didn't take long for Casey and Cricket to get going. For a few minutes, Rachel and I watched incredulously as they groped at each other. When their tops came off, we discretely left the room.

Thank you, Casey! This is precisely why I don't have a roommate!

Rachel and I strolled down the hallway to the back stairwell.

Rachel said, "I think that the beer, wine, and cookies are starting to have a weird effect on my stomach. I better call it a night."

I stopped at the stairway door and said, "Yeah, I know what you mean. Can I see you tomorrow?"

"You mean, like a date?"

"Kind of, we could…"

Think fast; she likes nature and activism, and I have little money. Hmm…

"How about I show you the world-famous campus, North Woods? We can bring a trash bag to clean up any litter we find along the way – to help make the world cleaner!"

She laughed and said, "That's a great idea!"

I said, "Meet me in the Dining Hall at 9:00 a.m. It would be nice to have a cup of coffee before we go."

"It's a date!" she said, then leaned forward to give me a quick kiss on the lips. "Good night."

Alrighty!

After Rachel left, I waited in Casey's and Don's room, watching Casey's TV until he finished his Cricket. I had mixed emotions. I was pissed that Casey had ruined the moment in my room with Rachel but happy that I would get to see her tomorrow!

Finally, Casey returned. I was ready to yell at him, mainly because I didn't want to hear any stupid, trivial details about Cricket's body, but Casey cut me short.

"Listen, Joe. I'm sorry I took over your room. It was your time, and I just butted in. I'll never do that again, man. I owe you one. Say,

JUST MISSED THE SIXTIES

I'm really tired. I'm gonna hit the sack right now. Good night, Joe." Then, he began changing into his night clothes. I left without yelling.
What? No stupid, trivial details? Why is he different this time?

The Date

I set the alarm for 8:00 AM to make my 9:00 AM date with Rachel. After washing and dressing in my favorite jeans, I arrived at the Dining Hall to find it practically deserted.

I bet 99% of the students are sleeping off their first Friday night parties.

I spotted Rachel, dressed in bib overalls, sitting at a table and sipping a mug of hot chocolate. She was paging through the campus newspaper, *The Pointer*.

"Good morning, Rachel!" She set down her mug and gave me a big, bright smile. It knocked my socks off.

"Good morning, Joe!"

"Wow! Uh… well. I'll grab some coffee and be right back."

When I returned, she said, "So, are you ready to go out and pick up some litter in the woods?"

"Oh! Yes! Sure! I have a blanket, a couple of joints, matches, and the leftover wine from last night. Pretty good, huh?"

"What about a… you know… a garbage bag?"

She got me! What is that? Does she have a cute little smirk on her face?

I paused and said, "Right… just a second… I'll be right back after I go to the bathroom".

OK, think fast.

Walking into the men's room, I saw the answer: a trash bin containing a freshly installed, empty plastic garbage bag.

Thank you, janitor-guy, wherever you are!

I twisted off the top of the garbage bin, one of those large metal torpedoes, and yanked out the bag. The can fell to the floor. CRASH!

When I returned, proudly displaying the bag, Rachel smiled and asked, "Are you okay? I heard a really loud noise!"

"No problem! I just slipped on some wet floor and knocked over a garbage can, but I'm okay! Somebody should invent a little sign that warns people if the floor is wet! Anyway, I've got a garbage bag, see? Let's finish our drinks and get out to the woods, shall we?"

Soon, we were walking past the dorms and into the North Woods. There was plenty of work for us to do right there along the road, filling the bag with litter that motorists had chucked out of their car windows.

Picking up a soda can, Rachel said, "This makes me mad that some stupid slob has to throw his empty soda can out of his car window instead of taking it home and putting it into the trash. I mean, how hard is that?"

"I know! It's ridiculous! Sometimes, I'd like to follow the dude home and throw all the garbage on his lawn. Let's see how he feels about that!"

"Hah! That's a great idea. Say, Joe, when I'm doing this kind of stuff, you know, like we're doing, making the world a better place and all that… I get a good feeling, making me want to get more involved. Do you ever feel like that, Joe?"

Like, since I was ten.

"Yes. Yes, I do!"

"So, what's something we can do?"

That's an excellent question. There's not much going on in Point. What in our world is an issue? Hard classes? Dormitory life? Wait, I remember that QP thought the mandatory dorm time was stupid.

"Rachel, I think we need to fight for student's rights!"

"Student's rights? What do you mean?"

"Did you know that when you attend the University, they can tell you where to live for your first two years? Tell you… heck, they force you to live in their dormitories for your freshman and sophomore years! They say, 'You have no choice; you live where we tell you.' Well, I say, what the hell does that have to do with getting an education?

Absolutely nothing! That's what! It's wrong! It's a form of repression, and it should be stopped right now!"

Hmmm...I think I sounded pretty dramatic!

"You're right, Joe. I hadn't thought of it before, but you're absolutely right! We should organize! Organize to protest the oppression by our school!"

"Right, we'll start a movement – power to the people and all that. Hey! Look! Here's the path that leads to the Clearing!"

"The Clearing? What's that?"

"Well, Casey, Don, and I discovered it last year when we were looking for a nice place to toke up, and we took this very path into the woods ..."

And then I told Rachel the story of the Clearing, the lean-to, Gary, and the Woodcocks. As we entered the Clearing, I pointed out the triangle trees and the location of the lean-to.

"Well, just like Don said, the lean-to is gone."

Rachel said, "Say, Joe, maybe someday we could rebuild something here, maybe something a little bigger than a lean-to, like a hut!"

"A hut! I like how you think!"

I spread the blanket out on the grass. We sat, sharing the wine and reefer.

Looking around, Rachel said, "This is just like paradise."

I said, "Well, let's hope they don't take paradise and put up a parking lot!"

She laughed and said, "No, really. I love the woods."

"Me too! I do, too! Last year, I was a forestry major! But, after one semester, I changed my major."

"Really? You were a forestry-major? Okay, what were some of the things you learned?"

Pointing at some nearby trees, I said, "See that tree? That's a Red Pine, and that one's a Jack Pine, and that one's a Scots Pine, and that's a White Pine."

"Really? What's the difference?"

"Actually, I have no idea. I'm just happy to know that they're pine trees. Oh, and we also learned how to look at any tree and calculate, in our heads just by looking at it, how many boards you could get from the tree."

"Okay, smarty-pants," she said, pointing at a towering White Ash. "How many boards can you get from that tree?"

"I'm afraid it would be just one."

"One? That tree is huge."

"Yes, that's true. It would be one giant toothpick for a really, really big dude."

Rachel laughed, crawled close to me, and kissed me. We kissed lightly for a good thirty seconds.

Wow, her lips are soft. This is nice.

Then, she pulled away and said softly, "So, Joe, what's your major now?"

"Biology."

"Okay. Tell me something you've learned in Biology."

"Well. I learned the four things life is made of; do you know what they are?"

"Hmmm, let me think about that for a second. Is the answer love, music, chocolate, and kittens?"

"Well, that sounds like an enjoyable life, but, and this is very important, you forgot one thing."

"Oh yeah? What did I forget?"

"Me." I pulled her close and resumed the kissing. She responded with a higher level of intensity. A level I'd never encountered previously

Wow! It's time to go for broke!

"Hey, Rachel, let's make out."

"Sounds like fun. Do you have any protection?"

Crap! She got me again! I don't suppose I can find anything in a restroom in the woods?

"Oh. No, I don't. I'm sorry."

I must have looked incredibly bummed because Rachel laughed and said, "Well, you'll just have to settle for a hand job!"

JUST MISSED THE SIXTIES

I'll settle! I'll settle!

JUST MISSED THE SIXTIES

Within You, Without You

She said, "Lie back on the blanket, relax, and you can smoke this other reefer all by yourself."

I lay back. She struck a match, started the joint with a big puff, and passed it to me. "It's all yours now. Enjoy. I'll be down here."

I looked up at the blue, blue sky.

It's cobalt, just like her eyes!

A few tufts of white drifted high above us. I exhaled and blew the smoke up to join the clouds. After watching the tendrils of smoke drift away, I shut my eyes.

I imagined I was far, far away, in an ancient mystical land in the Far East. Beautiful sitar music could be heard in the distance. I was walking through a fog that swirled as I passed. Treading a narrow path of small, polished stones lined with bamboo shoots, I began climbing a small hill. At the top, I spied, through the mist, an ancient Buddhist temple. A curtain of beads hung from an arched doorway. I pushed through the beads. A single figure was seated before me, in the lotus position, on a rice mat. He was surrounded by smoking incense sticks and burning candles. He had no hair, a large belly, and wore only a thong.

He said, "Namaste. I am Far East Man."

I said, "Namaste to you, Far East Man. I am Joseph.

He said, "Joseph, may I ask what you seek?"

"Yes, you may."

"Do you seek knowledge, enlightenment, or maybe... you are just looking to get your rocks off?"

"I seek... um... that last thing you mentioned."

"I see."

"But, you know, someday... I'm sure I'll be looking for those other things too."

"Very well, then. Do what I say. Please turn around and look back through the entryway."

I turned around. Parting the strings of beads, I looked over the treetops at the surrounding countryside. I could feel that something was happening out there: Something big.

"Joseph, soon you will see a volcano emerging above the trees, rising towards the heavens. This is what you must do. Run to the volcano. And when you reach the volcano, you must fling yourself upon it; when it erupts, you too will erupt. You must erupt with the volcano. That is my message. That is all I have to say."

I turned to say "Thank you" to the Far East Man, but I saw he was gone. In his place, also in the lotus position, was the Fonz. He gave me a thumbs-up and said, "Namast-Ehhhh!"

I spun around and followed the Far East Man's instructions, running to the volcano.

Afterward, I opened my eyes. Rachel was looking at me.

"Oh my God, Rachel, that was amazing! I was a freaking volcano!"

"Yeah. I noticed. Next time, bring some protection!" And then I remembered.

Kerry's got some protection sitting right there on his dresser!

Campfire Stories I

On Monday, I ate dinner at the Dining Hall with QP, Chuck, Casey, and Don and told the boys about my date with Rachel.

"We picked up some litter on the roadside and then took the path to the Clearing. And that's where we shared some pot and talked and stuff."

Casey said, "And stuff? I know what stuff is! Heh! Heh! Heh!"

I said, "Yeah, yeah, yeah..."

QP said, "Hey, look! Joseph is blushing! Wait a minute! Say, guys, I just had a great idea! Why don't we take all the freshmen out tonight and show them the Clearing?"

Chuck said, "Yeah! Let's do it!"

Don said, "Wish I could be there, guys, but I'm off to work."

After dinner, we went to K-Mart and bought some cold brew. Then, back at the dorm, we met Al in the hallway.

QP said, "Hey, Al, are you interested in joining us for a beer in the woods?

Al said, "Does the Pope shit in the woods? Are bears Catholic?"

Next thing you know, Al was going door-to-door with us, knocking and yelling for all the wingmates to come out and have a beer in the woods like real men. He wouldn't take no for an answer.

Spitz tried to say no. "Sorry, Al, I can't. I've got to do some reading for tomorrow."

"You can read later after you've gotten wasted in the woods. You'll probably read better that way. Hell, I know I do! Now get your candy-ass out of that room before we have to go in there and drag you out! We're all out here waiting just for you!" The door opened, and Spitz stepped into the hall.

Oh yes, there's nothing like a little gentle peer pressure!

Our numbers grew. When it was time for our gang of recruits and volunteers to move towards the stairwell, we met Rachel coming down to our floor.

"Where are you guys going?"

I said, "Hi, Rachel! We're going to show the Clearing to the new freshmen. Wanna come?"

"I don't know…"

Tim said, "Come on, Rachel, you're one of us now: an honorary Second Easter!"

"Okay, sure!"

As the gang from Second East, plus Rachel, filed down the stairway, I didn't notice Casey turn around at the top of the stairs and walk back to his room.

Rachel was by my side as I hiked up the road to the woods. I let QP and Chuck catch up so I could share some of my plans for the evening.

I said, "We can build a fire in the old fire pit… by the three pines. Then we can tell jokes and stories and stuff like that. Sound okay? Just follow my lead, okay? Here, let me help you carry some of that beer!"

Chuck said, "Aye, aye, sir. No problem, Captain."

Captain? Yeah! I like that! And QP, Chuck, and Al are my lieutenants!

I laughed and said, "This is our chance, guys! Our chance to mold these tiny little freshmen minds to our wills!"

Rachel pointed and said, "It's a little hard to see in the dark, but… look! I think that's the path to the clearing."

Turning to hike the path into the woods, I looked back at our crew. I noticed Al was wearing a black, early Dylan-style, working-class hero cap. William was decked out in his cowboy hat, vest, and boots. Chuck and QP were carrying a couple of cases of beer, and Jay was toting a leather pouch.

Oh yeah! I bet he's got something good in that pouch!

JUST MISSED THE SIXTIES

Rachel and I led the way up the path to the Clearing and the fire pit. I turned and ordered everyone to gather a load of firewood. Once the wood was gathered, William whipped up a nicely burning campfire like he'd been doing every day of his life.

Al said, "Just like out on the trail, eh, cowboy?"

William said, "Yeah, right. Something like that."

I said, "Everyone, let's all sit around the fire. I was going to say that QP and Chuck should pass around the beers, but it looks like they're already doing it! Anyway, welcome to the Clearing. I want you all to know that this is a special place, a sacred place."

Al said, "Sacred place? No shit!"

"Yes, shit! You see, for many years, UWSP students have been coming to this very spot in this clearing to celebrate nature's gifts." I held up a beer in one hand and a joint in the other. "So, let's celebrate again tonight to honor the many students who have been here before us."

QP and Chuck said, "Here, here! Let's have a beer! A toast! To the many students who have been before us!" they held up their cans.

Everyone toasted.

I said, "There's another special thing about this place in the woods. Once upon a time, in years past, there was a little wooden structure right here. We called it the Hut. It was built of logs, branches, and rope. It was, one could say, a home away from the dorm. Here, at the hut, students could escape the stress of campus life and relax in the peaceful woods. They could even stay overnight in the hut if they felt like it. It was great. But, alas, the Hut, for unknown reasons, ceased to exist last summer. Well, I'd like to fix that. I propose that we rebuild the Hut this semester!" I looked at QP.

QP paused momentarily before realizing he should follow my lead and said, "Uh... I second that motion!"

Chuck said, "Yeah, right... I third it!"

Jay and William were much more enthused and planned to come out the next afternoon to start the rebuilding. Yay! Most everyone caught the spirit and agreed to help.

Al said, "I wish everyone would shut the fuck up and pass me a joint!"

Soon, with the consumption of beer and pot and the passage of time, the campfire took on magical qualities, dancing hypnotically before our eyes.

I broke the silence and said, "Let's take turns telling jokes, or stories, or anything else you might want to say about yourself. Who wants to go first? How about you, Rachel?"

"Okay, Joe. I'm Rachel, and I'm here to become a teacher. Someday, I'd like to help teach Indian children living on a reservation."

Al said, "Really? What are you, some kind of goody-two-shoes?"

Tim said, "No, Al, look. She's wearing Earth Shoes, not goody-two-shoes."

Al said, "What the fuck are Earth Shoes."

Jay said, "You don't know what Earth Shoes are? Look at how the soles are designed differently than regular shoes. It's supposed to be good for your arches."

Al said, "Looks like the heels are in the front! Anybody wearing those things is going to start walking backward!" Then he snorted and said, "The way I see it, if I'm lucky, I'll be walking backward by the end of the night, if I'm walking at all!" Then he took another toke and said, "Jay, since you know so much, why don't you go next."

Jay said, "Cool! Anyway, Rachel, those are some nice shoes."

"Thanks, Jay!"

Jay had a story to share. "Once a couple buddies of mine drove to Tijuana to score some Gold (you know Acapulco Gold), and they had the trunk loaded up with about five keys (you know kilos). They cost about three grand, and they were trying to cross the border, in my 4x4 that they'd borrowed, through the desert at night, and this rancher dude sees them crossing his land and thinks they're some cattle rustlers and starts shooting his shotgun. Man, they were freaked! BBs were zinging all around them! But they cleared out to the highway and got away! Check it out sometime - my Jeep still has some BBs stuck in the bumper! Good thing nobody got hurt, except one of my buddies lost an eye, no big deal."

Silence around the campfire. Looking over at Tim, I saw his eyes were wide as saucers.

Tim said, "What a fry!"

Al said, "That's fucking insane, Jay, did you just make that shit up?"

"No way, man! You're smoking some of it right now! Pretty good stuff, eh?"

Al said, "Yeah, I still don't believe it. What about you, Joe? Do you have anything normal to say? What brings you here, to the University of Wisconsin, Stevens Point?"

"Well, I came here to be a forest ranger last year. I figured that's a good job for someone who wants to smoke pot in the woods. But then I realized I was terrible at forestry and liked my biology classes better, so I switched to biology. And you know what? It turned out okay because even biologists can smoke pot in the woods, right?"

Al said, "So you want to be a biologist, eh? So, tell us, Joe, what's something you've learned in Biology Class?"

I said, "Okay. I learned that all living things are made of the same four basic components. Do you know what they are?"

Jay chimed in, "I know! The four basic components are uppers, downers, hallucinogens, and opiates."

Tim laughed, "Jay, those are four kinds of drugs!"

Al said, "Well, I guess that's Jay's life in a nutshell."

Jay said, "Oops! I forgot about the cocaine-derivatives. That would make five components."

Al said, "That's enough from you, Jay. Okay, Joe, we're stumped. What are the four basic components of all living things?"

"Al, the four basic components of all living things are sugars, proteins, fats, and nucleic acids."

Al said, "You know what, Joe, I'm sorry I asked because I don't give a rat's ass. This brings me to my next question: what the hell will you do as a biologist?"

JUST MISSED THE SIXTIES

"I'd like to get a job with a pharmaceutical company, researching to find new drugs."

Al's face lit up, "New drugs? Now you're talking! Count me in, Joe! Listen, when you get this drug research job, look me up. I'll be one of your guinea pigs. All you got to do is feed me, give me a place to shit, sleep and listen to music. Then, I'll take any damn thing you want to give me."

I said, "Okay, Al, I'll remember to look you up!"

"Cool!"

Man, this guy's serious! I'd love to know what he told his guidance counselor!

Then, Tim said, "Well, I'm sitting next to Jay, so I'll go next. I have a riddle for you guys. We like to tell this one to the customers at the resort. Let's see if anyone can figure it out.

One day, three guys are checking into a motel. They're going to share one room. The man at the front desk says the room costs 150 bucks. So, they split it 3-ways, each guy putting in $50. They get the key and go to the room. Later, the man at the desk realizes he overcharged them because the room should only cost $125. So, he sends his son to the room with five five-dollar bills. The kid decides to get into the action and cut himself some of the money, so he gives each man back one of the fives and pockets the other two. So, here's the mystery: each man paid $45 for the room, right? And so, three times $45 is $135. The kid kept two fives, so $135 plus $10 is $145. Where did the other five dollars go?"

Al said, "How the fuck do you expect us to figure out that shit? We're all stoned!"

Then, the Professor said, "Oh, I get it, it's easy! The motel got $125, the kid got $10, and the guests got back $15. One hundred twenty-five plus ten plus fifteen equals one hundred and fifty! The concept of adding the ten dollars to the one hundred and thirty-five dollars is just a ruse so that you'll think…"

Al cut him off, "Oh, shut the fuck up and tell me some other time, like, when I'm straight. Actually, don't ever tell me because I don't give a rat's ass."

William said, "Yeah, because who needs to know arithmetic when you're a guinea pig for a drug company?"

Al said, "Well, well! So, the cowboy speaks! Howdy, partner! Golly gee, I reckon you can talk next! What do ya say there, Hop-A-long?"

Dead silence. Then William said, "Are you talking to me, Al?"

"You see anybody else here dressed up like a fucking cowboy? Hey, desperado, shouldn't you be out mending some fences? It's your turn, Tex!"

Dead silence, once again. Then William yanked a cigarette off his ear and shoved it in his mouth. Next, the CLICK of his silver Zippo echoed in the woods. WHOOSH! He took a puff and looked at Al. "I got a story for you, boy."

"Well then, let's hear it, cowpoke."

William said, "One day, I found out my girlfriend was cheating on me with some other guy. So, the next Saturday night, I staked out her house. I was sitting in my car when I saw some dude drive up and park in her driveway. Minutes later, she comes running outside and hops into his car. They took off, and I followed them. They drove to a bar, parked, and went inside. Looking through the window, I spotted where they were sitting. So, I got a baseball bat out of my car and hid it under a long jacket. I snuck inside the bar and stealthily snuck into the men's room without them seeing me. I hid inside a stall for about 15 minutes before the dude finally decided he had to pee. I watched him walk up to the urinal. Then, while he was pissing, I stepped out behind him and beat the shit out of him with my bat. End of story." Then he stared at Al. Al stared back.

Tim said, "Oh my God! What a fry!"

I said, "Remember, dudes, it's make love, not war!"

Still staring at Al, William said, "You know, Al, I've got that bat back in my room, right here at Hyer Hall. Maybe someday I'd like to... *introduce* it to you."

Al said, "What are you, some kind of fucking psycho? Well, you don't scare me!"

William said, "And why's that, Al?"

JUST MISSED THE SIXTIES

Then, I yelled, "Because both your boots are on fire!"

While those two had been engaged in their little stare-down, I'd taken a long stick, lighted the end in the fire, and used it to light the stubble of dry grass beneath their feet. With all the smoke going up, it appeared that their shoes were actually on fire.

Al and William both shouted, "You fucker!" and began quickly patting down their footwear, just to discover that only the grass was burning. Everyone laughed, and the tension was relieved. Rachel commented that I had a knack for doing the right thing at the right time.

Yeah, but how long can I keep that up?

QP went next. He asked, " Have you ever watched *The Twilight Zone*?"

Al said, "Who the hell hasn't watched *The Twilight Zone*?"

QP said, "That's true, Al. One of my favorite episodes is about the pocket watch that stops time. The episode is a good one, but what's super freaky is what happened after the show aired – and it's a true story! Anyway, here's the plot of the episode.

This dude gets a letter telling him that a distant uncle has died, and he has to travel across the country to pick up an item that was left to him in his uncle's will. When he arrives, the estate executor hands him a little box and says, 'That's it.' That's all his uncle left to him, just one little box. So, the dude says 'Thanks' and returns to his hotel room. Once he gets to his room, he looks inside the box and finds, apparently, just an ordinary pocket watch. It has a button on the top for winding - pull the button out and turn it to set the time, you know the drill. So, he pulls it up and sets the time. Then, he pushes it down to wind the spring but accidentally pushes the button even further in the winding process. There's a loud CLICK, and then... he notices everything is dead quiet. It's weird because the hotel is in a large, noisy city. There's no traffic noise. He can't hear TVs or people talking in the other rooms. Nothing. So, he pushes the button again, and all the noises are back: TVs, honking horns, talking, and even a helicopter flying by the window. So, he jumps off the bed and goes to the window. Looking at the helicopter, he presses the button again. The helicopter stops, the

JUST MISSED THE SIXTIES

noise is gone; it appears to be hanging in mid-air! He can clearly see each propeller blade, and they're not moving! He presses the button again, and the helicopter flies away as if nothing has happened. He presses the button several more times to convince himself that it's really happening. Stop the world and start the world, etc.

He's amazed at first but then slowly realizes the potential of his new possession. If the watch can stop time for everyone and everything except him, it also means that when time is stopped, he can do anything he wants! So, he stops time once again and goes down the stairs to the hotel's kitchen. He walks in and sees all the staff frozen in place. He grabs a cart used for bussing tables and exits the hotel to the city sidewalks. About a block away is a bank. He pushes the bank door open, wheels the cart behind the teller stations, and begins to help himself to the cash in the drawers. What luck! He notices the bank vault is open and grabs some bags of money. Soon, the cart was heaping full; he'd have to buy another suitcase to hold all his loot! As he's pushing the cart back to his hotel, he hits a crack in the sidewalk. The pocket watch he'd set on the cart flies off and smashes down on the concrete. It's broken! Does it work? He tries a quick push, but nothing happens. Nobody moves. The cars in the street all stay still. Frantically, he keeps pushing and pushing the button. Panic ensues. He approaches people and shoves them, screaming, 'Wake up, wake up!' The show ends with a shot of him running down the street, yelling, 'Noooooo!'

Well, most people, including myself, thought that guy blew it. What a dummy he was to put the pocket watch on top of the cart!

So, anyway, there was this one dude in Alabama who saw the show, and weirdly enough, he'd just inherited an identical pocket watch from his grandpa! Well, he was a superstitious guy, so he thought the show was a message to him from his dead grandpa. He turns off the TV, removes the watch, and presses the button. It just so happens that his hound dog, barking at a raccoon, stops barking at that exact moment. He presses the button again just as the dog sees the raccoon and barks again. Well, that was good enough for him; he thought he had a genuine, fucking, time-stopping pocket watch, just like on TV! So, he gets excited, jumps into his car, and heads to the local bank. He'd be smart and not put the watch on the cart. Instead, he'd keep it in his pocket, where it would be safe.

Unfortunately, he's so excited that he flies through the local speed trap. An officer of the law pursues him, and he pulls to the shoulder. As the officer walks up to the car, the dude decides this is an excellent time to stop time so he can get away. He yanks the watch from his pocket, points it at the cop, and starts pushing the button. The officer sees the movement and a flash of light reflecting from the metal on the watch and thinks the dude is pulling out a weapon. The officer pulls out his gun and shoots the dude dead. Later investigation reveals the dude was holding a harmless watch, and the officer is demoted.

Tim said, "What a fry! Is that for real?"

"Oh yeah, and that's not the end of the story! The cop who shot the guy becomes the subject of relentless taunting by his fellow police officers. Some days, he'd walk into the station, and the other officers would pretend they were shooting each other with their wristwatches. And then, one day, he'd had enough teasing. He pulled out his weapon and slaughtered everyone at the station before shooting himself in the head."

Tim said, "What a fry! It's an evil pocket watch!"

QP said, "That's right. And another thing: the pocket watch that caused all the problems... disappeared and was never found. Who knows where it will pop up next?"

Jay said, "Wow, it was never found. That is a fry!" And then he looked deeply into his leather tote and said, "And by the way, I can't find any more joints."

I said, "Well, ladies and gentlemen, no more pot, no more beer. I think it's time to get out of here!"

Rachel said, "Wow, Joe, I didn't know you were a poet. But wait! What about the fire? We can't leave it burning here like this, right?"

I said, "Rachel, don't worry. You might want to look the other way for the next couple minutes as... us guys have a way to put out fires if you know what I mean."

JUST MISSED THE SIXTIES

"Ewww, that's gross!"

Building the Hut

William, Jay, Rachel, Tim, and I met the next afternoon at the Clearing for the construction of a new hut.

I said, "It would be nice if we could build it larger than the old lean-to so it's more, you know, hut-like."

William said, "If we could find a long log, long enough to go between those two pines, we could set it on the lower branches and have a great hut!"

"Super idea! Okay, Tim, Rachel, and I will look for a log. Jay, you find something for a roof, like branches to make roof beams. If you find enough, we could make it almost rain-proof. William, find some pine boughs to cover the roof for camouflage."

Rachel said, "And please, everybody, let's do this ecologically. Don't harm any living things."

Jay said, "Cool," and we spread into the woods.

After about 30 minutes, we found the perfect log. Tim and I hefted it back to the job site, where Jay and William were waiting for us. Together, we set the log into the forks of the lower branches of the two trees. Jay laid down the ceiling beams. William chopped them to size with a hatchet he produced from a leather holster tied to his thigh. Then, he tied the beams to the main log using a rope that had been looped around his shoulder.

Note to self: Sometimes, having a cowboy with you is handy.

I said, "How can we make this thing rainproof?"

Jay said, "Look! I've got this huge plastic sheet!" Jay held up the sheet. It must have been 20 feet square.

I said, "Where the hell did you find that?"

"Oh, it was just in some garbage by the side of the road."

JUST MISSED THE SIXTIES

Rachel said, "Oh! That makes me so angry that people would throw it by the side of the road! I'm glad we can put it to good use. So now, we've both built a hut *and* cleaned up some litter, too!"

Jay said, "That's a win-win!" Then he laid the sheet over the ceiling beams, and our hut had a roof. William secured the corners with more rope.

I said, "Great! Now, we have to camouflage the Hut so nobody sees it. It's got to blend in with the surroundings."

William pointed to a pile of greenery and said, "Look! I found all of these pine boughs on the forest floor."

Rachel looked at one bough and said, "Are these hatchet marks? Are you sure you didn't cut this down?"

"Oh, no, no, no! That's the way I found it. Some animal must have chewed on it."

I said, "All right, let's get this hut covered!"

When we were finished, it looked gorgeous and very natural. For a finishing touch, we cut a hole in the plastic at one end and put a small fire pit below—a built-in fireplace! We admired our handy work for 15 minutes and returned to the dorm.

On the way back, Tim said, "I'm looking forward to showing it off to the wing!"

Back at the dorm, we split our separate ways. I promised Rachel I'd be sure to include her anytime the wing returned to the Clearing and the Hut. Then, I decided to visit Casey and Don to see what they were doing. Casey was there by himself, playing solitaire.

"Hey, Casey, you want to play a little cribbage?"

"Sure, Joe." Casey got out the cribbage board, and I dealt the first hand.

Casey looked at his cards and said, "I got knobs!" He moved his peg a notch on the board.

I said, "Where's Don today, work?"

"Oh yeah, I hardly ever see him anymore. By the way, I got 18 points in my hand. Looks like you got five." And Casey moved the pegs.

Shit!

"Say, Casey, I thought you were going to come to the woods with us last night. What happened?"

"Oh, I was just about to go, but then I remembered I had a study date with a girl from my history class. Let me tell you, we did a lot more than study history! Oh yeah, we made some history!"

Did he make that up?

"Hey, man! What about Cricket? Remember, you made out with her in *my* room?"

"Oh well, you know me, I can never be monogamous. By the way, I've got a double-double run for 26 points. I am kicking your ass, brother!"

Sensing that Casey didn't like the wing as much as I did, I decided to see if my instincts were right and said, "So, Casey, what do you think of our new wingmates?"

Casey paused a moment and said, "You know what, Joe? I'm a little concerned about them; in fact, I'm very concerned about a few of them. For example, Jay is heavily into the drug scene, and William has a violent side, but most of all... Oh, hey, look! I got a triple-run. I won! I'm especially concerned about Al. He's scary in a weird way. You better watch out for that guy."

Nothing I can't handle. I wonder... when did Casey become such a pussy?

Campfire Stories II

A couple of days later, we roused the wing for another trip to the Clearing. Al did his usual encouraging of wingmates, and soon, we had a quorum. William, Jay, Rachel, Tim, and I were eager to show off the new Hut and see everyone's reactions.

Spitz looked at the Hut and said, "This is far out. It blends... with nature, you know?"

Tim said, "Look, it's waterproof and has a built-in fireplace!"

Al said, "No shit! Where's the bar and hot tub? Ha! Ha!"

I said, "Funny, Al. Anyway, there's not enough room for everybody in the Hut right now, but feel free to come out and use it by yourself or in smaller groups anytime you feel like it. We can have the fire at the fire pit tonight like we did last time."

When everyone was settled around the pit with their refreshments, I said, "Tonight, we should hear from anyone who didn't get a chance to talk last time if you feel comfortable, of course. How about you, Chuck?"

Chuck smiled and said, "Hello, my name is Chuck."

Al said, "We know who you are, douche-bag."

Chuck said, "Fuck you, Al."

William said, "Hey, Chuck, you can borrow my bat anytime you want to!"

Chuck said, "Thanks, William, but that's okay. We got our ways to deal with varmints where I come from."

Al said, "Oh, no! Now, the cowboy and the farm boy are teaming up on me! I'm so scared! For Pete's sake! Come on, you sod-buster, say what you gotta say!"

Chuck said, "Don't push me, Al! Anyway, I just wanted to tell you guys a funny story I heard about this guy who was tripping on acid. He was feeling a little hyper, so he drove to the store for some beer to help him mellow out a little. He knew he had to drive extra, extra carefully. He didn't want to get pulled over by the cops and then they'd see that he was as high as a kite. So, he's driving along and being super careful, but still, despite his best efforts, he gets pulled over.

So, he rolls down his window and says, as respectfully as possible, 'What's the matter, sir? I wasn't speeding, was I?'

The officer doubles over laughing. Minutes tick by before he can stop laughing and compose himself. Finally, he sticks his head in the window and says, 'Sir, you weren't speeding. You were driving five miles an hour!' Can you believe it?"

Tim said, "What a fry!"

Spitz said, "That's funny. Hey! I've got a joke! When Adolph Hitler blows his nose, what does he blow into his handkerchief?"

Al replied, "Okay, Spitz. We give up. What does Hitler blow into his handkerchief?"

"Snotzies!"

Chuck said, "Oh! Groan!"

QP said, "Hey, Spitz, just for that, we're taking away one of your medals!"

Al said, "Hey, Professor, what about you? What's the deal with the nickname?"

The Professor said, "Oh, I like to tinker around and make stuff. I like fooling around with electrical components, you know, like transistors, circuit boards, light boards, recorders, radios, and other fun little gadgets. Oh, and I like making firecrackers, too!"

Al said, "Well, I'll be sure to look you up on the Fourth of July!"

I said, "Al, you've had plenty of comments for everyone else, but you never got to talk about yourself. Why don't you tell us something?

"What the fuck do I have to talk about?"

"I don't know... what's your philosophy of life?"

JUST MISSED THE SIXTIES

"Philosophy of life? You want to hear what the fuck I think about life?"

"Yeah, I do."

"Okay."

This is going to be good.

"Life is a shit parade."

"A what?"

"You heard me. Life is just one piece of stinking feces after another. Sure, there's a little variety in the turds. Sometimes, there's a dry one, sometimes a wet one, sometimes a gassy one, or a long one. Yeah, life provides an interesting variety of shit, but in the end, it's all shit."

Spitz said, "But don't you think we're here for a purpose?"

"Purpose? Really, Spitz? I'll tell you what your purpose is. You're here to amuse God. That's right! He gets his kicks watching us suffer. Hah! In a way, we're like God's little ant farm of torture. He's got us in a little plastic case, sitting up there on a little shelf in heaven. Occasionally, he gets bored, so he taps on the glass to watch us run. Sometimes, he shakes the farm, and WHAM! There's an earthquake, and there's 100,000 dead and mangled bodies. What fun! Sometimes, he pours water down the top, and SPLASH! There's a tsunami, and another 100,000 are drowned. Good times! He's a sick sadistic fucker is what he is. That's the only thing that makes any sense to me."

Jay said, while passing a joint, "But, Al, remember, he also provided us with some far-out ganja, just for our pleasure. Relax! Have a toke and enjoy his gifts!"

I said, "Al, why are you so cynical?"

"Why am I so cynical? Have any of you fuckers ever come home from school to find your mother lying on the floor, overdosing on barbiturates? I bet none of you, right?"

Jay said, "Oh, man, I'm so sorry, Al, what happened?"

"Well, I called emergency and held her hand 'till they came. What else could I do? She made it through all right. Later, she told me that she got her pills 'confused'. I don't believe her. I think she wanted to check out."

"How did your father take it?"

"How the fuck would I know? My father ditched us when I was ten—the usual story: he went out for a ride and never came back. I tell you what, after that day with my mom, I realized there is nothing certain in this world, and the less I think about it, the better I feel. Anyway, that's why life sucks. Hey, Tim, quit freaking out and get me another beer!"

This would be a good time to say one of those right things!

"Hey, Professor! Do you have any firecrackers back in your room?"

"Sure. I got a bunch."

"Hey, guys, let's go put some firecrackers under the doors of those dudes on Second West! What do you say? Sssssss-Bang!"

Everyone was enthusiastic. We quickly extinguished the campfire.

Once again, Rachel said, "Ew, gross!"

Upon returning to the dorm, The Professor handed everyone a fire-cracker, and we stealthily snuck down the hallway of Second West. We were in luck; the Second West dudes were all sacked out for the night. With a few giggles and shushes, the crackers were set in place, one under every door. We lit the fuses and ran. The fuses were extra long, allowing us plenty of time to escape.

We waited anxiously in our rooms, ears pressed against the doors. Then they blew: BLAM! BLAM! BLAM! BLAM! Sixteen times. We didn't realize how loud the blasts would seem in the quiet of the night. We dared not leave our rooms.

The next day, people said, "Wow! Practically, the entire dorm went to Second West to see what had happened. But, funny thing, there was nobody there from Second East! Hah! *Tell me that didn't look suspicious!*"

The English Assignment

Meanwhile, in my English class, Professor Bray assigned the task of writing a short story. I hadn't put much thought into it. In fact, I hadn't thought about it at all until he reminded us about the assignment the day before it was due.

Oh, man, what am I going to write about?

I couldn't stop thinking about the last campfire and everything Al had said.

That night, Rachel and I were doing homework together in my room, and I said, "Rachel, I'm racking my brains for a short story, and all I can think about is what Al said last night and how cynical he is."

"Well, why don't you write about that? Think about it. In the meantime, you can fold up your laundry. It's not very nice seeing all your dirty old undies lying around the place!"

"They're not old! Look! This one still has its label!"

"Well, that's just lucky."

"Well... yes! That's my lucky underwear! I only wear it on special occasions. And, of course, that's much better than having holy underwear because I can only wear holy underwear to church. Get it?"

And then I was inspired.

JUST MISSED THE SIXTIES

Joseph Roman
English 102
Short Story
Sept. 25, 1973
Dr. Bray

C'est la Vie, C'est la Guerre, C'est la Underwear

I knew there was something special about that pair of underwear because it still had on its label. All the other pairs had lost their labels in the wash a long time ago. That's why I wore that pair on the big test day. I'd been studying for weeks, studying hard. I'd read and reread every note I took in class. I even borrowed notes from my classmates. I studied the textbook, and if there was anything I didn't understand, I asked the professor for help. I was completely ready. Still, when it was time to get dressed that morning, I put on that pair of underwear because I wanted that little something special that the underwear had to help me do even better. I aced the test. The underwear went into my dirty laundry at the end of the day. I washed it on Saturday, my normal laundry day, and I decided while putting away the clean laundry, to set that pair to one side in the underwear drawer and not to wear it again until it was needed for something special.

There was a girl in my class that I found to be quite attractive. I wanted to ask her on a date but I was nervous. Maybe I could ask her if she wanted to go out for some coffee after class. Perhaps if I wore the underwear, I would have the courage to ask. Well, I did, and she agreed to go. We went to the student union, had coffee, and discussed the last test. She was impressed with how much I had prepared for the test. She had studied much less than I had and received an average grade. I found out a lot more about her, too. I was thrilled when she said I could call her sometime. It was great. Life was good, and I thanked my underwear, my "Lucky Underwear."

JUST MISSED THE SIXTIES

Because I saved the Lucky Underwear for special days, I began to find that special things only happened when I wore them. I wore my Lucky Underwear on the day I asked the girl from my class to be my girlfriend.

She said, "Of course. Why do you think I've been seeing only you for the last two months?"

One day, I had a terrible sinus infection. I wore my Lucky Underwear to the doctor's office and subsequently to the pharmacy to pick up my prescription for antibiotics. The infection cleared up the next day—thank you, Lucky Underwear (LU)! Who can doubt the healing powers of LU?

Bad things usually happened on days I was not wearing the LU. Once, when I was not wearing the LU, I got a speeding ticket. I was hurrying to class, knowing I was way over the limit. Usually, on days when I wore the LU, I made sure to drive at or below the posted speed.

Once, oddly enough, something good happened when I was not wearing the LU. The professor gave a surprise quiz. I knew I would do okay because I was keeping up with the material in class, but I was a little concerned because I wasn't wearing the LU. Yet I scored 100% on the quiz, and I think I know why. On the last laundry day, one pair of regular, not-so-lucky, no-label underwear had nested itself inside the pair of LU while the clothes were spinning in the dryer. I bet I'd been wearing that pair! Somehow, the LU knew I needed some luck that day and knew I wasn't planning to wear it, so it transferred some of its power to the nested pair. I am so thankful for the extraordinary powers of the LU!

I graduated with full honors and had immediate job offers. I'm sure the LU had something to do with that! A funny thing happened at my first job interview. While parking, I noticed a billboard for the company that made my LU was next to the office building! I knew right then that was a sign from my LU. How wonderfully clever that the LU gave me a sign, on a sign! Of course, I did great at the interview, as I had been getting interview coaching from a placement agency. I knew all there was to know about the company and the position. I knew I would be a great fit. And, of course, I took the job when it was offered. My LU is awesome!

A week later, I was driving to visit my girlfriend. I was taking an engagement ring and was planning to ask for her hand in marriage. I was very nervous. Of course, I was wearing my LU! Yet, somehow, I was in a terrible car accident. Another driver ran a stop sign and crashed into my driver's side door. I was rushed to the hospital.

As I was being driven away in the ambulance, my last thought before unconsciousness was, "How could this happen when I'm wearing the LU?" Honestly, I almost lost my faith that day.

When I awoke in a hospital bed again, I wondered how this could have happened, and then I felt shame. How could I question the LU? Perhaps it knew something that I didn't. Possibly, if not for the accident, I would have been hit by a train at the next crossing, and so instead of being in a hospital bed, I would be in a funeral home! No one should question the mysterious ways of the LU!

Well, my girlfriend accepted the proposal – right at the hospital! The staff had just brought out my personal effects in a bag that contained the ring and the clothes I'd been wearing the day of the accident. She'd been hinting about a wedding for months, but when I saw that, in the bag, the box containing the wedding ring had fallen deeply into the crotch of the LU – I knew it was a done deal! I found out later that I had emptied my bowels during the accident. The hospital had washed my LU. After I was released, the hospital received a $10,000 donation from an anonymous donor. Again, I could only stand back in awe of the incredible power of the LU! Another thing I learned is that the LU can be defiled in the coarsest of ways and still retain its special powers.

After we were married, we started sharing our laundry duties, so I had to tell her about the LU. I had to convince her of the powers of the LU, and perhaps, somehow, she could benefit from them, too. She confessed that all her life, she carried a lucky penny wherever she went. I realized there were several options at this point: I could change to the lucky penny belief, she could convert to the LU, or somehow, we could blend the two. I listed everything the LU had done for me, and she listed everything the penny had done for her. It wasn't a perfect comparison as she always carried the lucky penny, and I wore the LU only once a week. Once she considered that since I had better grades and a better-paying job, all of that had happened despite my LU being worn less than 1/7th the number of days that she'd had the penny with her – well, she converted. The proof was overwhelming. I offered up the idea that perhaps the penny had done its job of leading her to me and, ultimately, the LU. She liked that. I winked at the LU because we (the LU and I) knew that was hogwash, but it didn't matter as long as she was now an LU believer.

I was immensely relieved that she'd left her false beliefs behind. Deep down, I was sure we were on the right path. I would have said anything to convince her. How could anyone not be sure after hearing all that the LU had done for me? We put the penny into a display frame and hung it over her dresser. [Note: Much later, when we moved from an apartment to a house, the movers "lost" the penny (wink, wink)].

Now, the question was: How could she share the power of the LU? I told her about the nesting incident, and she thought we could use that. We'd balled up her undies, put them inside the LU, put rubber bands around the LU to keep them from falling out, and washed and dried them together. It worked great; she enjoyed the remarkable power of the LU every day with her nested undies.

The downside of all the repeated washings was that, eventually, the LU began to wear out. Once it fell apart, we put its pieces into unique underwear-shaped lockets with the letters LU engraved on the front. That way, we could wear the locket on a necklace and clutch it if we needed reassurance. We made 50 lockets with bits of the LU and sent them to family members.

The LU may be gone, but I don't worry because its special powers live on in my wife's nested undies. I told my friends they, too, could have the power of the LU if they washed their underwear nested inside my wife's underwear. Afterward, their underwear could be used to nest other underwear; in that way, we could spread the power of the LU into eternity.

I contacted all my friends and encouraged them to come to my house during the week and wash their underwear inside my wife's underwear. I was amazed - the response was terrific!

My wife said, "You've done me a favor, you know. I would have thrown away that penny years ago if it meant I could get lucky with your friends every day while you're at work!" She has a funny way of phrasing things.

I thought, "Why should our friends be the only ones to share the power of the LU?" So, I said, "Honey, is there some way that we can reach out and share the LU with more than just our friends but with strangers too?"

She replied, "Sure! There are lots of guys at the corner bar that are desperate for a little... luck."

"Can you help them out too?"

She looked up, and I saw a fire light up her eyes at the prospect of spreading the LU.

"I'm on it!" She leaped to her feet and grabbed her car keys.

"Don't forget some extra undies!" I yelled as she raced down the hallway.

"I'll just use the ones I got on!" She is so resourceful!

This morning, I approached my best friend, Alan, and asked, "Alan, have you been feeling the power in my wife's underwear?"

At first, he seemed startled by the question, but then he gazed into my eyes for a minute, took some deep breaths, and replied, "I AM feeling that power. Thank you so much for sharing!" Sharing with friends and sharing with strangers, thank you, LU, for showing us the righteous road!

I also tell my friends that when their nested pair wears out, I'll provide them with an underwear-shaped locket engraved with "LU" to always keep a piece close to their hearts. And I can do all of this for you, too! For just $499.95, I can provide you with your own personal Founder Underwear (FU), which traces its nesting washings back to the very first LU! Also included is an authentic paper that documents the nesting lineage of your special FU! And there's more! You'll receive the special bands of rubber necessary to keep underwear nested in your FU during the transfer washing procedure. And there's even more! You'll receive a beautiful locket with your choice of engraving, either LU or FU, and a necklace for you to preserve the final pieces of your FU after it's been used hundreds of times to spread the extraordinary power of the LU to your underwear.

Once you start using the FU LU system, you will notice little signs that it's working. There are no setbacks, as everything happens for a purpose that hasn't been made clear yet. You will lead a richer and more fulfilling life thanks to the LU.

You may wonder, "How did anything special happen to me before LU?" Soon, you will see clues and signs that the LU is taking care of you, too. Perhaps you will see an advertisement for your brand at a meaningful time, such as on your birthday, and you will know that the LU is watching you. Use your imagination. I'm sure you can make up signs as well as I can!

Everyone needs a reason for life. Everyone wants a purpose. Your purpose can be to help keep the power of the LU alive. It's something special, something to give your life meaning. If you have other beliefs, that's OK. You can slowly transition to LU at your comfort level. Hang on to those lucky pennies, rabbit's feet, or whatever it is you cherish until you are fully ready to embrace LU. It's not too big a sacrifice. After all, the LU made the ultimate sacrifice for everyone – becoming threadbare.

I have been asked, "Is there one LU or many LU?" The answer is: both are true! There is only one true LU; all that come afterward are manifestations of the one. And so, you see, the many are one. Most importantly, you must remember that the only way to know the LU is through your FU. This message is so important that sometimes I write "FU" on a large piece of cardboard and display it at sporting events.

I envision a future where entire neighborhoods will come together weekly on Wash Day. The ceremonies will be wonderful as generation after generation passes on the knowledge of the LU. Together, families will watch their FU spread the power of the LU to newly "Transformed Underwear" (TU), and the followers will chant

JUST MISSED THE SIXTIES

FUL-U-TU, FUL-U-TU (pronounced "fool u too") in rhythm to the turning of the giant washers and dryers at the special FULUTU Houses. Someday, there will be a FULUTU house in every neighborhood worldwide.

Other special ceremonies will occur, such as when your FU is determined to be "locket-ready." Youngsters can attend classes to learn the stories of the first LU, where to look for signs, how to overcome doubts, and how to spread the word.

One day, missionaries will cross the world requesting only to wash the underwear of non-believers and amaze them when their lives are transformed by the extraordinary powers of their own personal FU.

All we ask is for you to give us a try. After all, what if we're right? Eventually, I am sure you will discover that we can FULUTU!

The End

My story amused Dr. Bray. I know he was because he put a little smiley face next to the big D+. He also wrote these comments, "Short story or sales pitch? You might try wearing your Lucky Underwear when you write your next English assignment."

About three months later, Dr. Bray became renowned for his famous essay, "Why Today's College Students Can't Write". I saw it published in the Milwaukee Journal. I wonder if I was inspirational.

The Chess Tournament

I locked my door before heading off to morning classes when Kerry, the Wing Director, caught me in the hallway.

He loped up to me, flashed his toothy grin, and said, "Hey, Joe, do you have a second? Come on into my room. I got a question for you."

I said, "Okay, just for a second." I walked in and sat on the other bed. Looking over at Kerry's dresser, my eyes locked onto the box of condoms, and I remembered what Rachel had said on our picking-up-litter date at the Clearing.

Protection! I've got to get some protection! That'll be nice... when she's lying there all ready to go, and I pull one of those beauties out of my pocket and say, "Looky, looky!"

Then Kerry spoke, knocking me out of my daydream, "You sophomore guys have done a groovy job of making the new freshmen feel comfortable here. Now, I'd like to do some activity as a wing that would be fun for everyone. So, anyway, I'm trying to think of ideas, and I wonder if I could ask you to help me think of some ideas too? You don't have to come up with anything right now, but keep your mind open. What do you say?"

As my eyes drifted away from the box of condoms, the next thing I saw was his chess board lying there on the dresser. I was inspired.

"I've got an idea. How about a chess tournament?"

"You ever played before? And I mean, really played, not just fooled around."

"Oh. Yeah. Sure. I took lessons!" *When I was in fifth grade!*

JUST MISSED THE SIXTIES

"Yeah? Well, I was the high school state champion. Pretty groovy, huh? Anyway, I think that's a far-out idea, Joe! Why don't you go around the wing today and put anyone who wants to play into a bracket-elimination tournament, just like the NCAA basketball finals? And, Joe, since you took a chess course, put me down to play you first tonight!"

Yikes!

So, after my morning classes, I went around the wing, signing wingmates to fill the brackets of a one-game elimination chess tournament. Most everyone wanted to be in the tournament. The exceptions were Don and Lewis, whom I couldn't find because they were hardly ever around the wing.

When I asked QP, he said, "Oh, I see Kerry's got you working on a wing activity. He asked me to gather ideas for a design for a Second East t-shirt. You know... something that truly captures the spirit of the wing. He thought maybe we could have a mascot, like the Second East Eagles or something like that. Anyway, Joe, I'll be in your tournament if you help me think of a t-shirt."

"Deal."

Night-time arrived, and I was in Kerry's room, watching him grab his chessboard off the dresser. I saw the box of condoms.

That's good. The box of protection is still there. I could grab one at an opportune moment.

I sat on his bed with my back to the dresser. Kerry sat at the other end and put the chessboard between us. As he set up the pieces, I tried to recall some strategies from my long-ago chess class.

Okay, I remember: Start the game with a middle pawn. Develop your power pieces slowly. Don't bring out the queen too quickly. Don't surround yourself with yourself.

Kerry quickly praised, "Nice opening move, Joe." Several moves later, he said, "I like how you're positioning your bishops and knights."

Okay. Now I've cleared the pieces between my king and rook so I can castle.

I said, "I'm going to castle."

JUST MISSED THE SIXTIES

I picked up the king. As I moved it towards the rook, Kerry said, "Good job, Joe, that's a great way to give your king more protection!"

He said protection!

My hand twitched. The bottom of the king hit the rook and sent it flying off the chessboard. It rolled off the bed, onto the floor, and deep beneath the other bed.

Kerry quickly got onto his hands and knees and said, "Let me get that for you, Joe! You'll need the protection!"

He said it again!

Impulsively, I spun around, grabbed three condoms from the box, and shoved them into my pocket.

That's right, Kerry, I got my protection!

Still on his hands and knees, Kerry backed out from under the bed and returned my rook to the board. After that, I played the game with reckless abandon.

My mission is done here.

"Careful, Joe, you shouldn't attack so much with your Queen so early in the game! Just look at all these pieces I'm developing to attack your defenses in front of your king!"

I don't care.

I doubt Kerry had ever seen such a free-wheeling style. Thinking I was in folly, he ignored my Queen and continued his methodical piece development.

Then he captured the pawn directly in front of my king with his rook and said, "Check."

All I could do was move the king to one side. On his next move, he aimed a bishop at the spot just vacated by my king. He was setting me up for the kill. He would put me into check-mate if I didn't take immediate defensive action. He had a confident look in his eye.

Oh well. I don't give a shit. Wait a minute – did he leave his back row open for my queen?

I said, "Look, Kerry! I can move my queen back here. Check!"

"What the f...?"

Kerry had to stop his offensive movements to play defense. He moved his king out of check. I followed with my queen for another check. Move after move, I stayed in pursuit, putting him in check five more times until suddenly and incredulously, he was cornered. I yelled, "Checkmate!"

He looked so dazed and confused that I almost felt sorry for him.

He was the champion of which state?

I was surprised and pleased about the win but felt a little like a thief. Mostly, I wanted to see Rachel as soon as possible.

The Art of Seduction

After eliminating and demoralizing Kerry in the Second East Chess Tournament, I flew quickly up the stairs to Rachel's room. I knocked, and she opened the door. She was holding a handful of colored pencils.

"Hi, Rachel. What's going on? Are you doing an art project? I thought you were getting a teaching degree."

"Yes, I am, Joe, but I'm also minoring in art. I like being creative, but now I'm starting to think it was a bad idea. My God, they give us so much homework!"

"Oh, sorry, I'll let you get back to it. I was just wondering if this Friday you might want to listen to some music in my room again with some wine like we did before."

"That sounds nice."

"Oh, and by the way, I have some – protection."

"Oh, I see. What if your little buddy Casey decides to drop by again?"

"Don't ever call him little buddy. He really hates that."

Man, if I only had a necktie!

"Don't worry, I won't. Well? How will you keep Casey (who I can't call little buddy) away from your room?"

"Hmmm. Last year, a roommate put a necktie on our doorknob when he wanted privacy. I used to complain to Casey about it every time. We could do that now, but unfortunately, I don't have any neckties."

Rachel looked at the colored pencils in her hand and said, "Don't worry about it. I'll see you Friday night."

JUST MISSED THE SIXTIES

Friday Night arrived, and my room was set. The lights were low, the candles lit, and the fan was spinning. The three packages of protection were lying on my dresser top. The musical selection was ready. The first song, of course, was George Harrison's sultry "I'd Have You Anytime".

I started the music the moment she knocked on my door.

"Come in! It's open!"

Rachel entered. She was wearing a tight pink top and looked good. Then, I noticed she was carrying a manila folder and a roll of Scotch Tape.

"Hi, Joe. Gosh, it's been a long week. I'm ready for some of that wine you promised."

I got a bottle out of the mini-fridge and unscrewed the top.

I said, "This is an upgrade from last time. Look! MD 20-20."

She said, "Wow, it's kosher for Passover! That sounds perfect!" She laughed.

I poured two mugs of wine and asked, "Are you Jewish?"

"No, no, my family is Holiday Catholic. They only go to mass on the two big holidays, Christmas and Easter. I'm more into a kind of universal energy of life. How about you?"

"I don't know. I believe in my Lucky Underwear."

"What?"

"Just Kidding! However, I wrote a funny story about Lucky Underwear for an English assignment. You can read it tonight if you like. My teacher didn't think it was funny, though. Say, what's in the manila folder?"

"I thought you'd never ask. We can tape this picture to the door to keep Casey away!"

JUST MISSED THE SIXTIES

An hour later, Casey came walking up the hallway, cribbage board under his arm and holding a steaming mug of coffee. "Hot Joe" was written on the side of the mug. He stopped in front of my door and looked at the picture.

"Oh damn! A necktie. I guess I'll be playing solitaire tonight."

Back inside my room, I was slowly reaching for the third protection package.

I said, "Say, can't we just enjoy the afterglow?"

Rachel replied, "I tell you what. What you call afterglow, I call burning desire."

JUST MISSED THE SIXTIES

Thirty minutes later, I was ready to sleep. Lying on my side, I looked over at my pile of clothes and the contents of my pockets, such as keys, wallet, and loose change. I saw the back of a quarter with this design:

Suddenly, I knew what the design of our wing t-shirt should be.

"Rachel, wake up! Look at the back of this quarter. Can you draw that?"

"What, the eagle with the arrows and the olive branch?"

"Yeah. Except where it says Quar. Dol. Write Second East and replace the arrows with a firecracker and the olive branch with a marijuana sprig. Voila! We'll capture the true spirit of Second East!"

The next day, Rachel drew it perfectly. On top, she wrote, Fly like an Eagle – to be free! We submitted the drawing to QP. He loved it. A couple of days later, QP distributed our new t-shirts at no charge,

JUST MISSED THE SIXTIES

thanks to the print shop at the Student Union and the Campus Student Activity Fund. After that, the college never covered the costs of wing t-shirts again.

Student Activism

When Jay burst into the door, Rachel and I were sitting in my room, admiring the new t-shirts. He was waving the campus newspaper, *The Pointer*.

"Look, guys! You've got to see this!"

He opened the paper and pointed to a small announcement on the back page. It read:

ATTENTION STUDENTS OF STEVENS POINT:
Are you interested in making a difference on your campus, our country, and our world? Join us to help promote **peace, equality, and justice**.
Where: Student Union, Meeting Room 2
When: September 23rd at 7:00 PM
Who: Students for a Democratic Society

"Look, Joe, there's an ad in the paper recruiting students for the Students for a Democratic Society!"

"Oh man - the SDS! Way cool!"

Suddenly, in my mind, I was back on the couch in my den, watching the student demonstrations on the evening news. Students were singing, chanting, waving signs, and throwing rocks. The police were in riot gear with face masks and big shields. The cops shot tear gas canisters at the mob. Brave students stepped forward, picked up the canisters, and lobbed them back at the police. Smiling coeds flashed peace signs for the cameras. *Oh, Man! That's the way to be part of something meaningful, something important!*

"That's tonight, Joe. What do you say? Want to go?"

JUST MISSED THE SIXTIES

"Yes! Definitely! Rachel, do you want to go?"
"Cool! Yes! I'm very excited!"

We arrived at the Student Union and found Meeting Room #2 that evening. A couple of grizzled old dudes were seated at a table that reminded me of Jerry Garcia. Their curly hair was dark black with a touch of gray. Lying in front of them was a collection of clipboards and folders with yellowed and battered paper corners protruding from the edges.

Grizzled Old Dude #1 rose and shook our hands, "Hi, I'm Phil, and this is Ron, but everyone calls him 'Pig-Sty.'"

Grizzled Old Dude #2 waved hello.

"Welcome to the first meeting of the UWSP-SDS. UWSP-SDS, man, that's a mouthful, eh? Anyway, we just drove up from Madison, where we're trying to reestablish the Wisconsin headquarters for the SDS. We hope to have chapters in all the extension schools, like in Stevens Point. So, take a seat. We'll wait another five minutes to see if anybody else shows up before we begin."

Five minutes later, after three more students had joined the group, Grizzled Old Dude #1 began. "Okay, everyone, again, welcome to our local chapter of the Students for a Democratic Society, also known as the SDS. I hope this is the beginning of something good here in Stevens Point. Let me begin by telling you some of the history of the SDS. The SDS of today evolved from a group that started way back in 1905. That group was called the Student League for Industrial Democracy, aka SLID. In 1960, they changed the name to SDS because industrial democracy sounded too much like a labor union, making it challenging to recruit new students. Later, SDS split away from the old SLID organization, which was more interested in promoting socialism.

SDS first met in 1960 at the University of Michigan in Ann Arbor. They elected officers and created their first political manifesto: 'The Port Huron Statement.' The statement criticized the international policies of the US, which, at the time, were the Cold War and the mutual threat of nuclear annihilation. The statement was critical of the large amounts of money wasted on the arms race. Domestically, it was against racial discrimination, economic inequality, and big business, especially the heartless corporations that saw people as cattle to be used for making money. It suggested that people band together to make their voices heard. It said people should demand more public works programs to fight poverty. It advocated non-violent civil disobedience to make our country more peaceful and caring.

Early in the Sixties, the group was very active in support of civil rights issues and later became heavily involved in organizing student protests against the war in Vietnam. University involvement in the war effort, such as ROTC facilities or supplying class rankings to determine draft eligibility, was protested by student groups with building takeovers and sit-ins. That's when things started to get out of hand. A splinter group, the Weathermen, which advocated violent protest, was kicked out of the SDS. Most core members of the SDS were committed to Gandhi-style non-violent tactics. By 1969, there were so many splinter groups it was impossible to hold a democratic-style meeting to create national policy. The last known actions of the SDS were the rallies at the political conventions of 1972. Many of the Weatherman leaders were forced to go underground because of outstanding arrest warrants. Since then, and up till now, there have been no meetings and no activities. The SDS ceased to exist.

So, that brings us to the present: trying to organize local branches on various campuses. Local branches will feed into a state organization and a new national one. Pig-Sty and I worked in the state organization back in 1970, just before that stupid campus bombing forced us to disband. So, anyway, I know that was a lot of information to absorb at once. Does anyone have any questions?"

I was pumped up. "Hey! When can we have our first demonstration?"

Jay was excited, too, "Yeah! What are we going to blow up first?"

I spun in my seat and stared at Jay in disbelief. "Blow up first? Jay, we can't have violence, man! Remember, we make love, not war!"

JUST MISSED THE SIXTIES

Jay said, "No, no, no, Joe. We got to fight fire with fire, man! Remember this song?" Jay started singing, "Tin soldiers and Nixon's coming…"

"No way, man! Neil Young does not approve of violence! What happened to sticking flowers into gun barrels as a sign of peace?"

Jay said, "Well, you can't stick a flower into a gun that's shooting at you! And that's actually what happened, man! Hey, there's only one way to get the power to the people: *you don't need a weatherman to know which way the wind blows*!"

Not knowing the meaning of that, I started singing, *"Come on people now and smile on your brother. Everybody get together and try to love one another right now!"*

Jay started singing louder than me, *"Stop! Hey! What's that sound? Everybody look what's going down."*

Grizzled Old Dude #1 had heard enough, "Hey, you two, settle down! We're trying to run a meeting here!"

Suddenly, Grizzled Old Dude #2 groaned, "Oh, man! I can't take it! I'm having a heavy deja vu! It's just like the 1969 convention all over again! This is some heavy shit – I got to get a hit of some fresh air." He stood and left the room.

Grizzled Old Dude #1 was worried, "Sorry, guys, I've got to go check on Pig-Sty. This concludes today's meeting. I want to see you all for a week from now, at the same time, at the same place, and please, bring some ideas for projects. We'll discuss your ideas at the meeting. And most importantly," he looked directly at Jay, "No blowing stuff up! I'll see you next week." He gathered his clipboards and folders and rushed out to find his comrade.

Next week, the Grizzled Old Dudes were no-shows at the second meeting of the UWSP-SDS.

Gosh, I hope they weren't disappointed in us! I tried not to sing out of key.

Nevertheless, despite Grizzled Old Dudes #1 and #2's absence, we continued the meeting. It was a good time. We drank a few beers and talked about our ideas. Ultimately, we narrowed the suggestions down to two projects. Both were petitions. One was a call for the impeachment of President Nixon. Recent revelations about the cover-up of the Watergate break-in were pointing toward the involvement of high-level White House staff, likely all the way to the President. A couple of journalists at the Washington Post were getting incredible scoops from a source they called "Deep Throat."

The second petition was more local. It was directed at the Campus Housing Department and called for the end of mandatory dormitory housing for freshmen and sophomores.

We decided to collect signatures by sitting at tables near the dining halls' entrances during mealtimes or hoofing it through every dormitory on campus and knocking on all the doors. It would take some effort, but we were up for the task.

After getting as many signatures as possible, we'd send the first petition to our congressman and the latter to the University Housing Department. We felt cool. We had a plan, and we were moving forward.

The Meeting at Gertrude's Apartment

The next day, Gertrude Kaiser sent a notice to the residents of Second East inviting them to her apartment for a meeting. It was mandatory.

I found the notice taped on my door upon returning from classes.

It read, "Your attendance is required at a meeting in Gertrude Kaiser's apartment tonight at 6:30 PM."

I looked down the hallway and saw similar notices posted on every door in the wing. Kerry was walking towards me, holding a roll of tape.

Kerry said, "Hey, Joe, make sure you attend the Kaiser's meeting tonight. It's important!"

"What's it about?"

"I don't know. We'll find out when we get there. All I do know is that she's got something special to say, just to our wing. If you see anybody from the wing, please remind them to be there too. Okay?"

"Sure."

At that night's dinner, everyone tried to guess why she wanted to see us. What was she going to say? Were we in trouble?

Spitz said, "Maybe she wants to nominate us for the 'Best Wing on Campus'!"

"Yeah! Right!" said Tim. "That would be a super-fry!"

Al said, "Congratulations, men, I think we just won the 'Most Fuck-ups on Campus Competition'!"

JUST MISSED THE SIXTIES

At 6:30, Kerry mustered the wing and led us down the stairs to the lobby, where we gathered in front of the door to Gertrude's apartment.

Kerry knocked, "Gertrude! Second East is here for our meeting!"

The door opened. Gertrude was standing there, dressed casually in jeans and a sweatshirt.

"Come in, everybody! Please find a place to sit in the living room on the couches, chairs, or the floor."

Everyone found a seat. I took some time to survey the digs of our dormitory leader. It was a modest flat with one main living area containing the kitchen, dining, and living room (that now contained my tightly packed-in wingmates). Down a short hallway were two doors that, I guessed, were the bathroom and a bedroom. The walls were gun-metal grey. The color in the room was provided by the avocado curtains and matching shag carpet. The living room furniture was early American. Gertrude pulled over a chair from the dining room table and addressed the wing.

"First off, I want to thank you all for being here this evening. I'm sorry this had to take you away from your valuable study time."

Did I hear Al snort?

"Before I get into the real reason I called this meeting, let's go around the room and say our names and where we're from. I have a policy that I want to get to know all the students in my dormitory. I know many of you already, but let's go around the room and have everyone say their name anyway, so no one gets left out."

Then, everybody took turns saying their name and hometown.

After I said, "I'm Joe, and I'm from Wauwatosa." It was William's turn.

But, just before William could open his mouth, Al said, "Oh, that's Buffalo Bill, and he's from the last century!"

William said, "Shut up, Al! I'm William, and I'm from Brown Deer."

After everyone said their name, Gertrude got to the point. "The reason I called this meeting is, very early in the semester, your wing has come to my attention, and not in a good way. There was an incident with firecrackers that appears to be the work of some of your wingmates. Maybe all of you were in on it. Kerry showed me your new wing T-shirt, and it's evident that you are very proud of what you've done. How do I know this? Because you put a picture of a firecracker on the shirt! Whether anyone here was responsible for the bombings or not, it doesn't matter: I will be getting a similar message out to everyone in the dormitory, and that means not just your wing. Here's the message: This kind of behavior will never be tolerated! I want to put a stop to these activities right now. We will be forced to take punitive actions if there are any more incidents.

Also, I saw a picture of a plant on your wing t-shirt that resembles marijuana."

Several wingmates casually folded their arms in front of their new wing shirts.

"Let me remind you, marijuana is an illegal substance, and if we catch you in possession of any amount of this material, you could be expelled from the dormitory. And, if the circumstances warrant it, you could be dismissed from the University. Do I make myself clear?

Oh, and by the way, the other floors are complaining that your music is too loud. Please turn off your music systems after 9:00 pm. There will be no exceptions.

Despite everything I just said, I want you to know I am here to help you. So, let's open up the discussion. Does anyone have any questions?"

Jay said, "Gertrude, do you believe that freshmen and sophomores should be forced to live in campus housing?"

"Jay, it doesn't matter what I believe – those are the rules, and we must live by them until the rules change."

"Well, I'm determined to change those rules. You wait and see!"

"Jay, I wish you all the best, sincerely."

Gertrude continued, "You should all try to remember what you are here for—an education. You are not here to party and have a good time. Now I understand. Sometimes, you need to release a little tension and have some fun."

Al said, "I know a good way to avoid the tension – don't go to classes!"

"Seriously, Kerry tells me that Joe just organized a chess tournament in your wing. I think that's a great idea. Chess is a good, clean kind of fun that's also good for your mind. I'd like to see more of those kinds of activities."

Al said, "Gertrude, will you answer a personal question?"

"I don't know. I'll let you know after I hear the question."

"Tell me honestly, do you like your job?"

"Of course I do. I wouldn't be here today if I didn't like my job. Why do you ask?"

"I bet you'll hate this job after a semester with our wing."

What a fry! I can't believe he just said that!

Gertrude said, "That's up to me to decide, isn't it, Al?"

"Gertrude, I wish you all the best, sincerely."

I looked at Tim, and his expression said, "What a fry!"

And then it was over. Gertrude ushered us out of her little home, and we returned to our wing. I thought the meeting went quite well. Nobody was in trouble; it was just a general warning to all. Al's comments were irreverent and amusing without going too far. I got a little teasing about being presented as a role model.

If she only knew the truth!

We made a few jokes about the questions we should have asked Gertrude, such as, "Why aren't you married?" or "When's the last time you got laid?" or "Where's your torture chamber?"

Perhaps Gertrude's little talk worked. There were no more (intended) firecracker incidents in the dormitory. Jay, Rachel, and I resumed our student activist work. Al resumed doing whatever it was he did to amuse himself.

JUST MISSED THE SIXTIES

Activism and Al

The work began on the petitions for our new UWSP-SDS. We determined the text and formatting. Rachel typed them up and Jay did the photocopying on a machine at the campus library. We started getting signatures at mealtimes and later went door-to-door in the dormitories. Many students were eager to sign both petitions. A few called us crazy to think our little petitions could change anything.

I felt pretty cool, sitting at our petition table at the entrance of the dining halls. It wasn't as glamorous as a street demonstration, but it beat getting hit on the head with a riot stick. That's right, we were activists and doing activist stuff.

Look out, Mr. Jones!

The activist work kept me away from some of the wing's latest antics, although I heard stories—mainly about Al. Once, Spitz was driving Al to get some beer, and Al thought it would be funny to moon a couple of nuns walking on the sidewalk.

Ewwww! Gross! Al's butt cheeks touched his windshield!

Tim told me Al took a couple of super-stoned freshmen to an intersection and convinced them that traffic lights were part of a government conspiracy of thought control.

Al said, "It is always the same: green is go, red is stop. They're training us, just like rats in a cage!"

Another time, Al took a group to K-Mart and bought some cap guns. Then, they went to a small diner frequented by the locals.

Al flung open the front door and yelled, "This is for stealing my girl!" Then, they all aimed their toy guns inside the door and pretended to shoot up the joint. Al thought it was hilarious to see the waitresses and customers all screaming, ducking, and scrambling for cover.

JUST MISSED THE SIXTIES

Wow, he's a menace to society! I gotta get back to the wing and take charge. If left on his own, who knows what he'll do next?

My question was answered when Al, inspired by our work with the SDS, decided to try his hand at a little social activism with his unique style of a social outreach program.

I was wearily walking up the hallway after another evening of door-to-door signature collecting when I spotted Don exiting Al's room.

Wow! A Don-sighting! Now that's a rare event.

Don was grinning, and his eyes were bright red.

Stoned again!

"Hey, Don, what's going down? Did you just come out of Al's room?"

"Hey, Joe, you wouldn't believe the scene in there. Al invited Lewis and a couple of his friends to his room to pass the peace pipe or something like that. Anyway, they're all in there getting stoned. It's a fry."

"Ha! I'll have to check it out! Where are you off to?"

"Work, as usual."

Oh my God, he's stoned and going to sort packages? I hope he doesn't send them all to Salinas, where everything slips away.

When I entered Al's room, I saw Al, Jay, Spitz, Tim, Lewis, and two black friends sitting on the left-side bed. "Everyday People" was booming from Al's stereo.

> *There is a yellow one,*
> *That won't accept the black one,*
> *That won't accept the red one,*
> *That won't accept the white one.*
> *Different strokes for different folks.*

Al said, "Hey, it's our wing brother, Joseph! Joseph, you gotta meet my new soul friends. This is our wing brother, Lewis Washington, his soul-brother, Lundees Jefferson, and his soul-sister Lynette Roosevelt."

JUST MISSED THE SIXTIES

Sounds like Mount Rushmore.

"We've been sittin' here smoking the peace pipe. Can you dig it? Right-on! Right, Lewis?" He reached out to Lewis for a fist bump. Lewis reluctantly bumped back.

Oh my God, Al's being weirdly performative!

Al mused, "Yep, yep, smoking a peace pipe, you know, it's too bad William's not here. Then we could've had Cowboys and Africans! Snort!"

Please stop, Al!

Spitz laughed and said, "That's funny, Al! Hey! Maybe, someday, there could be a musical group with a cowboy, an African-American, an Indian, and, I don't know, a fireman, a policeman..."

Al cut him off and said, "Sure, Spitz, and they'd all be a bunch of those homosexuals too!" Turning back to Lewis, Al said, "Seriously, Lewis, I invited you and your friends here tonight to show you how tolerant I am."

I grimaced. "Oh God, Al, please stop!"

Ignoring Al, Lynette reached out to shake my hand and said, "Nice to meet you, Joseph."

I said, "Nice to meet you too. What's your major?"

"Biology."

"Hey, that's mine too! How's it going so far?"

"Not bad. I like the new science building. It's got some cool new gadgets like that electron microscope – I hope I can take the course next semester."

I said, "I know, it's amazing to think about it. I can't even imagine what it's like to see every tiny detail inside a cell!"

I asked Lewis what he was studying at Point. Lewis laughed and said, "You may think this is funny for someone who grew up in the inner city of Milwaukee, but I want to be a forest ranger."

Lynette said, "It is funny, Lewis. What the hell do you know about forests?"

Lewis replied, "I know that the conservation of forest land is essential for watersheds to be efficient aquifers to preserve clean water, and..."

JUST MISSED THE SIXTIES

Al interrupted, "I want you people to know that, just like you all, I too believe in 'sticking it to the man' and look at me! I'm wearing my Super Fly sweatshirt!"

Lundees said, "That's, uh, funky, Al."

"Does this mean I can be a soul brother too?"

"Sure, Al, you can be a soul brother too."

"Good! Because I'm getting hot. I'm going to take off this sweatshirt right now."

Al removed the sweatshirt to reveal his t-shirt underneath. On the front of his shirt was a Confederate Flag. Beneath the flag, it read: *Never Forget.*

Lewis, Lynette, and Lundees gasped.

Al was confused, "What? I don't get it."

I said, "Al, your t-shirt! Look! It has a Confederate flag on it! You know, Dixieland, slavery, Jim Crow, and all that bad stuff?"

"Oh, shit! Tell you what, I will take off this shirt right now and put it in the trash!"

Spitz said, "Hey, Al! Why don't you burn it?"

Al said, "Cool!" He removed the shirt and tossed it in the trash, followed by a lighted match.

Spitz, Jay, and Al chanted, "Burn, baby, burn!"

Al said, "Holy shit, this is making a lot of smoke!"

Jay said, "Move it over by the fan!"

Al touched the can and said, "It's fucking hot, man!"

Lewis and his friends were cracking up. Tim looked at me with his "What a fry!" face. Perhaps this was a good time for me to leave. I didn't know how much more I could take of topless Al and his awkward, one-man social outreach program. I slipped out the door.

I'll sleep well tonight knowing that the country's race-relationship issues are in Al's capable hands!

It was time for me to regain control of the wing. Time for some fun and games!

Wing Games

Second Summer in Wisconsin, it's that last gasp of wonderful Fall weather before the cold Canadian winds blow in and stay put, usually until late April. The leaves had turned – gold and red were everywhere. There was a hint of that cool, wintry smell in the air. Once again, the wing was taking an evening hike to the woods.

Before dinner, I'd found Al in his room and said, "Hey, let's take the wing back to the clearing tonight. I want to teach them some games we played during my freshmen year."

"Far out. Games. Hmm. What kind of games are you talking about?"

"The kind that is only fun to play when you're stoned."

"Well then, fuck! Count me in!" He jumped up to start knocking on doors and recruiting wingmates.

"Spitz, Chuck, QP, Jay, William, Professor, Tim, you better get your asses out here after dinner tonight; we're gonna get fucked-up and play some games!"

Jay popped his head out his door and said, "Cool! I just got some dynamite hashish."

Al and I said, in unison, "Bring it."

Once again, walking down the road into the North Woods, I looked back at the crew before turning onto the deer path. Most everyone was wearing a light jacket or sweatshirt. Al wore a blue denim jacket that was so washed-out it was practically white. William was wearing a dark brown leather jacket that matched his Stetson hat. Jay wore a black jacket and was carrying his leather tote. QP and Chuck wore sweatshirts and held the beer.

Chuck said, "Next time, someone else has to bring the beer!"

JUST MISSED THE SIXTIES

I was holding 10 Frisbees, stacked together, and a pocket full of cloth strips for the games. As usual, Casey and Don were no-shows. Casey told me he was seeing a girl from one of his classes.

I wonder what happened to Cricket?

Don was at UPS again. And then I realized I'd forgotten about Rachel.

Oh shit! Well, I'll remember her next time.

Arriving at the fire pit in the Clearing, everyone grabbed some firewood and sat.

Wow! Everybody's sitting in the same place they always sit!

Chuck and QP started passing out beers. It didn't take long for Al to get started.

"So, William, you got any stories about the cattle drive?" Then Al began to sing, "Rollin' rollin' rollin', keep them doggies rollin'!"

I better take charge of this scene, and quickly!

I said, "Okay, dudes, now listen up! I thought that tonight, I could teach you a game or two to help you all unwind a little. You know what I mean, to help you to relax from the stress of your classes and..."

QP said, "Classes? What the fuck is he talking about? Do you know Chuck?"

"I don't know, QP. Maybe William knows something about these things called *classes*."

William shrugged and said, "I don't have a clue what he's talking about. What about you, Jay?"

Jay said, "You know, I think it might have something to do with those other buildings on campus. You know what I mean, the ones that aren't dormitories or dining halls - those *other* buildings. Have you gone inside one of those buildings, Al?"

"Hell no! Classes are for losers, right, Spitz?"

"Speak for yourself, Al."

Al said, "Oh shit, Spitz, way to fuck up the joke! Did you hit your head on the end of the pool again?" Everyone laughed.

They're bonding again! This is so cool! But now it's time for the first game. I've got to get them away from this fire pit.

JUST MISSED THE SIXTIES

"Okay, everyone, we're going to do a little warm-up activity before the main game. I call this exercise 'The Stoned Charge'. Everybody, line up over there at the edge of the clearing."

They did as I commanded.

Wow! Cool! I feel power!

"Now, Jay, light up your hash pipe. Then, go down the line and give everyone a bowl-blast."

Jay lit the pipe and then walked up to Tim. He cupped his hand over the top of the bowl, put his mouth to his hand, then blew smoke out the stem – right down Tim's throat."

Tim said, "Oh my God! What a fry!" And then he made a silly grin.

After Jay dosed the entire troop, I began my *"Patton"* spiel.

"Okay, men! Pretend you are under my command. You are now in my unit. Here's the drill. Men! We've got to take the ground on the other side of the clearing. It won't be easy! When I yell, 'Charge,' I want you to scream as loud as you can and run as fast as you can to the other side. At any time during the run, I want you to yell, 'They got me', and fall dead to the ground. Do you understand your mission?"

"Yes!"

"Say, 'Yes, sir'!"

"Yes, sir!"

"I can't hear you!"

"Yes, sir!"

Look at them – they can't wait for me to let them go!

"CHARGE!"

"AAAAAAAAAAAAAAAAAAAA! They got me! They got me!"

Then, I joined in the run. I died close to the other side. Lying down in the tall grass and looking up, I saw a woodcock wheeling about in front of the harvest moon.

This is very relaxing, but I need to get to the next game.

"Okay! Good job, everyone! Now, everyone, please get up and cluster closely together in the middle of the clearing. Closer! Closer!"

Al said to Spitz, "Not so close, dude."

JUST MISSED THE SIXTIES

William said, "Spitz, tell him to fuck off."

Why do they make this so hard?

"Okay, Jay, everyone needs another blast from your magic pipe. You got any more ammo?"

"Sir, yes, sir!"

Jay re-blasted each wing-mate, and then I covered their eyes with a blindfold made from the strips of cloth.

Tim said, "Oh man, a blind fry!"

When all were buzzed and blind, I pushed them tightly together and gave everyone a Frisbee.

I said, "I call this game Stoned Blind Frisbee. Here's how you play. I'll count to three. At three, everyone throws their Frisbee straight up in the air. Of course, the Frisbees will fall back to the ground. Anyone who gets hit by a falling Frisbee is out of the game. If you are out, remove your blindfold and help pass out the Frisbees for the next round. The last one to survive without getting hit is the winner. Got it?"

Al said, "Yeah, we got it."

"Okay. Here goes. One. Two. Al! You shot your Frisbee already!"

QP said, "Al, you asshole, can't you count?"

Al said, "Not after that hash."

I said, "Okay, Al, here's your Frisbee. This time, wait for three."

Al said, "If you say so, chief."

"One. Two. Three! Fire!"

Everyone launched their discs and immediately started shouting.

Tim said, "I don't want to get hit!"

Spitz said, "No! No! Don't hit me!"

Chuck said, "I'm scared!"

Al said, "Shut up, you pussies! You sound like a bunch of little girls! Ow! Ow! Ow! Ow! Ow! They're all hitting me!"

Euphoria erupted. It was unstoppable laughter. We were rolling on the ground and clutching our sides. We fed off each other's hashish-induced giddiness until we were exhausted.

JUST MISSED THE SIXTIES

"Hey! Let's do that again!"

Al said, "I think I'll sit out this one."

I said, "You have to, Al, you got hit!"

"Well, that's one good thing about this fucked-up game."

The game continued until everyone was hit except for Tim. We crowned him the winner of the first Second East Stoned Blind Frisbee Event and returned to the dorm. While walking back, I suddenly remembered I had a chemistry test the next day.

Oh shit! I want to do well on that test! I like chemistry. I like atoms. Atoms are cool. It's so crazy. Everything is made of little, tiny atoms. Little atoms are constantly bouncing around. Look around you. In the air, little atoms are bouncing everywhere. Bouncing off you and bouncing off me, look, they're bouncing off that tree!

As we entered our hallway from the stairwell, I said, "Have you guys ever wondered what it would be like to be an atom flying around in the air? You know, you'd just be moving along until you hit something and then bounce off, like a pool ball, and just going again until you hit something else and bouncing again and going and bouncing and going..."

I began walking stiffly, robotically, down the hall - chanting, "Atom! Atom! Atom! Atom!" Then, I hit a wall, bounced, and continued chanting.

It was contagious. Soon, the entire wing was bouncing around the hallway, off the walls, off each other, chanting louder and louder.

"Atom! Atom! Atom! Atom!"

Eventually, everyone bounced into their rooms. As I bounced into mine, I glanced up the hallway and saw, standing at the end, three students from Second West in their bathrobes, clutching their toilet kits and washcloths, mouths agape.

Fighting Fascism

The next afternoon, I was just back from classes and unlocking my door (still thinking about the morning's chemistry test) when I heard a commotion coming from QP's and Chuck's room.

QP said, "You think you got it bad? Look at this!"

Tim said, "What a fry!" Laughter.

Chuck said, "How the hell did you get it there?"

QP said, "I don't know! I must have gotten it on my hands and then spread it around!"

I've got to see what they're talking about!

I quickly walked down the hallway and peeked into their room.

Chuck saw me, pointed, and said, "There's the guy who did this to you!"

I said, "What? What did I do?"

I looked at QP. He was holding his shirt in his hand.

QP said, "Well, hello, Joe, or should I say, General Patton? Thanks! Thanks for this!" He pointed to a red rash on his arms, shoulders, back, and chest.

Chuck laughed, "It looks like QP charged right into a patch of poison ivy!"

I said, "No shit!"

Chuck said, "Yep. Some guys have some on their arms and legs, but QP is the worst! I just got back from K-Mart with some calamine lotion." He set a paper bag on the dresser.

I said, "Well, let's start treating the troops! Everyone, line up for your medicine!"

The injured troops formed a line.

I've never had a calamine lotion party before.

JUST MISSED THE SIXTIES

Jay suggested that grass was also a good therapy. "Hey, boys, this will help relieve the itching. Close the door, Chuck. Turn on the fan, QP. It's time for the medicine that's sure to heal."

Tim said, "Hey, Jay, I hear that stuff cures almost everything."

"That's my philosophy."

Tim said, "By the way, Jay, how's that SDS thing going with the petitions and all that?"

Jay said, "Way cool, man. We're pretty much done getting all the signatures."

Spitz said, "What were the petitions again?"

"Well, one was to impeach Nixon, and the other was to allow freshmen and sophomores to live off campus if they want to."

I was starting to apply calamine to QP's back with a rag.

I said, "Yeah! That mandatory housing rule is so repressive, it's almost fascist!"

I drew a calamine lotion swastika on his back.

I said, "This represents the fascist Campus Housing Department!"

I drew a pink line through the swastika.

"This line represents the SDS – fighting the repression!"

Jay said, "Yeah, that's right, Joe! We're fighting the fascists!"

Soon, everyone got into the spirit and started decorating their bodies with crossed-out swastikas.

Then, QP started chanting, "Fight the fascists! Fight! Fight! Fight!"

The chanting reminded me of last night, so I yelled, "Atom! Atom! Atom!

Everyone chanted, "Atom! Atom! Atom!"

The door opened, and we spilled into the hallway. Once again, we were bouncing off the walls and each other, chanting, "Atom! Atom! Atom! Atom!"

Then, I saw Lewis and Lynette standing at the end of the hallway, staring, shocked. They spun around and walked away.

I shouted, "Lewis! Lynette! It's not what it looks like!" But they didn't stop.

JUST MISSED THE SIXTIES

*I wonder... what the hell **did** it look like?*

A couple of days later, at lunch, QP shared a rumor.
"Guys, I heard that Lewis just moved off our wing!"
I said, "Really? Why's that?"
"He said the wing was too weird."
Chuck said, "What? Where did he get that idea?"
QP said, "I don't know. I don't understand it."
Chuck said, "Or maybe he just needed an excuse to move into the same dorm with Lynette."
QP said, "Yeah. That's probably it."
Oh no! We've lost our first wingmate!

The Music of Second East

The Second Summer ended, as it always does, followed by a stretch of cold and rainy weather, keeping us indoors and away from the Clearing. Al unwittingly inspired a new game.

Saturday morning, he was at my door.

"Hey, Joe, you gotta come to my room and listen to this song. It will blow your mind!"

"Sure, Al, I'll be right there."

I grabbed a shirt and went to Al's room. Half the wing was already there. Moments later, a couple more arrived.

QP said, "Okay, Al, what's the big deal with this song?"

"It's so cool, you'll love it. But first, you've got to get into the right frame of mind. Jay, can you help me out here?"

"Sure, Al, turn on the fan."

We toked, and Al played the tune "OD'd on Life Itself" by the Blue Oyster Cult. When the song finished, Al asked for feedback from the group.

Al said, "Well? Pretty cool, eh? I love that song!"

Tim said, "Yeah, Al. It's got some nice changes."

OD'd on life itself. Oh my God! That pretty much sums up Al!

Jay said, "That was pretty heavy, Al. But wait! I got a song I want to play for everyone, too!"

I said, "Me too! Hey! Why don't we make this into a competition? We could have a Best Stoned Song Competition?"

Al said, "Okay, that could be interesting. How do we play?"

I said, "Well, first, we need a prize, so... everybody put a dollar into the pot. Then we play our songs. We need some judges to select a winner."

Al said, "Why the fuck would I want to be a judge? Then I can't play a song!"

I said, "The judges will be super stoned throughout the competition."

Al said, "Oh! Well... now I'm torn!" He continued, "I know, let's make QP and Chuck the judges. QP only likes that old fifties crap, and Chuck thinks the mooing of cows is music."

Chuck said, "Shut up, Al... oh, what the heck. Give me a joint and play me some tunes!"

QP said, "Yeah, boys, we want to hear the best you got! Bring it on! And don't Bogart that joint, Chucky!"

Jay said, "I better win this pot – just to help pay for all the pot I share with you guys!"

Al said, "Oh, Jay, you know you share it because you love us so much – kissy, kissy, smoochy, smoochy."

Jay said, "Oh, Al, that's so gross!"

I said, "All right then! Everyone, go to your room and pull out your winning tune! Try to be back here in 10 minutes!"

Everyone ran to their rooms. I shuffled through my record collection at top speed and pulled out a few solid contenders and a last desperation album.

Soon, the wing was reassembled in Al's room. The judges sat directly between Al's massive speakers. Al handled the turn table. Jay hovered close to the judges to monitor their dosing. The rest of the contestants drew numbers from a hat to determine the order.

QP said, "Okay, guys. Who's up first? Play your song!"

The Professor stood up, album in hand, and walked to Al.

Chuck said, "Stop right there, Professor. Is that a Moody Blues Album?"

"Why, yes. It is!"

"You weren't thinking of playing 'Nights in White Satin,' were you?"

"Well, yes, I was absolutely thinking of playing 'Nights in White Satin.'"

"Just a second, Professor. We're going to have a judge's conference." QP and Chuck exchanged a few guarded whispers. QP turned back to the Professor.

"Okay, here's our ruling. We're going to give you a second chance at a different song. Try to find something unique, different, perhaps something not as well-known. Listen, the only time I ever want to hear that song is with a girl parked on Lover's Lane. Can you dig that?"

"Sure. No problem... wait! I've got an idea!"

The Professor flew to his room and back in record time. He handed Al an album and told him which track to play. It was "White Bird" by It's a Beautiful Day. It was rock, like I'd never heard before.

Holy shit - violins! Wow, this arrangement is highly intricate. Very cool, Professor.

But, when I looked at the judge's faces, I saw confusion.

Oh, man. Those are harsh judges!

Chuck said, "Who's next?"

William stood and handed his album to Al.

Al said, "Oh no. Now, we'll have to listen to 'Home, Home on the Range.' What? Wait a minute. What's this? Is this Arlo Guthrie? Isn't he a folk singer?"

I said, "Hey, Al, he's cool. He did 'Alice's Restaurant' and 'Coming into Los Angeles'."

Al said, "I don't know."

I said, "Really! He's cool. He was at Woodstock."

Al said, "Oh! Well, that's different! You should have said that in the first place."

Al started the cut: "Running Down the Road".

Oh shit! This one's good too! The false ending is far out!

When the song ended, the judges nodded and exchanged some whispers.

I think they liked it.

QP said, "All righty then. Who's next?"

Jay stood up and handed Al an album and a joint to the judges.

QP grabbed the joint and said, "Ah gee, thanks, Jay!"

JUST MISSED THE SIXTIES

I said, "No fair! That's bribing the judges!"

Jay argued his case, "Wait a minute, they're supposed to be stoned, right? I'm just making sure they don't start crashing! You know, Joe, since you haven't gone yet, this can only help you too!"

I relinquished, "Okay! Okay! Toke away!"

Jay's song was a strong contender; 'Heroin' by Lou Reed.

Oh my God! We're looking into the mind of a heroin addict! Was it Nietzsche who said, "When you look into the abyss, the abyss looks into you?" What happens if you quote Nietzsche? Does Nietzsche quote you?

Jay's selection blew the judges away.

Chuck turned to QP and said, "Wow!"

The bar at the Stoned Music Competition has just been raised!

QP said, "Gosh! We should take a little break after that tune, but no, we'll carry on! So, who's next, and what do you have?"

Spitz handed his album to Al. Al looked at the cover. His eyes went wide open.

"It's Pink Floyd! We're all doomed!"

Spitz, Jay, and I were on our feet. "No, not fair! You can't pull a Pink Floyd on us! Ringer!"

QP smiled, "The judges will decide if Pink Floyd will be allowed in the Second East Stoned Music Competition."

After a minute of whispering, QP said, "Spitz, it's okay. We will allow Pink Floyd into the competition on one condition: please don't play 'Money.'"

"Okay! I wasn't planning on it!"

Al started the track. It was "One of These Days". I couldn't believe my ears.

What! Not fair! I was going to play that! It's the best stoner song ever!

Now, I'll have to play my Hail Mary selection!

The song ended. The judges had silly grins on their faces.

I'm doomed. After that, I can only hope they're receptive to something completely different.

JUST MISSED THE SIXTIES

QP said, "Okay! Wow! Who's next? I almost feel sorry for the guy that has to follow that song. Hopefully, it's something completely different!"

That's my cue!

I stood and said, "Well, lucky me, I'm next." I handed my album to Al. The LP, *A Child's Garden of Grass: A Pre-Legalization Comedy,* is a humorous look at everything about pot. According to the record and agreed upon by many, the three best things to do when stoned are eating food, having sex, and listening to music. The album has a comedy track for each activity. I directed Al to play the track titled "Listening to Music When You're Stoned."

A narrator begins, "Listening to music while stoned will open your mind to a whole new world. Every kind of music sounds great! You can listen to Acid Rock!" And then you hear an awesome riff of psychedelic, wailing fuzz guitar.

The narrator continues, "Or Bluegrass." Followed by a short bit of expert finger-picking on mandolins, banjos, and guitars.

The narrator says, "Or Jazz." And then the smooth sounds of sax, bass, and keyboard.

Lastly, the narrator says, "Or even…Classical Music." 'The Hallelujah Chorus' performed by a kazoo and tuba duet.

It's a hilarious concept that sounds hilarious.

QP said, "Oh my God! What a fry!"

Then QP and Chuck doubled over laughing. They were wiping tears from their eyes.

Thank you, marijuana, for my victory!

Spitz, who thought he had the Stoned Music Contest wrapped up in a nice little Pink Floyd bow, said, "A comedy album? That's not fair!"

QP and Chuck, ignoring Spitz's protest, handed me the prize. "Here's the pot, Joe. Thanks for the laugh."

I said, "Great! Now I can buy some tickets for the Fleetwood Mac Concert!"

Yes, that's right. Fleetwood Mac was coming to our little campus on the edge of the Wisconsin North Woods.

Rock Concerts

The show was the following weekend. Monday, I went to the gymnasium, the site of the show, to buy tickets for Rachel and myself.

Approaching the box office, I was concerned.

I hope they have some good seats left!

"I'd like two tickets, please. I'll take the best seats available."

"There are no best seats. All the seats are the same."

"What? How can that be?"

"Well, we're trying a new idea called 'Festival Seating'. There are no reserved seats. It's the same price for every seat. That way, you can sit anywhere you want when you come for the show."

"Far out! That's cool! It's so much more equal that way."

When the night of the show arrived, everyone going to the show met outside Al's room to walk together to the concert. I was with Rachel. Spitz introduced us to a girl he'd met at the gym.

"Hey, Joe and Rachel, this is Sally. Sally and I ran into each other when we were running laps at the gym. I mean, we didn't literally run into each other. I mean…"

Al's door burst open, and standing in the doorframe was Steve, Al's party buddy from Tomah. He was holding a police car's roof rack, complete with lights and a siren.

"Hey there, dudes and dudettes! Look what I copped from the top of a fuzz-mobile! I think I plucked his cherry! Whee Haw!"

I was amazed, "How could you… Where could you…"

"I can't answer that, Joe! It's a trade secret! Anyway, we better get going to the show. Yee-hah!"

JUST MISSED THE SIXTIES

Steve tossed the rack on Al's bed. Al joined us, and we exited Hyer Hall.

Crossing the field to the gym, we could see about two hundred students milling about in front of the gym doors. There were five double doors, each separated by a yard of glass windows. We reached the back of the crowd. There was no line to queue up in. I wasn't sure how this was going to work. New arrivals massed behind us. There was a tension in the air.

Is this excitement for the show or concern about getting a good seat?

Steve said, "Look, guys. Watch me. When those doors open, I'm going to move like a banshee and get into the building. When you get in, look for me and Al. We'll have a row of seats reserved for everyone! Got it?"

"Yes! Yes!"

What's the worry? There are so many doors, they'll get everyone in really fast.

Suddenly, only the middle doors flew open. **ONLY THE MIDDLE DOORS**

Oh my God! Everyone is going to press into the middle!

Steve yelled, "Boo-yah!" And then, all I could see of Steve was a blur of blonde hair crisscrossing ahead through the crowd.

There was a scream followed by chaos. People were pushing from every direction. There was more screaming. It was a free-for-all.

Rachel said, "Joe! Help! My feet aren't touching the ground! Help!"

I said, "Hold my hand!" And she grabbed on tightly.

I said, "Grab anyone else you see!"

Luckily, our group was in the middle of the mob, so the tidal force of moving people swept us through the center doors and into the lobby. Looking back, I saw bodies and faces shoved up against the unopened doors on the sides.

Oh my God! Those poor people! Somebody is going to get badly hurt someday.

JUST MISSED THE SIXTIES

Once in the lobby, the crowd dispersed, followed by a mad dash to the front seats. The seats were simple folding chairs organized into rows. The neat rows vanished as chairs were hurdled, tossed aside, or picked up and taken closer.

Near the front, Al and Steve were waving at us. "Come on! Come on! We can't hold this row forever!"

Rachel said, "Wow, these are great seats!"

Twenty minutes later, the rush was over. The house lights dimmed. The band took the stage.

Standing at the keyboards, Christine McVie said, "Hello, Stevens Point! First, I'd like to say how wonderful it is to be here! I'm so excited! It's just smashing to travel, get away from the city, and visit someplace where you can look at the horizon and see trees and living things instead of buildings. I love traveling to wonderful places like Stevens Point, Wisconsin! Anyway, here's a number from our *Bare Trees* LP." And then she sang,

> "I want to sit at home in my rockin' chair,
> I don't want to travel the world,
> As far as I'm concerned, I've had my share...
> Buy me a ticket homeward bound."

Afterward, Bob Welsch sang his hit, "Sentimental Lady". That was followed by a weirdly entertaining bongo solo by Mick Fleetwood.

There was a moment of silence, then the stage lit up, and they launched into Peter Green's "Oh Well." The audience jumped to their feet. It was sing-along time. During the instrumental section, lights flashed, everyone cheered, the energy was high, and so was Second East.

After the show, ears still buzzing, Rachel and I walked arm-in-arm back to the dorm. During the exit, all the wingmates scattered their separate ways.

Rachel said, "Hey, Joe, thanks for saving me from the mob when they opened the front doors!"

"Wow! Yeah, that was crazy. I'm glad we didn't fall. We could have been crushed!"

"I know! I'll never forget how those people looked with their faces shoved into the windows!"

I said, "Yeah, I know, Rachel. It was so competitive. We were like wild animals! Whatever happened to the peace and love?"

"Apparently, peace and love are not as important as getting a good seat for a rock concert!"

I said, "You know what? The flower children of the sixties would not have been like this. They would have been, like, 'after you, brother and sister!' and 'peace and love'! Can somebody tell me? Where have all the flower children gone?"

"I don't know, Joe, to the florist?" Rachel laughed and said, "Really, Joe, I don't know. They weren't at the concert tonight! Speaking of concerts, would you like to see a Jethro Tull concert with me next weekend in Madison?"

"Wow! Of course! Yes! That sounds great! But, I'm a little short of bread right now..."

"Oh no, don't worry! I got some tickets from a friend, no charge!"

What kind of friend gives away concert tickets?

She said, "The show is next Friday. We can take the afternoon Greyhound down before the show, then return on the midnight run back to Point. It's just an hour and a half on the bus."

"Sounds like a great plan! But I have one little question about those tickets."

"What's that?"
"Are they festival seating?"
"No, they're reserved seats."
"Good."

Wednesday morning, we awoke to the first snowfall of the season. It was just a light dusting, but everything outdoors that had once been gray and dirty now looked white and clean. The boys of the Second East came to my door right after my last afternoon class.

Jay said, "Hey, Joe! Everyone wants to see what the Hut and the Clearing look like in the snow. Are you coming?"

"Sure! Yes, I'm coming!" I set down my books and spirals, grabbed my winter jacket, and joined the gang at the top of the stairs.

Walking along the deer path to the Clearing, I remembered.

Oh shit! I forgot about Rachel again! Oh, well, she's probably busy working on an art project.

Meanwhile, back at the dorm, Rachel was knocking on my door.

"Joe! Joe! Are you in there?"

Walking down the hallway, Casey saw her and said, "Rachel, I think Joe went with the gang to the woods again. I heard them say something about seeing the snow in the Clearing and on the Hut."

"No! That sucks! He promised me! I would have liked to see that, too! I helped build the damn thing, you know!"

"Oh. Sorry about that, Rachel."

Rachel and I rode the bus to Madison on Friday afternoon to see the Jethro Tull concert. Rachel was quieter than usual, so I talked about my favorite Tull songs.

"What's your favorite album? I like some of the stuff on *Benefit*, although I hope they play 'Bouree', which is on *Stand Up*. By the way, where are the seats located?"

Rachel pulled them out, "They're pretty good. They're about 12 rows back and to one side."

"Really! That is so far out! How did you get these seats again?"

"Oh. Ah. A friend gave them to me. Oh! It looks like we're here already! Let's go!"

The seats were just as good as Rachel had said. First, the band played some cuts from the album *Aqualung*. And then, I was pleased to hear them play "Bouree". But after that, band leader Ian Anderson announced, "And now, we're going to perform the entire LP of *Thick as a Brick*. Let me warn you, it's rather long, so after a time, you may find yourself shifting from buttock to buttock." The crowd cheered.

Oh yeah. We're all looking forward to a bit of buttock-shifting!

JUST MISSED THE SIXTIES

After the show, Rachel's concert and travel plans continued without a hitch. We briskly walked a couple of blocks to the terminal and caught the bus back to Point. I was still energized by the show.

"Wow! That show was great! And those seats were great! Thank you so much, Rachel, or rather, mystery friend!" Right then and there, I decided I would get some details about this mystery friend. "All right, tell me more about these tickets. First off, who gave them to you?"

"Oh. It was just some guy I met."

Some guy?

"Some guy you met? Who? Where?"

Rachel smiled. Although it was a little tiny hint of a smile, I could still see it.

Is she trying to make me jealous?

"Listen, it's no big deal. His name is Michael, and he sits next to me in Geology class. One day, we started talking about how much we both hate Geology. He's an English major. He writes poetry."

"Yeah? So why did he give you the tickets?"

"Well, he bought the tickets but later found out he couldn't attend the show. The English Department invited him to read some of his poetry at a departmental function. I think it's a dinner. He couldn't turn that down."

Wow! He must be a pretty good poet.

She said, "He's a pretty good poet."

"Yeah, right, he's good for Stevens Point. Did you pay him for the tickets?"

"No, he said I didn't have to give him money. But I did promise to study Geology with him."

"Oh, I see. So... have you had any study dates yet?"

"Well, maybe. I might have studied with him on one of the nights you went to the Hut, WITHOUT ME!"

Ouch. Touché.

I said, "Oh! Shit! I'm sorry about that, Rachel. I want to pay for my ticket, at least."

"Don't worry about it. His family is loaded."

"Okay, then."

"You should read some of his poetry sometime. It's pretty good. He read some to me, very romantic stuff."

Romantic?

"Oh, by the way, next Saturday night, Michael told me about a performance art presentation by the English department. Would you like to go with me?"

I said, "Sure. Sure. I'll be there for you."

I'll be there, especially if it means you'll forgive me for forgetting to ask you to the hut.

We sat quietly for the rest of the bus ride. Rachel fell asleep on my shoulder. I stared out the window. And the moon rose over an open field.

Second East Live

Once again, the following day, there was a commotion in QP and Chuck's room. I walked down to see what was happening. When I entered the room, Chuck told me the bad news.

"Joe! Guess what! QP's gonna drop out! He's going back to Racine!"

"No way, QP! You can't do that to us! Why are you dropping out?"

"I know, I know. I feel pretty bad about it. I don't like leaving you guys, either. But I just realized I'm doing nothing here. And I mean *nothing*. I'm doing nothing! I'm not going to classes. I'm not learning anything. Hell, I can do that at home! Who knows, maybe I'll find a job or something. I don't know. I've got to figure out what I want to do with my life."

I looked down at the floor.

Damn! I feel like I'm losing a little piece of myself.

QP said, "Hey if it makes you feel any better, it's been great! I don't remember ever having so much fun. Ever! Look, I even wrote a little song about my time in Second East!"

QP held out a sheet of paper. I grabbed it.

Chuck said, "Wrote a song? No, you didn't! You just took an old song from the Chi-Lites and changed the lyrics a little!"

Al said, "That's cool! Maybe you could make a career out of writing funny lyrics!"

Chuck said, "No! That's just weird, Al!"

QP said, "I like it! I'll call myself Crazy QP!"

JUST MISSED THE SIXTIES

I looked closely at QP's lyrics. "QP, you hardly changed anything! It's almost the same lyrics for 'Have You Seen Her' except for about, I don't know, three words?"

QP said, "But they're the perfect three words!"

Tim, Spitz, and Jay were getting anxious. "Come on! Come on! Sing the song!"

"Well, actually, I don't sing it. It's spoken, except at the end."

I said, "Well then, speak it!"

Professor said, "Wait a minute, QP! Let's record this on my new cassette recorder!"

I said, "Cassette recorder! That's cool. But don't they have problems with tape-hiss and background noise, compared to reel-to-reel tape recorders?"

"Not anymore, thanks to the new Dolby technology!"

The Professor zipped away to grab his recording gear. Soon, he was back, plugging it in and setting up a microphone on the coffee table.

"Okay, QP. Sit over here and project to the microphone. Three, two, one, you're on!"

"Okay. I will now perform 'Have You Seen Them' with apologies to Eugene Record and Barbara Acklin.

One Month ago today,
I was happy as a lark,
But now, I go for walks,
To the movies, maybe to the park.
I have a seat on the same old bench,
To watch Second East play.
You know, tomorrow's their future,
But for me, it's just another day.
They all gather 'round me,
They seem to know my name.
We laugh, smoke a few joints,
But it still doesn't ease my pain.
I know I can't hide from the memories,

JUST MISSED THE SIXTIES

Though day after day I've tried.
I keep saying, "I'll be back."
But today, again, I've lied.
Oh, I see Second East everywhere I go,
On the street and even at the picture show.
Have you seen them?
Tell me, have you seen them?"

He stopped, and the Professor clicked the stop button. There was a moment of silence.

This is a major bummer.

Spitz said, "Hey, Professor, can I say something on the tape recorder?"

"Sure, knock yourself out!" He held up the microphone and pressed the record button.

"Hi, everybody! I'm the Spitz! I can swim super fast. I can swim three-fifths of a mile in ten seconds!"

Then everybody started grabbing the mike and saying whatever goofy stuff came to mind.

Jay grabbed the mike and said, "Hey, everybody! Why don't we make some music - like a band?"

Spitz said, "Great idea!"

Jay said, "Okay, so... does anyone play an instrument?" Silence. "All righty, does anyone have any musical talent whatsoever?" Silence. "Okay then, does anyone own a musical instrument of any kind?"

I said, "I've got some kazoos."

Jay said, "That's great, at least that's something!"

Chuck said, "I've got some calls."

"Calls? What are calls?"

"You know, duck calls, crow calls, turkey calls, those kinds of calls!"

I said, "That's great! Has anyone ever heard 'Several Species of Small Furry Animals Gathered Together in a Cave and Grooving with a Pict?'" Nobody had heard it. "I'll play it! You'll find it very inspirational, and it's by Pink Floyd!"

JUST MISSED THE SIXTIES

Jay said, "Did you say Pink Floyd? I'll get a joint."

So, after the appropriate inspiration, the instruments were assembled. Tim designed a drum kit: a trash can for the drum and a fan grate for the cymbals. The Professor pressed record, and a cacophony of kazoos and calls were recorded for posterity.

Look out, Pink Floyd!

Man, how can QP leave all this behind?

Tim said, "You know what? After I heard that furry animal track from Pink Floyd, I realized what they said about the '60s was true."

Jay said, "What's that, Tim?"

"They recorded anything!"

Jay said, "Hey, guys! We have to give our band a name!"

I said, "How about Second East... Live!"

Jay said, "No! Don't get me started on that whole *live album* concept!"

"Why's that?"

"All right, here's a challenge for you. You have one minute. Can you guess the four reasons that I hate live albums? Time starting now - go!"

QP was quick, "They never have any new songs!"

"Ding! Ding! That's one!"

"Spitz said, "The songs are never as good as the studio versions!"

"Right again! I underestimated you guys! Got anything else?"

Tim said, "I hate it when the singer lets the crowd sing the song for him."

"I hadn't thought of that one. It's good, though, yet it fits in with number two. Hurry up! Time's running out!"

I said, "I hate the annoying crowd noises."

"Ding! Ding! Right again! Who wants to listen to whistles and hoots? One more! Anyone? Anyone? Tick, tick, tick..."

Tim started to panic, "What a fry!"

I said, "Let me think...The idea of a live album is that you're getting all the energy and excitement of a concert without actually having to go to the concert...."

JUST MISSED THE SIXTIES

"Close enough, and this is the most important point – you feel like a loser because you're not actually at the show! I hate that!"

I said, "Well, Second East Live isn't live, you see - we just pretend it is. Say, Jay, here's a question for you. Can you name a pop song recorded in a studio but pretended to be live? Hmm? Hmm?"

"That's easy. It's 'Bennie and the Jets' by Elton John."

"Oh wow! You're good."

"And don't forget 'Sgt. Pepper's Lonely Hearts Club Band!'"

"Oh, that's right – you're good!"

Spitz said, "So anyway, if we're called Second East Live and if we play a live show, would we be Second East Live, Live?"

QP said, "You're overthinking it, Spitz. The important thing is, thanks to the Professor, our sound is captured forever."

Yes! Second East Forever!

This Ain't the Hilton, You Know

Everyone helped QP take his stuff to the parking lot the next day. After packing his car, he shook our hands one last time. We were waving goodbye as QP backed up his battered old VW Bug. QP waved back and wiped his eyes.

CLANK!

Chuck said, "Oh shit! QP backed into Kerry's car!"

QP stuck his head out the window, looked back at their bumpers, and said, "Fuck it, it's only Kerry's car," and drove away.

William said, "Hey, Joe, aren't we supposed to play each other next in the chess tournament? I just beat Jay a couple of days ago."

"I think so. How was your game with Jay?"

"Easy. I told him he would play better if he got stoned, and he believed me. But damn, it took him forever to make any moves!"

"That's funny! You can't pull that trick on me! Okay, I'll stop by in a few minutes, and we can play. All right?"

"Far out."

I walked into William's room for the match a few minutes later. He had the game board and pieces on his coffee table, ready to go. A baseball bat was leaning up against the table, and William was holding out two fists.

That's the bat he used to beat the shit out of some guy! What a fry!

"OK, Joe, pick a hand; you go first if it's a white pawn. I hope you don't mind if my bat rests there. It's a superstition thing, you know, for good luck. I always like to have it with me if I can."

Yikes!

"No problem, William. I have superstitions of my own about my clothes when I take exams and stuff like that."

William said, "White pawn, Joe, you go first."

I made the standard opening: Move the King's pawn forward, two spaces.

"Say, William. That wouldn't happen to be the bat that you…"

"Beat the shit out of some guy with? You bet it is!"

Oh my God! The story was true! I must not freak out. I must focus on the game…

Ten moves passed, and I had no idea what I was doing. I kept glancing sideways at the bat, just resting there, so menacing. He started taking some of my pieces, a bishop and then a knight. All I'd taken was a stupid pawn that I never should have taken because it was a trap. Somehow, I had to change the mood.

"Say, William, did you ever get back with that girl in your story at the campfire?"

"No way! She was such a slut. I got a new girlfriend now."

"Oh! What's she like?"

"What's she like? Well… she likes my tongue! Ha! Ha! That's true. She likes my tongue in strategic places!"

"Oh! I see!"

"Seriously, Joe, she's smart and very nice. And most importantly, she's very skinny, just the way I like 'em. I don't like any fat to get in the way of my head when I'm down there in the womanly area if you know what I mean! Nothing but me and the lady parts and a little whipped cream to make it so sweet. Mmm, mmm."

"William, it's your turn."

"Oh! Yeah! That's right. For a second there, I was thinking about my little lady and her… You know, I think I'm gonna get this game over with quickly, so I can call her up and tell her to get her bony ass up here right away! It's been too long!"

"Sounds good, William. Hey, look! I just took your Queen, and you're in check. Say, when was the last time you saw her?"

"Oh. It was about three days ago."

"Oh, man! That's a long time! How can you stand it? It's your move."

With a tremor in his voice, William said, "A man's just gotta have patience, you know?"

"I see. Well, that's check-mate, William. Make your phone call. Don't worry; I'll put away the game while you're gone."

William dashed down the hallway to the public phone at the far end. He was lucky, it wasn't busy.

Jay walked into the room as I was cleaning up the chess pieces. He was holding a thick manila folder.

"Hey, Joe! This is cool. I just finished getting signatures on the petitions from the last dormitory. Why don't we put them together and send them off in the mail? Do you have time?"

"Yes. Bring 'em to my room. We'll get these out today."

We packaged the two sets of petitions into two large boxes. One was addressed to our Congressman in Washington, D.C., and the other to the Director of UWSP Campus Housing.

We walked to the campus post office and mailed the first box to Washington, D.C., using the slowest means and the lowest fare. The Campus Housing Office was a short block from the post office, so we hiked to the building.

Upon entering the Housing Office, we approached the front counter. Behind the counter were six secretaries doing paperwork at their desks. Behind the secretaries was a table, upon which lay a 3D scale model of the buildings on campus – done in white stone. Little trees and bushes decorated the scene. In front was a small aluminum sign; etched on the sign, it read: The University of Wisconsin – Stevens Point. Behind the miniature campus was the office of Mr. Phillips, the Campus Housing Director.

Jay and I stared at the cute little buildings and didn't notice the receptionist appear.

"Can I help you, boys?"

"Yes. Yes, you can. I'm Joseph, and this is Jay. We represent the UWSP chapter of the Students for a Democratic Society." She raised her eyebrows.

That got her attention!

Jay continued, "We'd like to submit this petition to the Director of Campus Housing."

I said, "Mr. Phillips!"

The receptionist looked past us and said, "Hi, Mr. Phillips!"

Jay and I spun around to see a handsome, well-dressed middle-aged man smiling and standing behind us.

"Well, well! What do we have here? Do you gentlemen have something for me?"

"Yes, sir. It's a petition, sir."

"Oh, I hope it's not another one of those demands for better toilet paper. This ain't the Hilton, you know? So, what do *you* want this time? Mints on your pillow? Turn-down service?"

I said, "Oh no, Mr. Phillips. It's nothing like that."

"Oh, that's good."

"This petition demands that the University allow freshmen and sophomores to live off-campus if they choose."

Mr. Phillips went pale. He stammered, "Off... off campus?"

"Yes, sir!"

"But what about our fantastic dorms, which, by the way, are coed now?" As he spoke, he walked past the miniature campus, indicating the dormitories with a wave of his hand. "That's preposterous!" And he stormed into his office, slamming the door behind him.

We left the box on the counter, waved farewell to the receptionist, and returned to Hyer Hall.

A couple of days later, shuffling down the hallway in my PJs to answer a much-too-early call of nature, I heard frantic whispering coming from the direction of William's room.

"Pssst, Joe! Over here!"

William's door was slightly ajar. Peeking through the crack, I saw that the room was dark. I thought I saw... something on a chair; it looked like a bare female foot. It was bare, except for the rope tying it to the chair!

"Pssst, Joe! I'm down here!"

Looking down, I saw William's face looking up at me. He was on his hands and knees. And, except for his big cowboy hat, he was naked. He held up a twenty-dollar bill.

"Joe, you gotta do me this big, big favor! Please run over to K-mart and buy me a can of whipped cream. I'm out! Oh, and a pack of smokes, too. You can keep the change. Okay?"

That's a lot of change!

"Sure, William, I'll be right back!" I grabbed the cash.

"I owe you, big time!"

As I jogged to the K-mart I wondered what I should do with my part of the twenty-dollar bill. I shivered and pulled my stocking cap down tighter against my ears. It was snowing, and the wind was gusting. I guess we'll be staying inside this weekend!

I hate winter. What can we do for fun?"

At the front of the store was a large display for the popular board game Risk. The sign said, "Play Risk and Conquer the World!"

That's a good idea! After all, everybody wants to rule the world! Sounds like a winner!

I checked out of the store with a can of whipped cream, a pack of smokes, and a dream of world domination.

JUST MISSED THE SIXTIES

Never Attack Russia!

I hyped the Risk game to every wingmate I encountered for the week.

"You gotta be there Saturday night for the big Risk game! It could go on all night! This is your chance to conquer the world! Be the master of Second East! Don't miss it! We'll start at 7:00 PM in the Common Room."

When the big day arrived, I spent the morning and afternoon at the campus library, getting my homework out of the way before the evening battles. For supper, I quickly gulped down a burger at the Student Union and hurried back to the dorm for game time. I grabbed the game from my room and went to the Common Room.

Al, Tim, Spitz, Jay, and Chuck were already there, waiting and partaking of beer and pretzels.

Chuck said, "Hey, Joe! Where have you been all day? Are you ready to play your Risk game?"

"Yes, I am, Chuck. I was at the library most of the day."

Chuck said, "Oh yeah. I've heard about that place..."

Al said, "No, you haven't."

Chuck said, "Yeah. You're right, Al. I have no idea what people do in a library."

Never argue with Al.

I noticed a few missing wingmates. "Jay, where's William tonight?"

"He's in Brown Deer this weekend, visiting his girlfriend."

"Wasn't she just here... a week ago?"

JUST MISSED THE SIXTIES

"Yes. She was. William must have had such a great time; he had to go down for more."

Yeah, that's right. He's going down for more!

"How about the Professor – he told me he'd be here, for sure!"

Tim said, "Oh my God! You didn't hear about what happened today!"

"What? What happened?"

Al said, "Oh man! It was crazy. You really missed it, Joe!"

Spitz said, "Didn't you notice that the wing smelled a little smoky when you returned from the library?

"Uh, no – our wing is always smoky. Come on, is someone going to tell me what happened!"

Tim said, "Well, the story is, at about 10:30 this morning, the professor was whipping up a fresh batch of firecrackers. Unfortunately, earlier, he'd been working with his soldering gun on one of his electronic projects, and the soldering gun was still pretty hot. So, picture this: he has the hot gun on his desk, and a bucket full of powder is below it. The Professor gets up to take a leak and slams the door as he leaves the room. The hot soldering gun rolls off the desk and right into the bucket of firecracker powder! BOOM! You should see his desk! It's totally fried!"

Al said, "Man, it was so loud! I fell right out of bed!"

Chuck said, "After the blast, the wing went nuts! Kerry was yelling, and Gertrude was up here asking questions. The fire department came, checked the room, and asked everybody questions. They took the Professor to see Mr. Phillips at the Housing Department."

I said, "Oh no. That means he's in big trouble!"

"That's right! And when Kerry and Gertrude saw all his bomb-making stuff, they put two and two together and figured he was also behind the blasting of the Second West doors!"

I said, "Oh shit! No! Now we're all in trouble!"

"No, amazingly, we're not! He took responsibility for the whole thing! So, we're okay! Anyway, it meant the Professor had an automatic two strikes, the bombing of Second West and the fire in his room, so they told him to pack up all his bombs and stuff and go home!"

I said, "Oh my God! What a great guy! He didn't tell on us!"

Al said, "Yeah, well, maybe he knew I'd cut off his balls if he squealed. But seriously, that's what real friends do for each other! They don't rat on their buddies. They take the fall like a man! He's a true, true friend! And he gets to keep his balls."

Yikes! I'll never, ever squeal on Al!

I said, "Wow, he is a true friend. So, what's he going to do now?"

Al said, "I don't know, and I don't give a shit."

Tim said, "Professor told me they might let him reapply for next semester. Perhaps they'll put him in a different dorm. But the Professor thinks he won't be coming back. He's seriously thinking about going into the recording business. He said he had a blast making those tapes of Second East Live. Oh, that reminds me, Joe, he left you this."

Tim pulled a cassette tape from his pocket. The Professor had written "Second East Live" on the cover.

I will keep this tape forever.

Al said, "Open up that damn game, Joe before I die of boredom!"

I opened the box, distributed the game pieces, and laid the board on the table.

"See the world here on the game board? It's been divided into exactly 42 territories."

Tim said, "Why 42?"

Al said, "Who the fuck cares? It's just a God-damn number, that's all!"

I said, "I don't know, Tim. It's just one of those mysteries of life and the universe. The important thing is that to win, you have to conquer every territory!"

I focused on my strategy after teaching everyone how to play the game. The plan was simple. Hide out in Australia, the Pacific

Islands, and Southeast Asia while everyone else fights each other for Europe, Africa, and the Americas. The vast expanse of Asia will buffer me from their battles. Meanwhile, I'll bide my time and build up my armies unnoticed by the others. Then, when the time is right, and they're weak from their wars, I'll emerge from my lair and defeat them all! The country I'll attack first Russia.

An hour later, I could see my plan was working! They were fighting amongst themselves and ignoring me.

As they fought their battles, I entertained myself by looking through the printed materials that came with the game.

I read, "The game of Risk was invented by French film director Albert Lamorisse and originally released in 1957 under the name La Conquête du Monde (The Conquest of the World). All rights belong to Parker Brothers, a division of Hasbro."

Interesting. A Frenchman invented the game. I remember learning about a famous Frenchman who conquered Europe – Napoleon.

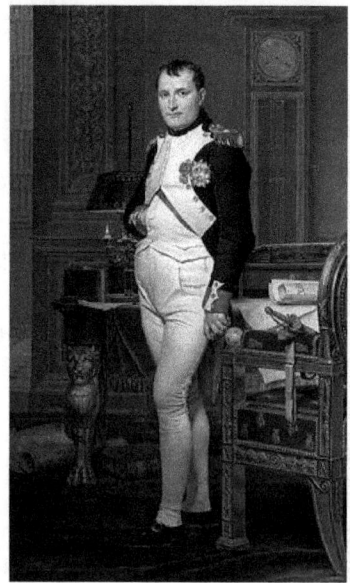

The Emperor Napoleon

JUST MISSED THE SIXTIES

I remember that things were going pretty well for Napoleon in his quest to conquer Europe until he attacked Russia. Napoleon marched into Russia on June 24, 1812, with an army of over 400,000. He was forced to retreat from Russia in December with less than 10,000 men remaining. A famous chart by Charles Joseph Minard illustrates the devastating loss of soldiers as the French Army moved in and out of Russia. It also depicts the temperature getting colder and colder as the army withdrew.

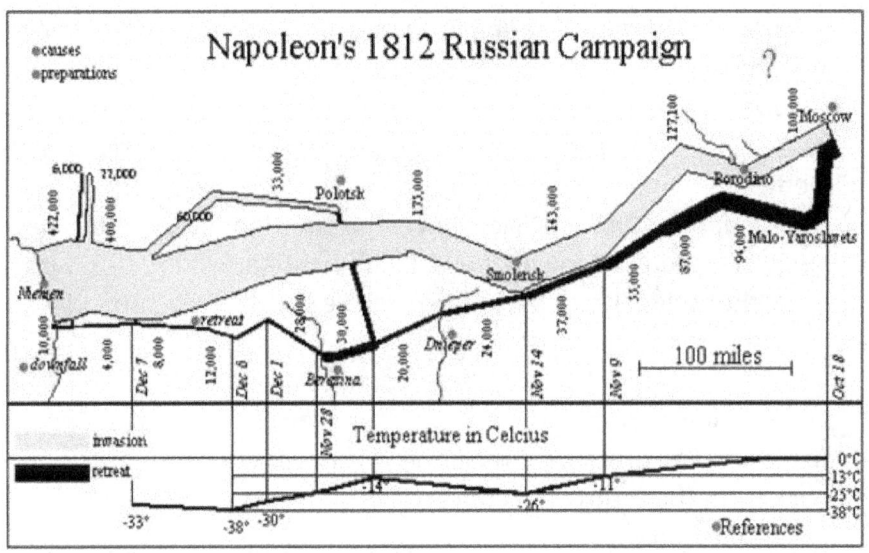

Napoleon's Grande Armée never recovered. In 1813, he lost a battle in Leipzig. The Coalition invaded France in 1814 and forced Napoleon to abdicate his throne.

I imagined how Napoleon must have felt when the French Army took Moscow. The city was empty; the Russians had evacuated to the East. The vastness of Asia must have looked overwhelming. They'd lost so many men, but what had they accomplished? I pictured him rattling around in the empty government buildings. Closing my eyes, I picture him pacing back and forth, head down. Suddenly, he spins about and shouts, "Never attack Russia!"

JUST MISSED THE SIXTIES

But I can do it, Napoleon! I know I can! I'm attacking from the other side!

Finally, it was my turn. Time to attack! Time to conquer the world! I pushed my colossal army pile to the Siberian-Mongolian border and said, "I'm going to attack with my entire army!"

Tim said, "Oh no! Joe's breaking out!"

Spitz said, "Look out! Here he comes!"

Al said, "Well, fuck me in the ear!"

I said, "Gentlemen, get ready to roll the dice for your salvation!"

Suddenly, there was a knock on the door. Rachel stuck her head in the room.

"Joe, come out here. I need to speak with you!"

Al said, "Oh my! It sounds like someone's a little pussy-whipped!"

I said, "Hey, Al – William gives pussy-whipped a whole new meaning." I smiled. "Hang on, guys, I'll be right back."

Rachel said, "Right back? No, you're not! You're coming with me!"

"Why? I can't! We're in the middle of a game!"

"Don't you remember? You promised to go to the English Department's Performance Art Show! You promised me on the bus ride back from the Jethro Tull concert!"

"What? I did?"

Al said, "Joe, get your ass back in here and finish your turn!"

Chuck said, "Joe, we're waiting!"

Performance Art Show! Oh yes! Oh no! Oh my God! I remember a show I went to last year. It was awful! A professor walked on stage, fully dressed as a Zulu warrior, wearing a shield and spear. He stood for five long, boring minutes and said nothing. Then he banged the bottom of his spear on the floor for another long, boring five minutes. Then he sang the Campbell's Soup jingle. "Hm, hm good, hm, hm good. That's what Campbell's soups are, hm, hm good." And then he left—end of the show. Oh man, that wasn't good! I gotta think of something. How can I get out of this?

JUST MISSED THE SIXTIES

"I'm sorry, Rachel, I can't go. You see, I'm just about to attack Russia!"

"Attack Russia? I don't care if you're attacking the moon! Seriously? No, Joe, you can't stand me up like this!"

More comments from the room, "Joe, what are you doing out there? Get in here before I steal your army!"

"Can you hear them, Rachel? I've got to get back to the game!"

"I don't care what they say; you promised to come with me."

"Well, they're my friends too. I can't just let them down! Say, why don't you go with that Geology poet friend of yours?"

Why did I say that?

"Well, maybe I will! I told you it was nothing to be jealous about, don't you believe me? I'm the one who should be jealous, jealous of your precious Second East!"

Al said, "Joe, this is your last warning! I'm counting to ten! If you don't get over here, we're splitting up your stuff!"

Turning back, "I'll be there, hang on! I've just got to deal with this little matter with Rachel."

Rachel screamed, "Don't worry, Al. This little matter is leaving right now!" She spun around and stormed down the hallway. I watched her leave with mixed emotions.

Returning to the room, I continued my northwestward assault on Russia. My plan worked to perfection. I swept away all the competition, taking their armies and all 42 territories.

Chuck said, "Well, Joe, it looks like you conquered the world!"

"Yeah, it looks like I did - doesn't it? Well, Chuck," I said, "You can get your revenge the next time we play."

"I don't know when we'll get to play again, Joe, because tomorrow I'm packing up to go back to the farm. Just like QP did, I realized I'm wasting my time here at Point."

Al said, "No, Chuck. We're not going to let you go!"

Chuck said, "Yeah, right, Al. Guess what? I just dropped all my classes."

Al said, "So what? You can drop out anytime you like, but you can never leave Second East!"

Chuck said, "Is that *your* plan, Al?"

"Plan? Who the fuck has a plan?"

Oh my God! Both QP and Chuck are gone! And with Casey and Don never being around, that leaves only me - as the sophomore to lead the freshmen! I am like Napoleon in Russia; the cold weather is here, and I'm losing my troops!

At the Hop

All next week, I tried hard not to think about everything that had happened last weekend: the Professor getting kicked out, Chuck dropping out, and the most challenging memory to suppress - my fight with Rachel. I tried to keep busy, focusing on classes and homework. I was vaguely aware of a growing feeling of unease and foreboding.

I gotta shake these bad vibes, man!

On Friday afternoon, I spotted flyers advertising a sock hop pinned on the wing bulletin board.

Sock hop? What is this – the fifties?

The dance was scheduled for Friday Night at the dining hall. A local band was booked for the event. I was reading the posting when I felt a sharp slap on my back. It was Al's party buddy, Steve.

"Hey, Joe, looks like they're having a little shindig down at the dining hall. We should go, and let's take a few of your Second East college buddies, too!"

Yeah, whoever's left!

"That sounds good, Steve, I'll see you at the hop!"

Actually, I thought it did sound good. This was a chance to forget about last weekend. This was a chance to pick up some cute little co-ed, and maybe it would make me feel better. Perhaps I'd stop thinking about my fight with Rachel.

I was walking into the dining hall/sock hop on Friday night when I spotted Al, Steve, and a few Second Easters. Steve was entertaining the gang by showing them how he could painlessly extinguish a cigarette in the palm of his hand.

JUST MISSED THE SIXTIES

"It hardly hurts at all! Look, you gotta twist it real fast. See! Now you try it!"

Jay was willing to try, "Okay, that looks easy enough. Here goes. OW! God damn it! Shit! That hurts like hell! What the fuck!"

Al and Steve laughed hysterically.

Steve said, "Oops, Jay! I forgot to tell you one thing - one tiny, little detail. See, I got this quarter in my palm. I put out the cigarette on the quarter - not my skin!"

Jay was upset, "Steve, I'm going to have a scar on my palm for the rest of my life!"

Tim looked at me, eyes wide open, and said, "What a fry!"

I left them and started to cruise the crowd for girls. I was working towards the bandstand when I saw her standing there, next to the sound table. She had long black hair, an oval face, and dark brown eyes. Her colossal breasts formed colorful mounds of her woven serape. She was so well-endowed that my wingmates had dubbed her B-52. I thought, "What the hell," and changed course to take a shot at B-52. I got her in my sights.

"Hello, would you be interested in a free body massage at my studio?"

"Really? You have a studio?"

"No, I don't, but I'd build one just for you. In the meantime, I'm working out of my dorm room right next door; you know the place, Hyer Hall."

"Oh, I see."

"Oh, and today, and for today only, there's a special—free wine and grass for all new clients. What do you say? Can I sign you up?"

"Okay. Fine. Let's go. This band is probably going to suck anyway."

Oh yeah! I can pick up the babes, just like the Fonz!

On our walk to Hyer Hall, we introduced ourselves. Her name was Brenda. She'd seen me around, too.

Brenda asked, "Did you really mean that about smoking grass in your room? I mean, won't we get caught?"

JUST MISSED THE SIXTIES

"No need for worry! I'll show you the trick! It works great!"

Once I got her in my room, I moved quickly to set the scene: wine, reefer, music, and turn on the fan. Brenda threw her colorful serape onto the other bed. Underneath the serape, she was wearing a white, turtleneck stretch top.

She said, "Wow, I like your room! You put a lot of effort into the decorations."

"Thanks! Now, here's a glass of wine. Drink up! And now I'll light this joint. Puff! Puff!"

She held up the joint and said, "So, what's the trick? How do you not get caught?"

"Look at the window. See the fan? It sucks the smoke right outside. It works like a charm! You'll be amazed."

She said, "Wow, this is much better than toking up outside in the cold."

We passed the joint back and forth. Then, I started rubbing her shoulders and back.

"Here's your complimentary massage."

"Umm, that feels nice!"

"If you take your top off, I can do a much deeper muscle rub."

"Oh yeah, that's a good idea."

Oh boy! This is going great!

Unfortunately, just as she started pulling off her top, there was a loud knock on the door. It was Kerry.

"Joe! Are you in there? Joe! Are you smoking marijuana?"

Brenda said, "Who's that?"

"Oh no! It's Kerry, our Wing Director!"

Brenda said, "Oh yeah, Joe, it's just God-damned amazing how great that fan works."

"Oh shit! What the fuck! It always works! Oh no! I forgot to open the stupid window! I'm an idiot! I turned on the fan and never opened the window! I'm an idiot!

"Joe, please open the door now!"

"No, Kerry, I can't right now."

"Are you smoking marijuana?"

"No, Kerry, it's just some incense that smells like pot!"

"Joe, if you don't open the door right now, I'm getting the master key!"

"Just a minute, Kerry!"

"Joe, I'm going to my room right now to get the master key. When I get back, if your door is still locked, I'll open it with the master key."

To Brenda, I said, "Quick, light this incense while I open the window – it'll clear out the smoke right away!" I opened the window and threw out what was left of the joint. Then I opened the door.

"Brenda, this is your chance; get out of here fast. I'm so sorry about this."

Brenda left without saying a word. Kerry returned to find my door wide open. I stood there trying to look cool, although a kilo of adrenalin flowed through my veins. I pointed to the burning incense sticks.

"See, Kerry, it's just some incense. I had a girl in my room, and we were having some tea."

"Okay, Joe, I don't smell the marijuana anymore, but I'm still going to have to report you to Gertrude for not opening the door when I requested."

The next afternoon, I was summoned to Gertrude's office. Kerry escorted me down the stairs to her pad and knocked on the door.

"Come in, please, take a seat, both of you. Joseph, I've asked you to come here today to help me better understand what happened in your room last night. Kerry tells me you refused to open the door for him when he first requested."

"But I did open the door!"

Gertrude said, "Now sit tight for a minute, young man; you'll get a chance to tell your side of the story. First, Kerry will tell us his story. Right, Kerry?"

"Yes, Gertrude, well, it was about 8:00 PM, and I was sitting in my room doing homework with my girlfriend. I had to take a bathroom break, and when I got into the hallway, I thought I smelled marijuana.

I located the source of the smell: Joe's room. I could even see smoke coming out from under his door...." That's when I tuned Kerry out of my head.

I must think of a good reason for not opening the door! I've already got one strike for alcohol at Knutzen Hall. One more strike, and I'm doomed!

Suddenly, Gertrude was talking to me, "So, Joseph, why didn't you open the door when Kerry requested? Let me remind you that when you agreed to live in a campus dormitory, you also agreed that Wing Directors have certain rights, including access to your room. So, once again, why didn't you open your door?"

Wait a minute; wasn't I forced to live in a dormitory?

I said, "Because I didn't want to embarrass the girl I had in my room."

"Kerry, did you see a girl in Joseph's room?"

"No, but she could have left when I went to get the master key."

I said, "She did."

Gertrude said, "Tell me, Joseph, why should this girl be embarrassed?"

"Well, uh... because she needed to put some clothes on."

Gertrude said, "What?"

And then, it was like someone had sucked all the air right out of the room. I had a feeling I was screwed just as badly as if I'd said I'd been smoking pot.

Gertrude said, "Joseph, you should have known that it's against dormitory rules to have sexual activity in your rooms!"

But what about Kerry and his condoms?

"I'm sorry, Joe, but this will have to count as a strike in our two-strike system."

Oh my God! I'm toast!

But then, I got a lucky break.

"So, Joseph, consider this to be your strike one. One more infraction of the dormitory rules will be considered a strike two, for which serious consequences will occur. Please obey the rules from now on; hopefully, we won't have another meeting like this. Do you understand everything I have just said, Joseph?"

"Yes, I do."

We left the office. Kerry looked pleased. I was counting my lucky stars. Thankfully, the information about my strike at Knutzen hadn't reached Hyer Hall.

Woo-hoo! I'm still a Second Easter!

semester has been one of the best times of my life ever! Can't you see it? It's been amazing! We, sophomores, took those little freshmen and taught them everything we learned last year, and we've molded them into our minions!"

I laughed and held up a fist, "I am Lord of the Wing! We tell them to come, and they come. We tell them what games to play, and they play! We tell them to hit themselves with a Frisbee, and... they do it! I can make them throw their bodies into walls... for me! I am the general, and they are my troops! Can you believe it?"

"No shit."

"But don't worry. I got this whole power thing under control. We have a lot of fun, man! We play games and listen to music. It's so cool! We made some recordings, too!"

"Joe, I've known you a long time, like since third grade, right? And I've never, ever seen you like this before. I'm worried about you."

"Casey, you know what? This is the first time in my life that I've been a leader and not a follower. My older brother and sister always bossed me around when I was little. Then, with my friends, I'd fall into the same pattern. I always did what my friends wanted to do. But now it's different. We're the sophomores! This is our chance! This is our chance to call the shots. And you know what? It feels great! But don't worry, I can handle it. Oh damn! I'm out of smokes! Casey, do you have a cigarette I can borrow? I'm like, really, really tense!"

"Sure, Joe. I'll light it for you."

"Oh, thanks, man; my hands are a little shaky today."

"So, Joe, does this mean you and Rachel officially broke up?"

"I don't know. We haven't seen each other... lately... since the fight."

"Oh. Well, that's okay. In fact, that's fine because Kathy has a girlfriend that you should meet. Her name is Terry. Would you be interested in coming by my room tonight to meet her? We could hang out, have a smoke, and watch some TV."

"Sure."

What do I have to lose? Maybe I won't crash and burn as I did with B-52.

*If They Ain't Gonna French,
They Ain't Gonna Fuck
Joseph Roman*

To Boldly Go

After dinner, I knocked on Casey's door.

"Come on in, Joe. The ladies haven't arrived yet. I'm gonna go brush up. I'll be right back. Can you hang out in my room in case they come while I'm in the bathroom?"

"No problem."

I saw Don's half of the room: empty.

Shit! I feel a little emptier just looking at it.

Then, I perused Casey's record collection to check out his new tunes. Casey had some new Poco and Pure Prairie League country-rock fusion.

Casey returned from the can just as Kathy and Terry arrived. I quickly assessed Terry's appearance and gave her a passing grade. She was on the short side, about five-two, with short black hair, a cute little nose, and bright green eyes. Casey's girlfriend, Kathy, was a little taller than Casey (as are most 8th-grade females, lol). She was thin and had light brown hair and freckles. I recognized her from English class.

I said, "Hi, Kathy. How do you like English so far and Dr. Bray?"

"Great! I've learned a lot this semester!"

"Are you sure we're in the same class? I'm just kidding. Well, not really; I'm barely getting by in there."

Kathy said, "I'm sorry to hear that. So, Joe, this is my friend, Terry; she's also from my hometown, Crandon."

"It's nice to meet you, Terry. Wow, Crandon, that's a long way from Milwaukee."

Terry said, "That's right, it's almost at the very top of the state."

Casey pulled out a beer for everyone. Casey and Kathy sat on one bed, and Terry and I sat on Don's old bed. Casey and Kathy began a private, whispered conversation.

Well, that's annoying. I guess it's time to make nice-nice with Terry.

"So, Terry, tell me all about life in Crandon, Wisconsin."

We chatted for a good ten minutes. I learned that Crandon is very small and surrounded by a National Forest. Her father works for the Forest Service. She enjoys snowmobiles and horses. I smiled and nodded a lot.

Casey said, "Hey, guys, let's watch some Star Trek!" He hopped up, walked over to his little TV set, which was sitting on Don's old dresser, and turned it on. "It comes on next, right after the Farm Report."

I said, "Star Trek? Do you mean that outer space show from the '60s, the one that no one ever watched?"

"That's right! Now it's in reruns, and it's a big hit! Everybody's watching it!"

"No shit!"

"Really! Go check out the TV room in the basement right now; I'll bet you'll find at least half the dorm is down there watching the show!"

So, that's what everyone else does while we're getting stoned in the woods.

Casey said, "The show's cool, in a fun way! I think you'll like it. It's got this funny alien guy named Spock, who has really big ears and is a Vulcan. Vulcans never show emotions; they're always logical. But Spock is half-human, so he's always fighting an internal battle, and the Captain is always trying to get Spock to show some emotion. Meanwhile, Spock is always trading insults with the ship's doctor, who's called Bones. Also, there's an African communications officer, a Russian ensign, and a Japanese lieutenant."

JUST MISSED THE SIXTIES

Oh my!

"Joe, why don't you and Terry pull up those bean bag chairs so you can sit in front of us and face the TV."

Terry and I grabbed the bean bag chairs and plopped ourselves in front of Casey's bed. The Farm Report wrapped up and segued into the opening monologue of Star Trek:

Space, the final frontier…
These are the voyages of the Starship Enterprise.
Her five-year mission: to explore strange new worlds.
To seek out new life and new civilizations.
To boldly go where no man has gone before.

Kathy said, "Oh my God! Dr. Bray would hate that last sentence!"

I said, "Huh? Why's that?"

"Because", she said, "it has a split infinitive! To boldly go is a split infinitive! He hates them. He also hates it if you end a sentence with a preposition."

I said, "All I know is, I can never figure out what to fucking write about!"

We watched the show. In this episode, the starship was being overrun by cute little creatures that looked like adorable, fist-sized balls of fur. It was like no outer-space show I could have ever imagined. I turned around to comment.

"Casey, this is a funny…"

I never finished. I saw Casey and Kathy under the sheets, making out. I nudged Terry and nodded back to the bed. She looked and scowled.

I nodded to the door and mouthed, "Let's go."

She nodded, "Yes".

Now I can get her to my room and have my way with her.

Walking down the hallway, I mentally set the scene: start the music, turn on the fan, have a doobie, have some wine, and make my move. We entered my room.

JUST MISSED THE SIXTIES

She said, "Oh, I see you've got birch logs, just like Casey!"

"That's right! We found the logs at the end of last year and hid them in the bushes to save them for this semester."

I started the record player.

"Would you mind if we don't have music? Do you have a TV?"

"Sorry, I don't. Would you like to smoke a joint? I've got a fan to take out the smoke."

"No thanks, but you can."

No, the idea is for us to get stoned together.

"How about some wine? I've got some strawberry or grape."

"No thanks."

"Tea?"

"Sure."

Finally, there's something I can do for her.

I heated some water in a hot pot and put a tea bag in a mug.

"I liberated these tea bags from the dining hall."

"I do that too!"

"So, Terry, your dad works for the Forest Service. My major was forestry when I started college here last year. I wanted to help all the forest animals like deer, owls, bobcats, and beavers. Have you ever seen a bobcat?"

"Oh yeah, we see them all the time."

"Has one ever pounced on you... like this?"

I grabbed her shoulders and planted a kiss on her lips. She didn't fight, so I lingered. Then I tried the tongue. Her lips remained sealed. It was like a rainbow trout ramming headfirst into Hoover Dam. I leaned back, defeated. I remembered an old saying that I just made up.

If they ain't gonna French, they ain't gonna fuck.

Then I said, "I've got an idea! Let's go to the basement and watch the rest of the Star Trek show with those cute little Tribbles!"

"Yeah! That's a great idea!"

Casey was right; the TV room was full of Trekkies. After we watched the rest of the show, I walked her back to her dorm.

JUST MISSED THE SIXTIES

I said, "Goodnight, Terry, nice to have met you," and gave her a peck on the cheek. "Maybe someday, I'll see you at a Trekkie convention."

She laughed and said, "Goodnight, Joe."

Well, Casey, thanks for nothing, as usual.

Walking back through the campus on the walkways between the snowbanks, I wondered if I'd ever have any luck with the opposite sex for the rest of my life. The lights along the walk illuminated swirls of falling snowflakes. Looking ahead, I spied a familiar female figure stumbling my way.

It was Cricket, a very drunk Cricket, weaving side-to-side on the walkway, practically tipping into the snow.

"Hey, Cricket! Where are you going?"

"Oh, hi! It's you! Schmoe! I mean Joe! I just called you Schmoe, Mr. Joe!"

"That's okay, Cricket. Where are you going?"

"Back to the dorm. You know, Hymen Hall! Ha! That's funny, Hymen Hall!" She whispered, "You know I don't have mine anymore."

"I know. Remember, I was in the room with you and Casey that night."

She swung around, fists clenched by her side, "Oh, that Casey, he makes me so mad! He says, 'He has to sow his wild oats,' and all that guy crap. You tell him this, okay, Joe? Next time you see him, you tell him you saw Cricket at a party, and every guy there wanted to fuck her! Okay?"

"Sure, Cricket, I'll tell him that."

"Tell him I could have had them all!"

"Hmmm... so... did you?"

"Did I what?"

"Have all those guys at the party?"

"Almost...I didn't have that last guy, though; he smelled funny. And did you know he has a birthmark on his belly that looks just like a potato? Or is it Ireland? I don't know. I always get those two things confused."

Oh my God. Cricket and Casey are perfect for each other.
"No joke?"

"No jokey, Mr. Schmokey! Anyway, you just let Casey know, okay?"

"Sure, Cricket, I will tell Casey."

"Thanks, Schmoe. You're a good guy, you know? You and Rachel make such a nice couple."

"Well, Cricket, there's some bad news there. We fought and haven't seen each other in a while."

"Well, that sucks! Hey! Maybe I can help! I'm gonna help you, Joseph, help you get her out of your heart!"

She leaned into me, much too close for comfort. I got a strong hit of beer and tobacco smell.

Ugh!

She said, "I'm gonna help you get her out of your...BLUARG!" And she puked on my shoes.

"I'm sorry about that, Schmoe. Did I get your shoes wet?"

"Don't worry, Cricket, it's alright. I'll clean it off later. Say, Cricket, let's get you back to your room so you can get a nice sleep."

"Thanks, Schmoe. That sounds really good. You're a good guy, you know?"

I put a supporting arm around her and guided her back to the dorm.

I don't think she can do the stairs. I better carry her up to her room.

I laid Cricket on her bed and pulled up the covers to keep her warm. As her head sank into the pillow, she murmured, "Goodnight, Schmoe."

I slipped into the hallway, attempting to close the door behind me as quietly as possible. And then I heard another door opening further down the hallway. I turned to look. It was Rachel!

She saw me closing Cricket's door and said, "Oh my God! That's so disgusting!" And then she went into her room, slamming the door behind her.

I said, "Rachel! It's not what it looks like!"

JUST MISSED THE SIXTIES

I don't know how I did it, but I screwed up again!

Three days later, I was still replaying my fight with Rachel, over and over again, in my mind.

How can I get these images to stop?

Nothing was working. I tried listening to my favorite tunes on the headphones. It didn't help; I couldn't relax - I was so wired. I was chain-smoking again and unable to concentrate on my studies. I didn't feel much like socializing.

My brooding was interrupted by Al and Steve knocking and shouting at my door. I had to let them into my room.

"Hey, Joe, get your ass out here, we're taking you to a concert!"

"Another concert? Who is it?"

"It's Wishbone fucking Ash!"

"Wishbone Ash, oh yeah, I've heard of them; they've got some good riffs. But you know what, guys? I'm just not feeling well tonight."

Steve said, "What's the matter? You look fine! Anyway, there ain't nothing bothering you that Al can't fix!" Putting his arm on my shoulder, he continued, "You got the fever; he's got the cure! So, what are your symptoms, little buddy?"

"Oh, I don't know. I'm just anxious and wired all the time. I can't sleep; my brain is racing."

Steve looked at Al, "You hear that, Doc? Can you fix him up?"

Al said, "Oh yes, indeedy. Joe, take one of these blue pills, and your worries will disappear! No problems anymore! Relax, I got them from a pharmacy."

Then, they gotta be safe, right?

"Okay. Okay. Give me one of those pills, Al. It'll be nice to get out of my room... I guess."

Steve said, "That's the spirit, Joe! Yee-haw! We're gonna see some rock and roll!"

I took the blue pill and followed them to the gym for the concert. By the time we took our seats, I was in a very mellow place.

Ah... it's so lovely. I feel like I'm floating. Look! There's a band and they have guitars. Wow, they're playing music. Wow! I hear music.

JUST MISSED THE SIXTIES

I may not have been happy as a lark, but I was comfortably numb.

The Final Daze of Second East

The following day, I was sleeping in, recovering from Al's little blue pill. Loud banging noises started penetrating the fog that filled my head. I wished they would stop. They didn't. They got louder.

What is going on? Oh shit, it's Tim, pounding frantically on my door.

"Joe, Joe! Wake up! It's registration day! You got to get up!"

Oh shit! I've got to register for next semester!

"I'm coming, I'm coming," I mumbled as I shuffled to the door. Tim burst through like a jack-in-the-box. He was holding the school catalog and a registration schedule.

"Joe! I've got to register, but I don't know what to do! How do I do it? What classes should I take? Where do I go? What if I don't do it? Then I won't have any classes! Oh my God! I'm so fried!"

"Tim, Tim, relax, it's okay. I know what to do. You're a biology major just like me, so you can take all the same classes I took in my second semester."

I am lucky he woke me up so I could register!

"Teach me, Joe!"

"Sure. It looks like you brought everything you need. Look in the catalog to see the courses required for your major. Cross out the ones you've already taken this semester. Now, look and see what they're offering in the spring semester. Pick the ones you need. Put together a 15 or 16-credit schedule, and you're set! Of course, now we have to go to the gym and pull the cards for the classes we want – and hopefully, there will still be some openings!"

"Oh my God! Openings! Please let there be openings!"

JUST MISSED THE SIXTIES

"Okay, Tim. Let's get to work. I still have to put my schedule together, too. And then we'll go to the gym and register."

So, Tim and I survived the registration experience – and most importantly, we put together reasonable class loads. Walking back to the dorm, Tim looked like he had a weight lifted off his shoulders. For a second, I was feeling a little better, too. But then I looked at our wing from the sidewalk.

"Tim, do you notice anything different about our wing?"

"No, Joe, not really, it's just a bunch of windows."

"It's just a bunch of windows that, about a month ago, were full of window fans! Look at it now! How many fans are there? Only about two on a side! Tim, it's so, so... symbolic of the loss of our wingmates!"

"Am I going to learn about this symbolism in my English class next semester?"

"Seriously, Tim! We've got to do something to save what's left of our wing!"

"Sure, Joe, whatever you say."

"No, really, Tim. Next week is finals week, and everyone has to buckle down and hit the books if they want to make it. Tim, we have to encourage more studying!"

"Studying? How are we going to get this wing to start studying?"

"Uh, let me think. I know! I'll pull the long table from the common room into the hallway and call it... a study hall! We'll encourage everyone to join us at the table for a group study-in!"

"That sounds... groovy."

Tim and I pulled the table and some chairs into the hallway. I lit a candle in the middle of the table. Next to the candle, I placed a file card on which I wrote: CANDLE OF KNOWLEDGE.

We grabbed our study materials and started the study-in. Casey walked by.

"Hey, Casey! We're having a study-in for the finals. Care to join us!"

"Uh, thanks, but no thanks, guys. I'm going to Kathy's dorm to study."

Next came Spitz.

"Hey, Spitz! Get your textbooks and class notes! We're having a Second East Cram-for-Exams Hallway Experience!"

"Ha! That looks like a gas, guys! But, sorry, I'm meeting Sally in the library. Maybe I'll join you later, though!"

Al poked his head into the hallway and said, "Hey! Could you guys keep it down out there? I'm trying to sleep!"

"Al, it's four o'clock in the afternoon! You'll miss registration!"

"The only fucking class I'm registering for is called bedtime. Now quit making so much God-damned noise!"

Al shut his door just as William and Jay left their room. They approached the study table. William said, "So what are you fellows doing out here?"

I said, "We're trying to get the wing studying! Finals are next week, you know!"

Jay said, "So, how's your studying going, Joe?"

"Oh, man, not so good. I can't seem to concentrate. I'm so tired. My mind feels all foggy! I'm worried about statistics and all the formulas I have to drill into my brain! What I need is more energy."

"Have you tried the White Cross?"

"What's that? A religion? A pastry? A religion that eats pastries?"

"No, man, it's speed, amphetamines, you know, uppers! They're guaranteed to get your circuits buzzing!"

"Wow, that's just what I need. Can you give me enough to get through the week?"

Jay handed me a bottle. "That'll be twenty bucks."

This guy doesn't need college; he's already got a career.

I counted out some bills and about six dollars of change from my pockets.

"Thanks, Joe. Hey, what's this CANDLE OF KNOWLEDGE?"

"Well, if you study here at the table, then the light from the candle is symbolic of the light of knowledge!"

JUST MISSED THE SIXTIES

Tim said, "Man, he's been talking like that all day."

Jay said, "Say, Joe, you won't mind if I light one of these on the CANDLE OF KNOWLEDGE?" He pulled a joint out of his pocket and lit it on the flame from the CANDLE OF KNOWLEDGE. William laughed.

I said, "I think that's symbolic of something completely different! Now get out of here before you stink up the place! You can't get stoned at the CANDLE OF KNOWLEDGE!"

William said, "It doesn't matter, Joe. Jay and I aren't coming back next semester. We're taking a trip out west to find ourselves."

You're not lost! You're right here at Second East, where you belong!

They started walking down the hall, and then Jay turned back and said, "One more thing, Joe, about the White Crosses. Once you start taking them, you can't stop until the exams are over. Otherwise, you'll forget everything! Oh, and then, be ready to crash really hard afterward."

They exited down the stairwell. Tim and I lit some incense. An hour later, we were eating dinner at the dining hall.

"Say, Tim, since there's not very many of us left in Second East, maybe we survivors should stick together. Sort of, you know, like circling the wagons. Would you be interested in rooming together next semester?"

"Sure, Joe. That would be cool."

"Let's go to the housing office tomorrow and reserve our room. Tomorrow night, I'm starting the White Cross."

Jay's White Cross prescription worked well. I crammed and the formulas stuck in my head. Sitting in the exams, I could feel my brain's circuit boards humming. Closing my eyes, I saw formulas floating by, ready to be retrieved. It was ditto for Chemistry, Biology, and the rest. And then the exams were over, just in time, because I'd run out of White Cross. It was time to crash. I was drained, lights-out.

"Joe, wake up!" It was Casey, shouting outside my door. "We got to catch the bus home for winter break!"

JUST MISSED THE SIXTIES

I threw some clothes in a suitcase, and we ran to the Greyhound station. On the bus, I resumed my hard crashing all the way to Milwaukee.

Winter Break

Casey's Mom picked us up at the Milwaukee bus terminal. She was driving a yellow Plymouth Satellite with a black vinyl top. I slid into the back seat. It was covered with towels to keep the fabric clean. For most of the ride, Casey talked with his mom while I fell deeply asleep.

"Joe, wake up! We're at your house!" I grabbed my backpack and slid out the door.

"Thanks for the ride."

Casey said, "Bye, Joe, take it easy."

They pulled away. Walking up the driveway, I noticed Dad had decked out the front bushes with Christmas lights, the big bulbs, which were his favorite.

Oh, man! It's Christmas! That means I have to think about gifts and stuff. But I'm so tired!

I walked through the front entryway and headed for the stairs. I wanted to do nothing but slink up to my room and crash. After four solid days of White Cross, a foggy haze penetrated so deeply into my brain that it felt like it would never leave. Besides that, I was anxious about other things. For example, what was happening to my wing? How did I mess up with Rachel? How come I was striking out with girls again? Why, when everything had seemed so great, did everything feel so wrong? I was feeling the plunge from soaring indomitability to unconquerable lethargy. When did the wheels fall off?

Mother heard me enter, and she shouted from the kitchen.

"Joe, is that you?"

"Yes, Mother, I'm home."

"Joe, could you do me a quick favor? Do you see the packages on the dining room table? They just arrived from your brother in

Germany and your sister in Florida. Could you open the packages and put the presents under the tree? Thanks!"

After opening the packages and stacking up the gifts for a trip to the artificial tree in the living room, I had a brainstorm or, perhaps, a brain drizzle because my brain was in no condition for a storm. I grabbed a pen from the credenza and wrote my name, as a co-gifter, on every one of the presents to my folks.

Alrighty then, shopping's done; time for sleep.

I put the gifts under the tree, went upstairs, and fell onto the old bed. Moments later, Mother knocked on the door, and I told her to come in. When she opened the door, I saw she was dressed up for the evening. I could smell her perfume.

"Joseph, your father and I are going to the Christmas party at the bank. There's a TV dinner in the freezer for when you get hungry."

I said, "Okay," and she shut the door. I could hear Mother and Father talking out in the hallway.

Father said, "It's awfully early to be in bed. Is Joe feeling alright?"

"You know how it is; he's tired from all his hard work this semester."

Two days later, it was Christmas. So far, I haven't left the house. I'd eaten, slept, and wandered around in my room. Once, I pulled out a pen and paper and started making a list of fun things to do with Second East next semester. I wrote, "Play Risk," but that made me think about Rachel, so I stopped.

Christmas morning, Mother made scrambled eggs. After polishing them off, we moved into the living room for the gift opening. I sat by the tree and opened mine. The folks gave me some shirts and cash.

Mother said, "Joe, you never told us what you wanted for Christmas. So, I figured you could always use a new shirt. Also, you can take the cash and buy something that you want. Oh, and Joe, thanks for the gifts you got with your brother and sister. Gosh, how did you work that out? What about one being in Germany and the other in Florida?"

"I know, right? I've got the best brother and sister in the whole wide world!"

The next day, I decided to get out of the house and spend some of my newly acquired Christmas cash. Maybe I could buy something that would make me happy – perhaps some new tunes. I took a walk west on North Avenue towards Mayfair Mall. It was a sunny, slushy day. About halfway to the mall, I heard a honk and saw a familiar yellow Plymouth Satellite pull to the curb in front of me. It was Casey behind the wheel of his mom's car. He was smoking a cigarette and blowing the smoke out the window. He waved me over.

"Hey! Joe! Where are you headed?"

"I'm going to Mayfair Mall. What about you?"

"I'm going to Brookfield to see a girl I met Christmas shopping. Hop in; I'll drop you off on the way."

What? He's got another girl? What? Did he go Christmas shopping?

"No shit, Casey! How in the world did you pick up a girl Christmas shopping?"

"Well, here's what happened. I was at the local Christian Science Reading Room to get my mom a book she'd asked for called *Cleanliness is next to Godliness,* and then I saw this girl, a really nice chick, sitting in one of the easy chairs reading the *Christian Science Monitor.* Joe, that's a great paper; you should check it out sometime."

"Nah, that's okay; I get all the news I need from the weather report. Anyway, go on. How did you pick her up?"

"Oh yeah, so I'm buying the book, and I look over at her, trying not to gawk, you know, and I see her pull out a bottle of aspirin. Right there in the Christian Scientist reading room!"

Even I, a devout Narcissist, understood the problem with that scene. "Noooo! Not in a Christian Scientist Reading Room!"

Casey said, "Seriously! That is not kosher at all. So, I walked over to her, bent down, and whispered, 'You know Jesus wouldn't want you to take those pills.' And she freaked! She was nervous, thanking

JUST MISSED THE SIXTIES

me, saying she forgot where she was, etc. So, I said, 'I got an idea; why don't we go somewhere and pray for your headache to go away?' Then she smiled and said, 'That sounds good, let's go to my place. I got a friend named Jim Beam that could help us with our prayers.' Well, long story short, the next thing you know, we're rolling around in her bed. Quite a gal, interesting; she likes to shave her pussy. Can you believe it? Anyway, I'm going to her place again today. How about you? Are you having a nice holiday?"

Yeah, right... doing nothing!

I said, "Casey, dare I ask, what about Kathy?"

"Oh, it's cool. Remember? Kathy lives on the other side of the state. Hell, they'll never run into each other."

"Speaking of running into someone, I never did tell you that I ran into Cricket one night on campus. She had a message for you. She wanted you to know that she was at a party, and she screwed every guy at the party except for one guy that smelled funny and had a funny birthmark on his belly that looked like Ireland."

Casey said, "Ha! I can appreciate that. So, Joe, what about you? Are you okay?"

"Well, not really. The finals were just a whirlwind. Now, I'm always tired, and I keep feeling like there's something I'm supposed to be doing, and I'm not doing it. Hopefully, I'll feel better when I'm back with the wing again."

"What wing?"

"You know... with all the dudes in Second East. You'll be there, right?"

"Sorry, Joe, I signed up to be in Kathy's dorm next semester. I didn't tell you about it at the time because you were too busy studying."

Napoleon! I'm losing my troops!

Casey said, "Say, Joe, are you and Rachel still broken up?

"Technically, yes."

"Well, maybe you should go makeup with her."

"Hmm, do you think so?"

JUST MISSED THE SIXTIES

"Why not? It might make you feel better. Anyway, here's the mall. Hey, tomorrow night I'll take you out to a movie. Sound good?"

"Sure."

I bought the new Todd Rundgren LP, *A Wizard, A True Star* at the record store. I took it home and plopped it on the folk's stereo console. Immediately, I realized the album was incredibly different from anything I'd ever heard. I couldn't quite wrap my mind around it. Then, it played this cut: "Never, Never Land" by *Peter Pan*.

There is a place where dreams are born...
Yes, I know that place- It's called Second East!

The next evening, Casey picked me up, and we checked out the new hit movie, *The Exorcist*.

Exiting the movie, Casey said, "Holy shit! That's not exactly family entertainment for the holidays!"

That night, I had the weirdest dream. I dreamt I saw Rachel walking up the hallway to the bedroom of Regan, the possessed little girl in the movie.

Don't open the door!

Rachel opened the door. The room was empty. She walked in and lay down on the bed. From the side, all I could see was her long blonde hair. Suddenly, she sat up and turned towards me, but it wasn't Rachel anymore. It was Al's friend Steve! He said, "Boo-yah!" and spun his head around 360 degrees. When the face returned, it wasn't Steve anymore. It was Al! Al laughed and puked. *Green Slime! Look out!* Then I woke up, shaking and sweating all over. I stared at the ceiling – afraid to go back to sleep.

What could it mean?

After three more nights and three more nightmares, I was back on the bus north to Stevens Point.

Oh, man! It'll be great to see the old gang!

I stepped off the bus in Point and felt like I just walked into the ice ages. *Holy shit, it's cold!*

JUST MISSED THE SIXTIES

Second Semester

Walking down the hallway of good old Second East, I noticed Tim had decorated the door of our new room with a bumper sticker:

TEENAGE WASTELAND

I walked inside and almost tripped over boxes full of stuff yet to be unpacked. They were mine. I dragged the boxes from my old room just before winter break.

Oh crap, I still have to put this shit away.

At least, I'd set up the sound system – a dude has to have some priorities. Tim was already using it to play some tunes: Loggins and Messina. He was busy organizing his dresser when he looked up and said, "Hey, Joe! Welcome back to Second East!"

"Hi, Tim! Thanks! I can't tell you how much I've looked forward to seeing the old wing again!"

"Really? You do realize, Joe, there's not much old-wing left?"

"I…. There's got to be someone left! Hmm… What about Al?"

"Hah! Al! He probably flunked out after the first day of class! And remember registration day? When Al slept in?"

"Oh. Yeah. What about Spitz?"

"Spitz moved to Sally's dorm. Casey moved to Kathy's dorm. The Professor got kicked out. QP and Chuck dropped out. Jay and William are traveling out West. I tell you, Joe, only you and I are left! Even our Wing Director, Kerry, has been replaced by some new guy, Jim."

"Holy shit, you're right!" And then I heard noises in the hallway. Voices, doors opening and closing – our wingmates! I stepped into the hallway and looked. Strange new residents were moving into the rooms of Second East. Who are these people?

Oh my God. It's like a whole new wing!

"Tim, you know what this means, don't you? It's up to you and me now! We've got to keep the spirit of the Second East alive! We have to mold the newbies to do our wishes. We have to take control!"

"Uh... Okay, Joe. Whatever you say."

Is he patronizing me?

A short, stocky dude with a crew cut stepped into the room. He had a round face and a no-nonsense look. He reminded me of a high school wrestling coach.

"Howdy, boys. There's a wing meeting in the Common Room in two hours. Please be there. By the way, I'm Jim, your new Wing Director."

Two hours later, Tim and I were sitting in the Common Room with a bunch of strangers. Jim stood up, introduced himself, had us say our names, and began his spiel.

"Okay, so I'm your new Wing Director. Feel free to see me anytime about anything. I plan on being here, on-wing, as much as possible."

Not at his girlfriend's dorm like Kerry?

"I know most of you are new to this wing, just like I am, but I still want to get one important message through to you. I heard that there was a lot of crazy stuff that went on in Second East last semester. So, I made a promise to Gertrude – it's not going to happen this semester, not on my watch! I hope you all can understand that!"

Oh my God! He's looking right at Tim and me!

The next day was the first day of second-semester classes. Unfortunately, I'd neglected to unpack my alarm clock. I mistakenly thought, "I'll wake up naturally." Wrong! When I finally woke up, I knew it was late because of the sun's position in the window. I flung myself out of bed in a panic.

"Tim, wake up! It's time to go to class!"

JUST MISSED THE SIXTIES

Tim's bed was empty. He'd left without me. I looked at my watch. It was one in the afternoon. Then the door opened, and Tim walked into the room.

"Morning, Joe! Rise and shine, eh? When are your classes? This afternoon?"

"No! They were this morning! I missed the first day of classes!"

"No shit! I would have woken you up if I'd known. But don't worry. You know they never do anything important on the first day."

"Yeah, yeah, you're right. I can relax, I guess."

"Speaking of relaxing, I forgot to show you. Jay left us a whole drawer full of, as he said, 'A little something to help us get through another semester.'"

I looked at Tim's desk and saw the little something was an entire drawer packed full of perfectly hand-rolled marijuana reefers.

Jay, wherever you are, I love you!

"Say, Joe, let's fire up one of these beauties to celebrate our first day of second semester."

I agreed. Thus, the first day of classes began on a high note after all. After the first reefer, Tim thought it would be a nice gesture to invite the new dudes directly across the hallway to share a second one. He left and soon returned with the two new, across-the-hall wingmates.

Tim said, "See, guys, we got a fan in the back of the room that takes the smoke outside. Trust me, Jim will never know. We just finished a joint, and you can't tell, right? Hey, Joe, meet the two guys from across the hall, Ed and Gary."

I nodded.

Gary said, "Hey, Joe, I like how you've decorated the room with boxes. That's a nice touch, heh, heh."

"Hey, Larry, that's not funny! You should have seen my room last semester; it was a goddamn love-nest man! You wouldn't believe how many chicks I had in that room."

Tim said, "Joe, his name is Gary, not Larry. Gary, Joe's a little tense because he just missed the first day of classes."

Gary said, "I was just joking. Okay, man?"

Ed said, "Bummer, Joe, bad way to start the semester."

I said, "Let me tell you something, Ned. From now on, I'm calling you Rubberhead because sometimes guys on Second East have cool nicknames, and Rubberhead is a cool nickname. And another thing, when it comes to classes, all you need are the classes Tim and I will give you here in Second East. You may think you're in Hyer Hall for a higher education! Oh, no! Think again! You're here at Hyer Hall to get higher! And what's going to be the first class of the day? Mindfuck 101, dudes! Right, Tim?"

"Um... Sure, Joe, whatever you say."

Did he roll his eyes and look at Rubberhead and Larry?

I said, "That's right! Tim and I are going to fuck with your minds! First, we'll light your shoes on fire, and then you'll hit yourselves with Frisbees because we tell you to!"

Tim just looked at them again! What's happening to me?

"Tim! Oh my God! I'm getting paranoid! You're not with me on this!"

Ed and Gary got up to leave the room.

Gary said, "Um... Nice to meet you, but we better get going. We'll see you around, guys."

Then, Ed leaned over and whispered to Tim, "Hey, it's okay. Sometimes pot can have that little side effect if you know what I mean."

After they left, Tim tried to comfort me.

"Joe, you're just tense, that's all. Maybe you need some more rest. I'll tell you what. You try to relax, and I'll grab you a sandwich at the dining hall."

"Okay, Tim. Thanks. You're a good friend. I'll go lay down here on the bed."

"Joe! Joe! Wake up! It's time for classes!
Wait a minute! I just lay down! Where's my sandwich?
Opening my eyes, I saw a sandwich on my desk.

JUST MISSED THE SIXTIES

"Sorry, Joe. I didn't want to disturb you—you were sleeping so soundly. And then, I fell asleep! Well, I guess you can have the sandwich for breakfast; it should be okay. I'm taking off for class now. See ya!"

So tired. I'll just shut my eyes for another ten minutes.

"Joe! Joe! Wake up! You missed your classes again!"

"Oh my God! This semester is turning into a train wreck! Oh, Tim, I'm sorry I was acting so strangely yesterday."

"That's fine, Joe. You gotta snap out of this big funk you're in. You gotta do something!"

"You're right, Tim. Tomorrow morning, I will wake up bright and early and… drop some classes."

Unlike the previous two days, I awoke before noon the next day. Yay! I dropped Chemistry and Calculus and visited the professors of my three remaining classes. I told them I had the flu. They were cool and got me up to speed. I was back in gear sort of, or at least partially engaged.

Upon returning to our room, Tim greeted me. He was holding up the latest printing of the campus newspaper, *The Pointer*.

"What a fry, Joe; you gotta see today's headline!"

What could there possibly be interesting in the campus newspaper?

And then I read:

ILLEGAL HUT FOUND IN CAMPUS NORTH WOODS

"Oh, my God!" *It feels like a dagger in my gut.*

Beneath the headline was a gorgeous, four-by-six-inch color photograph of The Hut.

It's so beautiful!

We read the text together, which stated in summary: The Hut was discovered by snowmobilers during winter break and reported to Campus Security. Security dispatched a team to confirm and demolish the illegal structure. During the dismantling, they discovered vandalized pine saplings (*William!*) and plastic sheeting believed to have been stolen from a nearby construction site (*Jay!*). Students are requested to please refrain from building illegal structures in the campus North Woods.

Tim thought it was funny. I was in shock.

"Oh no, Tim! Now I've lost everything!"

"What are you talking about?"

"I lost my girl; I lost my wing, and now… I lost my Hut! Augh!"

Tim exhaled heavily, looked at the floor for a second, and then said, "Joe, guess who I saw on campus yesterday?"

"I don't know, Tim, Gertrude?"

"No! I saw Rachel! And she asked how you're doing!"

"She did? Really?"

"Yes! You know she's still right here in Hyer Hall. She's still upstairs, in the same old room she was in last semester. You should go up and see her sometime!"

"Yes! Yes, Tim! You're right! That's what I need to make me feel better. I'll go to her room… tonight!"

JUST MISSED THE SIXTIES

The Poet

After dinner, I knocked on Rachel's door. I was prepared to eat crow for dessert. I planned to apologize profusely and beg for forgiveness. The door opened, and I began my pitch.

"Hello, Rachel, I must tell you how truly sorry I..."

She cut me off. "Joe! What a surprise! Come in! Come in! I want to introduce you to someone."

Introduce me to someone? Does she have a guy in her room?

"Joe, do you remember me talking about someone named Michael? You remember - he's the guy who studied geology with me. He's the guy who gave us the Jethro Tull tickets."

Oh shit! That guy? And he's here with Rachel at the same time that I want to get back together with her, and now I have to thank him for the Goddamned concert tickets.

Michael was sitting at Rachel's desk, forearms on the desktop, holding a manuscript. He looked like a college professor with his perfectly trimmed jet-black mustache and cream-colored cardigan sweater, complete with leather patches on the elbows. Lying near his elbow was a Sherlock Holmes-style calabash pipe. He looked at me and raised his right eyebrow.

I said, "Hi, Michael. Thanks for the tickets. It was a great show."

"So, that's what Rachel told me. I'm glad you could use the tickets. It would have been a damn shame for them to go to waste."

Awkward silence.

Rachel said, "Michael was just reading me some of his latest poetry. He even wrote a poem about me! It's called 'A Poem for You'."

Yeah, that narrows it down to just you.

I said, "Wow. A poem. That's really nice."

Michael said, "So, Joseph, Rachel tells me you've done a little writing too."

Huh? What's he talking about?

"You wrote a story about your lucky undergarments! Snort!"

Did he snort?

"Oh, yeah? Unfortunately, my English Professor didn't like it too much."

"Well, that's a shocker. And may I ask who your professor was?"

"Dr. Bray."

"Ah, Dr. Bray! The man's a genius. He just published a fantastic synopsis of the shortcomings of today's college students. Perhaps you were an inspiration for his efforts!"

"Genius? If he's such a genius, how come he couldn't understand a simple little poem I wrote for him?"

"Joseph, I don't know anything about this little poem you've written to have even the slightest clue what you're talking about."

"Well, lucky for you, I've got it memorized. Here goes:

Sand Castles are Concrete
By Joseph Roman

A wave rolled in,
And washed my sand castle away.
It was not a sin,
Because sand castles are concrete.

And that's it! Do you get it?"

Michael scratched his head and said, "Frankly... I'm lost. Sorry."

"You too?"

"Well, yes... seriously, who goes to the beach and makes concrete sand castles?"

"Nobody, of course! By concrete, I mean they're not abstract! You know the terms abstract and concrete, right? Concrete means real, something you can touch, like this chair. On the other hand, something abstract is something you can't touch, like an idea. So, it's okay if a wave can wash away something concrete, like sand, but if waves could ever wash away something abstract, like your thoughts... well, look out! We're all screwed! Just think about it; you could go for a swim and come back empty-headed!"

"I bet you like going to the beach a lot. Don't you, Joseph?"

Rachel said, "Listen to this, Joe. Michael plans to start a publishing company for his poetry *and* to help out other young, unpublished authors. Michael, maybe someday you could publish a compilation of Joe's stuff! He's already got the underwear story and the sandcastle poem, too!"

Michael said, "Great idea, Rachel, but I can't guarantee anything. What we publish will be based on a strict peer review system."

I see... if he doesn't like your stuff, he'll throw it off a pier.

"By the way, Joseph, what grades did Dr. Bray give you for the story and the poem?"

"I got a D-Plus for both of them."

"Wow, he's a genius and generous too!"

Rachel said, "After the poetry reading, Michael will give me a back rub. He knows some ancient Far Eastern techniques. He calls them Kama Sutra, right Michael?"

Back rub my ass! I know his little game. That's just a trick to get her to take her clothes off!

Rachel continued, "And then we might try some Transcendental Meditation. Michael learned a new meditation technique directly from the Maharishi Yogi! Isn't that right, Michael?"

Well, Rachel, it came to me via one of his disciples, an irrelevant detail.

Transcendental Meditation? What's that? Going into a trance and thinking about your teeth?

And then Rachel started her little record player. It was Joni Mitchell's "Chelsea Morning."

Oh no! That's our song!

JUST MISSED THE SIXTIES

Michael held up a leather pouch, "Say, Joseph, I've come across some extremely smooth yet compelling Cuban tobacco. I paid a premium for it. Would you like to try a bowl?"

"No thanks, Michael, I've got something more fun to smoke back in my room."

I'd seen enough. I didn't want to think another thought about Michael and Rachel rubbing each other, listening to our song, and thinking about their teeth - but I couldn't stop my brain! I couldn't get out of Rachel's room fast enough!

"Bye, Rachel and Michael. Have a nice evening."

I raced down the stairs, burst into my room, and announced, "Tim, open that drawer full of joints. We're gonna smoke 'em all tonight. I'm turning on the fan. I hope you don't have anything planned for, I don't know, the next century!"

I put an appropriate tune on the stereo, Country Joe and the Fish playing "Bass Strings." I sang along:

"I say, hey, partner!
Won't you pass that reefer 'round?
You know my world is spinning,
I just got to slow it down.
Oh, yes, you know,
I've sure got to slow it down.
I'll get so high this time,
I'll never come down."

Several hours and many reefers later, I said, "You know I can write poetry too! I just gotta put my mind to it."

"Sure, you can, Joe! What do you want to write about?"

"Right now, I just want to write the blues – you know? The 'College Blues'."

"Give it a shot, Joe!"

"Okay, here goes:

JUST MISSED THE SIXTIES

College Blues
By Joseph Roman

I watched the sunrise this morning,
Smoking the night away!
I watched the sunrise this morning,
Toking the night away!
But if I don't buckle down, baby,
I'll have the college blues every day."

"That's good, Joe, really good! Did you get any more ideas?"
"Well, I'm thinking, maybe I'd write something about that Michael dude. I could call it 'Cardigan and Calabash, I Really Hate Your Stinky Ash.' Ha! On the other hand, I'd like to write something about the winter weather - you know? I want to capture the feeling of snowflakes driven by the cold, cold wind biting into my face. Listen to this:
I look out the window and see the driving snow right between the fan blades; I can see it blow... Wait, what did I just say? I can see the snowflakes between the fan blades! Tim! The fan stopped! It won't start! It's busted!"
KNOCK! KNOCK! KNOCK!
"Joe and Tim, this is Jim, the Wing Director! I've got the passkey. I'm opening your door right now!" And that's how Tim and I got busted for smoking pot in our room.

The following day, our new wingmates, Rubberhead (the nickname stuck!) and Gary, told us about the incredible amount of marijuana smoke that was in the hallway last night.
Gary said, "We were just sitting in our room watching TV, and then Rubberhead said he could smell pot outside. So, he opened the door and, oh my God, I couldn't believe it! It was like a fog in the hallway!"
Rubberhead said, "Yeah, it was Purple Haze, man!"

JUST MISSED THE SIXTIES

All I could say was, "Oh, shit."

At about 10:00 am, Jim came to tell us that our meetings with Gertrude were scheduled for one o'clock this afternoon. Tim was first, and I was second.

JUST MISSED THE SIXTIES

How Does It Feel to Be On Your Own?

At one o'clock, Jim came and escorted Tim to Gertrude's office. About 20 minutes later, they returned, and it was my turn. But first I wanted to hear about Tim's meeting.
"Well, Tim, how did it go?"
"She gave me a strike one."
Strike one! Lucky guy! Shit, I'm screwed.

Gertrude was waiting for us outside her office door.
"Thank you, Jim, you can go now. Joseph, please come inside and take a seat in front of my desk."
This isn't going to be good.
"Joseph, I'm sure you know why you're here, so no explanation is necessary. I'm disappointed that we have to meet again under these circumstances. As I described at our first meeting, we have a two-strike policy regarding violations of the campus housing rules. Students who get two strikes face serious consequences.
But I just found out that the last time we met, under similar circumstances, when I thought I was giving you strike one, I was wrong. I learned you got your first strike at Knutzen Hall... last year! So now, you have three strikes!"
She held up three fingers. I stared at her hand. She spoke loudly. "This is unprecedented, Joseph Roman. You are in very serious trouble!"
She paused, collected herself, gritted her teeth, and continued.
"Joseph, here's my theory. I think you had everyone fooled this past semester with your chess tournament and your petitions. Now I've come to realize that, maybe, you were one of the ringleaders

behind ALL the shenanigans that took place on Second East! Perhaps YOU were the Master Manipulator!"

Once again, she paused to collect herself.

"Be that as it may, what I think doesn't matter. Your fate is entirely out of my hands now, Joseph. You have a meeting scheduled with Mr. Phillips, the Campus Housing Director. Do you know where his office is located?"

"Yes, I do."

"Good, because we're done here. Your meeting with Mr. Phillips is at 2:00 pm tomorrow. May God be with you."

"I'll wear my Lucky Underwear."

"What did you say?"

"I'll be there."

Returning to the room, I slumped down on my bed and said, "Oh my God, Tim, I'm really screwed this time! I've got to see Mr. Phillips!"

"What a fry!"

Once again, I was walking to the Campus Housing Department, but this trip wasn't for something fun like reserving a new room or turning in a petition.

After entering, I walked to the front counter and spoke with the receptionist. Upon hearing my name, she immediately ushered me back to Mr. Phillips's office, past the administrators at their desks and past the 3D small-scale model of the campus. She knocked.

"Yes, what is it?"

"Excuse me, Mr. Phillips - Joseph Roman is here for his appointment."

"Thank you. Let the young man in, please."

I walked in, and the receptionist closed the door behind me. Mr. Phillips looked sharp in suit and tie.

He could be a bank VP, like my Dad.

He motioned for me to sit in the chair before his desk. Resting his elbows on the desk, he put his hands together. Then he separated his palms and made a fingertip-steeple. He exhaled sharply and put down his hands.

"Mr. Roman, I know you know why you are here today, so I don't need to review any details. First, let me remind you that you are in a lot of trouble, Joseph, more than usual, because you earned three strikes in a two-strike penalty system. That's the first time that's ever happened since I've been the Housing Director."

He paused to let his words sink in.

"My first inclination was to have you expelled from the University, but then I looked at your grades. Joseph, you have a 3.2 GPA! Last semester, you had A's in organic chemistry, zoology, and statistics; I know those are not easy classes! The only class you had less than a B was Dr. Bray's English Class, but... I also know about Mr. Bray."

He cleared his throat, and for a second, there was a twinkle in his eye.

Did we share a moment there?

"So, I looked into your ACT scores and found that you had an overall score of 34, that's two points shy of perfect! Joseph, you could have gone to any school in the country, but you chose our little extension school. So, I wondered, why?"

I like the woods?

"Anyway, whatever the reason you came here, I know you're a smart guy, Joseph, and we don't want to lose you at UWSP. But you broke the rules, so there has to be a consequence.

Now Gertrude thinks you're some kind of master manipulator of your fellow wingmates. I agree with her assessment, but on the other hand, that also means you have leadership skills. And, leadership skills are a great thing to have, mainly if they're used constructively - like for this." He held up a stack of papers that I recognized immediately.

The Housing Petition!

"I know you were one of the leaders in the organization that circulated this petition to allow freshmen and sophomores to live off campus. Your group collected an admirable number of signatures, and you can bet we checked every name for its validity. So, Joseph, with all this in mind, I have two pieces of news for you.

One: Because of the overwhelming number of signatures you collected on this petition, the Board of Regents has reversed its opinion regarding mandatory dormitory housing for freshmen and sophomores. They've concluded that some individuals are not a good fit for the dormitory experience."

He paused, raised an eyebrow, and looked at me.

C'est moi?

"Two: Congratulations, you will be the first student to take advantage of this new opportunity. Well, you don't have any choice in the matter. You must leave Hyer Hall by this Friday at 5:00 pm and never return.

So, here's the deal for you. You may continue your enrollment in the University as a student but never live on campus again. You are forbidden to enter Hyer Hall for the next four years. In fact, you may never enter any UWSP campus dormitory for the next four years. You are forbidden from entering any dormitory in the University of Wisconsin system as well as in any state with which we have reciprocity, including all campus dormitories in Michigan, Minnesota, Iowa, Illinois, Indiana, and our sister campuses in San Juan, Puerto Rico and Hyderabad, India.

So, Joseph, that's it. You're officially off-campus now. You should be happy. You got what you were fighting for. If there are no questions, you may go."

But I want to stay with my friends on Second East!

I said, "No questions, sir. Thank you, sir."

I left the office and paused in front of the 3-D model of the campus.

It's all happening so fast – I'm not ready for this! Where am I going to live?

Suddenly, Mr. Phillips was standing behind me.

He said, "Well, Joseph, are you looking at all the buildings you can't go into anymore?"

How did he sneak up behind me again?

Then he took a black marker from his pocket and began slashing big black Xs on the rooftops of the little white dormitory buildings.

"Here's a place you can't go anymore, and here's another, and here's another..."

After he marked all the dorms with an X, he said, "Everybody! Look at all the buildings that are off-limits for Mr. Roman!" He then strutted back into his office.

Walking by the administrators' desks, I heard one call my name.

"Psst! Joseph Roman! Can I talk to you for a second?"

I walked to her desk and said, "Sure, why not?"

She looks like a nice lady.

"Hi, I'm Flo. You know what, Mr. Roman? You've made quite a splash around here!"

"I have? Really?"

"Oh yeah! Nobody's ever gotten three strikes before! Betty, over there, she said it's like you hit the trifecta – you know: alcohol, sex and drugs!"

Yeah, but I'm not sure I like the payoff.

"Then, on top of that little feat, you and your SDS group turned in a petition that helped change a campus policy that's been in effect for over 100 years!"

"That's all exciting and everything but... you know what? I don't have a clue where I am going to live. What am I going to do?"

"Well, Joseph, I want to discuss that with you. So, you say you have nowhere to go after leaving the dorm?"

"No! And I don't know what to do!"

"Don't worry, Joseph, we've got you covered. Did you know our office helps students find housing on *and* off campus? I bet you didn't know that, did you?"

"No, I didn't."

"Well, we certainly do. Now, the options are much more limited in the middle of the school year, but I just heard about an apartment close by with an immediate opening. One of the tenants had to leave school unexpectedly, and now they're looking for someone to replace him. Here, I'll give you the address, and you can look at the place and see if you like it."

I'll like it if it has a roof and a bed!

"That's great. I'll go right now."

"Good. I'll give them a call to let them know you're coming. Here's the address. It's on Main Street. Best wishes, I hope everything works out for you, Joseph Roman."

Gimme Shelter

Walking away from campus, I entered the town of Stevens Point. Narrow, two-story houses with wood siding and steeply pitched roofs lined the streets. These were the dwellings of the off-campus crowd.

Reaching Main Street, I quickly found the address. It was on a corner lot, and with three stories, the house was a little bigger than its neighbors. I approached the front stoop, walking beneath the limbs of a vast, old elm tree that dominated the lawn.

I wonder... will I fit into a new place with new people?

I rang the front doorbell, the door opened, and I was greeted cheerfully by a tall, heavy-set, bearded dude. He wore a big smile, a red flannel shirt, pajama bottoms, and fuzzy bunny slippers.

"Well, you must be three-strike Joe! I just heard all about you from my friend, Flo, over in housing! My name is Roger - we'll be roommates, that is, if you decide to live here. Come inside, Joe, and I'll give you the ten-cent tour. Our apartment is located in the top two floors of the house. That doorway leads to another unit on the first floor and the basement. We'll take the stairway up to ours."

We climbed the stairs. The railing was solid oak. Extensive wood molding and paneling finished the walls.

"It's an old house, but it's got sturdy bones - how they used to make 'em."

We entered a small living room on the second floor containing some tattered old couches and easy chairs. An old black and white TV rested on a side table. Aluminum foil hung from its rabbit ears. Taped on one wall was a yellowed poster with a drawing of a sunflower. Next to the flower, it read:

JUST MISSED THE SIXTIES

WAR
IS NOT HEALTHY
FOR CHILDREN
AND OTHER LIVING THINGS

"So, Joe, this is our common room - for hanging out or watching TV. Of course, you'll find everyone here at 4:30 pm watching Star Trek! Off to both the left and right are the bedrooms. That door leads to the commode, and this stairway leads up to the kitchen in the finished attic. There's a washer and dryer up there, too."

So far, it looks okay, I guess.

"Now, let me show you the bedroom."

I first noticed the triple-level bunk beds on the left and right walls when I entered the room. On the far wall, under a window, was a single desk surrounded by chests of drawers.

Oh my God! It's like living in a submarine!

Roger said, "Hey, look! There's Kevin!"

Kevin was lying in the bottom-left bunk, reading a magazine. He must have cut a hole in the cover because when we came into the room, he held up the magazine, put his face behind the hole, and smiled.

"Hey, Roger! Look! You wanna see my smiling face on the cover of the Rolling Stone?"

"Yeah, right. That's very funny, Kevin. You should buy five copies for your mother. Anyway, Kevin, meet Joe. Joe, meet Kevin. Joe's in the process of moving off-campus, and he's looking for an apartment. Flo sent him our way because of our… uh… sudden opening."

Kevin said, "Oh yeah, poor Brian."

Both Kevin and Roger glanced at the top-right bunk.

I said, "Nice to meet you, Kevin."

Kevin said, "Isn't this an odd time to look for an apartment?"

"Yeah, I'm in the process of leaving the dorms. Housing decided it would be better for everyone if I wasn't living on campus anymore. In short, I was kicked out."

"Wow! That's heavy! So, how do you like this place so far?"

"It's okay. I like all the wood. There are some nice hardwood floors in here."

"Yeah, well, Brian didn't like them too much when he fell out of bed - on his head!"

"What?"

Roger said, "Now, don't worry about that. After Brian fell, the landlord installed some new guardrails, see?"

I hope they're sturdy!

"How's Brian doing?"

"We'll know a lot more once he comes out of the coma, but I'm sure he'll be just fine."

"Oh, okay. It sure looks like there are a lot of people in here."

Roger said, "Don't worry, we got it all figured out. Everyone gets two dresser drawers – these two would be yours – oh look, Kevin! Brian's stuff is still here!"

Kevin said, "Oh, that poor dude!"

"What should we do with it, Kevin?"

"Pitch it."

"Okay, well, anyway, these would be your drawers. And for the desk, we all sign up for two-hour shifts—see, there's a little sign-up board on the wall here, and look, you can take Brian's slot of 2:00 a.m. to 4:00 a.m.

Let's go to the kitchen now; I'll show you how it works there."

The stairway to the kitchen/attic/laundry room was narrow and had a 90-degree turn about halfway up.

"Here we are. This door is for an extra bathroom, which is pretty handy sometimes. And see, we have plenty of cabinet space and two fridges, and there's the oven and stove – all gas, of course. Now you can put your stuff in this refrigerator, right on this little shelf on the door that says 'butter.' Just kidding! No, you get a whole shelf to yourself down here. See that ham sandwich with the bite out of it?

JUST MISSED THE SIXTIES

That was Brian's. You can finish it if you like. Ha! I'm just kidding again. Go ahead and throw it out. Anyway, that's the fridge. Over here are the cabinets. Your non-perishables go into this cabinet, on this shelf - as soon as you shop for groceries, of course."

I have to go shopping?

When we returned to the living room, three other residents were sitting on the couches with Kevin.

Kevin said, "Hey, this is Joe. He might be moving into Brian's old spot. He just got kicked off campus!"

"No shit! That's got to be quite a story! Tell us about it, Joe!"

"You really want to hear it?"

"Sure, anything's got to be more interesting than studying Poly. Sci. 303. Let's hear it!"

"Well, it all started my freshman year. We were doing shots in my room and..."

And I told them the story of the three strikes and the petition and how it all climaxed at my last meeting with Mr. Phillips.

"And so, here I am!"

"Wow, that's quite a tale. Well, Joe, you're certainly welcome to join us here."

"Thanks. I think I will."

When Friday came, Tim and I transferred my stuff from the dorm to my new apartment using Tim's car. Packing up my stuff didn't take very long since most of it was still in boxes from the end of last semester.

Tim said, "It's a good thing you never unpacked! What do you want to do with the fan and the logs?"

"You can keep the logs. Trash the fan. That way, it can never fail anyone, ever again!"

Carrying the first load up the stairs into the apartment, Tim was excited for me.

JUST MISSED THE SIXTIES

"Wow, Joe, this is so cool! You're moving off-campus! This place is far out. Is this the bed..." and then he saw the submarine bedroom, "...room?"

"Yeah, I know it's a little tight in here – but I'll find something bigger someday!"

"Cool. Hey, Joe, I'll try to visit sometime, okay?"

"That would be great."

And that's when it sunk in.

Tim can visit me, but I can never visit Tim at Second East!

After he left, I shoved my clothes into my new dresser drawers. Then, I sat on a bunk and surveyed my new digs. Once again, I thought about Napoleon.

When Napoleon abdicated the throne in 1814, the Coalition had to decide what to do with him. They decided against an execution for fear of creating a martyr. They didn't want him in prison for fear of a jailbreak, so they exiled him to Elba, a small island in the Mediterranean.

Napoleon on Elba, with the birds he shared this lonely view.

Like Napoleon, I was in exile—exile on Main Street. In 1814, the island of Elba had a population of about 12,000, and Napoleon quickly became their ruler. One hundred days later, he escaped, returned to France, and rebuilt his army.

*Where's **my** army? What can I do?*

When nothing exciting came to mind, I pulled out a textbook and started studying.

Check Mate

Saturday morning, I awoke hungry. I carefully descended from my lofty bunk and visited the downstairs facilities. When I returned, Roger was up and dressed.

He whispered, "Good morning, Joe! Welcome to your first full day of off-campus life. What are you going to do for breakfast?"

"Well, since I don't have any food yet, I thought I could buy something at the Student Union."

"Don't bother. I've got an extra egg or two. I was just about to fry some up. Join me. You ever fried an egg before?"

"Uh, no... my mother always made them for me. Or else I had cereal."

"Well, this is your lucky day, Joe. I'm going to teach you how to fry an egg."

"Let me grab a pencil and a notebook."

Upstairs in the kitchen, Roger opened a cabinet by the oven.

"Here are Brian's old pots and pans; why don't you just use his stuff? Have you ever cooked anything like spaghetti or tuna casserole?"

"Uh... no."

"Well, Joe, what *have* you cooked?"

"I've cooked TV dinners. You won't believe how well I can bake a TV dinner. Oh, man, the temperature and the timing are perfect every time!"

"I see. I'll dictate a few recipes to you, and you can write 'em down. Okay?"

JUST MISSED THE SIXTIES

A half-hour later, after Roger's culinary instructions, I was prepared to survive off-campus without spending a small fortune buying meals in restaurants. We were washing off our plates in the sink when Roger recalled a few more rules.

"A few more things to remember: always wash your dishes right after you're done, dry them, and put them away. And another thing, see that phone in the corner?"

He pointed to a phone sitting on a small table. A notepad lay beside the phone.

"Anytime you make a long-distance call, you have to jot down the date and time of the call on the notepad. That way, when we get the bill, we can figure out who pays for which call. Kevin will go around collecting what you owe when the bill comes."

Oh my God, that reminds me! I have to call home and tell the folks about my new apartment. I better do it right away!

A week later, I called home. Mother answered, in her usual way, "Mmmmm, hello?"

"Hi, Mother, it's me, Joseph. How are things at home?"

"Oh, we're fine, but I'm glad you called. Maybe you can help us to solve a few mysteries."

"Well, I doubt I could help you with anything, but what the heck, give it a shot."

"Okay, well, we just got today's mail, and there were some checks from your school. One said it was a credit for food and housing, and the other was a refund for seven-credit hours. Are you still living in the dormitory, eating at the dining hall, and attending classes?"

I guess I CAN help to solve their little mysteries.

"Oh that, yes, that's why I'm calling, um… Dad was right. The co-ed dorm was too much of a distraction, and all the new freshmen were driving me insane with their crazy uh… shenanigans. I even had to drop a few classes – it was affecting me so much! So, I talked to the head of the Housing Department, and they made a special case for me. They let me move off-campus, and now I'm in an apartment."

"Well, that was certainly good thinking on your part." I could hear her shout to Father, "Oh, honey, you were right – that co-ed dorm was too distracting for Joseph!" Then she spoke to me again, "Sorry, Joseph, I just had to tell your father. And he has a message for you about being careful about whom you choose for friends because your friends can get you into trouble. That's wise advice, right, Joseph? Anyway, is there anything we can do for you?"

"Yes, you know those checks you just got? Could you put them into my bank account so I can pay rent and buy groceries?"

"Yes, I'll do it right away. You know, this reminds me of the time I was taking classes at the University of Chicago. That was just before I met your father. My new roommate said she was working on a special project to build an atomic bomb. This was during World War II, you know. She snuck me into the lab one day to show me their work. There was raw uranium just lying all over the place. We didn't know anything about radiation back then. So, for years after that, I glowed in the dark! So anyway, now I'm radioactive, and we got in big trouble, and they started monitoring us all the time and..."

Oh, God, no! Not that radiation story again! Does every kid in my generation have to listen to boring atom bomb stories from their parents?

When the call ended, I was jotting down the date and time on the little notepad by the phone when I heard Kevin yelling for me from the bottom of the stairs.

"Hey, Joe! Are you up there? You've got company down here in the living room!"

Could it be Rachel? Yeah, right; what am I thinking?

"Hey, Joe! Come on down!"

What a surprise! It was three of my old wingmates: Tim, Spitz, and Casey. Tim was carrying a chess board.

I said, "Tim! You're visiting! Just like you promised you would! Spitz! Long time no see! Casey! It's so good to see you again!"

Casey said, "It's good to see you too, Joe. We had to check out your new off-campus pad!"

Spitz said, "So, this is what all the petitions were about."

JUST MISSED THE SIXTIES

"Oh yeah! This is the off-campus life, all right. Say, Tim, I see you brought your chess board. What's up?"

"Well, Joe, remember that little chess tournament you set up? I was cleaning up our, or I should say *my*, room a little bit, and I found the tournament brackets you'd put together. I saw that Spitz and I needed to play a match to see who'd play in the final round against *YOU*.

So, Spitz and I had a match, and I won. Tough luck, Spitz! That means you and I now have to play to determine who will be the chess champion of Second East! Are you ready for a chess battle royale?"

"You betcha! Where can we play?"

"It's your place, you tell us!"

I showed them the bedroom with the tall bunk beds.

When we entered, one of the residents was sitting at the desk by the window. He turned, looked at us, and said, "Hey! This is my time at the desk."

I said, "Guys, this isn't good. Let's go somewhere else."

We entered the Common Room and found five guys sitting on the couches watching Star Trek. I pointed at the stairway to the kitchen.

"It looks like we need to *boldly* go... upstairs!"

Tim and I set up our match on the kitchen table. Casey lit a cigarette. Spitz started looking through the cabinets.

Spitz said, "Hey, Joe, you got anything to eat here?"

I pointed and said, "No, don't go in there. That's my shelf over there."

Then, looking in my assigned cabinet, Spitz admired my collection of Spaghetti-Os and Beef-a-Roni.

"Oh, man!" he said, "this stuff makes dorm food look like fine dining."

"Hey, Spitz, anything tastes good when you're hungry. As you can see, I need to go shopping soon. That stuff, that's just my emergency food, and speaking of emergency food..." I reached behind the cans of Spaghetti-Os and Beef-a-Roni and pulled out a box of

JUST MISSED THE SIXTIES

Twinkies. "Check this out, guys!" I said and tossed the box onto the table. They tore into the box like a pack of zombies on a fresh kill.

Off-campus Survival Rule Number One: Never offer your favorite snack cake to a group of starving college students, even if they're your friends.

After the Twinkies had been devoured, Tim and I played chess for about twenty minutes, and I could see that we were pretty evenly matched. I thought, "In a close game like this, it only takes one wrong move, one tiny little mistake that gives your opponent just the slightest edge - and then you're toast." That's probably why Tim brought up the subject of Rachel.

"Guess what, Joe? I saw Rachel on campus yesterday, and she asked about you."

I moved my queen and said, "Really?"

"Whoopsie, Joe! I just took your queen. Yeah, she was excited about the housing petition and wondered if you liked your new place."

I moved a pawn and said, "She did? What did you say to her?"

"Checkmate, well, I didn't say *that* to her. Although I told her I was coming by to check on you today, no pun intended, and I'd let her know. By the way, I just won."

"Oh my God! What a fry! Yes! No! You won, didn't you? Well, that's okay. It seems right that you won since you're the last original wingmate on Second East. Tim, you are truly the ultimate Second East champion!"

Casey and Spitz said, "Congratulations, Tim!"

Tim said, "Cool, what do I win?"

I said, "I believe the champion wins a night of pleasure with Gertrude. Tim, I'd gladly take the prize for you, but I'm not allowed to enter the dorm, so it's yours."

"Wow, Joe, maybe if I'm lucky, I'll get kicked out before I can collect the prize!"

"If I were you, I'd quickly transfer to Casey or Spitz's dorm. By the way, Casey and Spitz, how do you guys like living in your new dorms with your chicks?"

JUST MISSED THE SIXTIES

Spitz said, "Well, it doesn't have the excitement of Second East, but it's nice to be close to Sally."

Casey said, "At first, it was nice to be close to Kathy, but lately… I think it's dampening my style."

As a slut?

I said, "Oh, that's too bad. I'm sorry to hear that."

Tim packed up his chess board to leave. I said, "Well, I hope you'll visit again sometime. It's always nice to have company. Say 'Hi' to Rachel for me."

JUST MISSED THE SIXTIES

Bad Company

It took a few weeks, but I started establishing rhythms in my new off-campus life. Different routines revolved around buying, organizing, and cooking food. Not to mention the after-meal clean-up: washing, drying, and putting away the dishes. And, of course, there were still classes, studying, and laundry to be done. Stability was starting to seem within my grasp until one quiet Saturday afternoon. Unpredictability returned with a knocking at the apartment door. It was Al and Steve.

"Hey, Joe! Mr. Campus Radical! Get your ass down here and open the God-damned door!"

"Yeah, you juvenile delinquent, we've come into your town to help you party it down! Now get down here so we can take you out and boogey! Yee-haw!"

Man, I better get down there before somebody calls the cops!

Letting them in, I said, "Hey, guys, welcome to my new off-campus home. How did you know I was here?"

Al said, "Well, first, we went to Hyer Hall but couldn't find anyone! Shit, there are all these new guys!"

"I know! That's so weird, right?"

"It freaked me out, man. I thought I was in the wrong dorm. But then we saw Tim walking down the hallway, and he told us about your new apartment. So, here we are! We asked Tim to come, but he's got some new girlfriend he's gotta go see – that pussy!"

Steve said, "Looks like it's just us three crazy hippie freaks! Let's go hit The Square!"

And then, like being in an irresistible torrent, I was swept along with Al and Steve. We practically jogged to the Square.

JUST MISSED THE SIXTIES

Back then, The Square was a solid block of college bars in downtown Stevens Point. We chose one establishment, the Yacht Club, and entered. Perhaps the Yacht Club got its name because of its proximity to the Wisconsin River, I don't know, but it was strictly a place for drinking and not for boating. There were a few hints of a nautical motif. The front door pull was an old boat wheel. The walls were decorated with model sailboats displayed on high shelving. Marine rope formed borders above and below the tiny ships. Behind the bar, a sign read:

DROP ANCHOR AT THE YACHT CLUB!

We slid into a booth close to the bar, and Steve went to fetch the first round.

"Hey, bartender! Three beers, please!"

Leaning back against the bar, Steve had a sudden epiphany.

"You know what would be cool? It'd be cool if we could live here, in Point, with you!"

Right. And there goes my stability!

"Uh... sure."

"I'm serious. Man, if we had a house, we could have some great parties and invite all your old college buddies. It would be far-fucking out! We just need to find some kind of job around here."

Al said, "Ha! What kind of idiot is gonna hire a bunch of chuckleheads like us?"

Then a guy in the next booth spoke up, "You dudes should get a job with the silo company!"

I looked at the guy. He might have been only a couple of years older than us, but the deep lines on his face made him look decades older. He was wearing a green John Deere Tractor cap over shaggy brown hair. Silver crowns on his front teeth sparkled when he smiled. Steve asked for more information, and he complied.

"Dig this, dudes. You only have to work about four months in the summer, and then they lay you off. So then, for the next nine months you don't have to do nothing but sit on your ass and collect unemployment until they hire you back for the next season. Get it? Four months on, nine months off!"

Apparently, math skills aren't a requirement.

"Hell, man, I'm getting paid right now for sitting here drinking this beer!"

Al and Steve were swallowing his spiel, hook, line, and sinker.

Steve said, "No shit, man, that sounds great!"

"Oh yeah," he continued, "and when you're working, you usually only work three or four days a week! You see, it's like this, every week, they send you out to a farm, and your crew builds a new silo. When the silo is done, you can go home! The beauty is that it only takes three or four days to build one, depending on the size."

They were enthralled. Al said, "Oh yeah, of course!"

"And, dig this: when you're out on a job, the company pays your motel bill and all the food you can eat! If you want to eat steak every night, you can eat steak every night!"

Steve said, "Whoa, Al, that's too good to be true!"

"Yeah, man, it's a great gig. You guys should check it out. Hey, last summer, we built a silo right by the Wisconsin Dells. One day, we took off and rode the fuckin' ducks, man! What a blast!"

Steve said, "Do you think they'd hire us?"

"For sure, they'd hire you! They're putting together more crews every summer. The place is just down Business 51 – you can't miss it. They got a little model silo right by the side of the road."

Steve was very excited. "Hey, bartender, change that order for our new friend here. Draw one, two, three, four glasses of beer!"

Several beers later and after a boatload of fantasizing about our future life together in Stevens Point, Steve started talking in his redneck farmer character.

"Hey! Looky there, Martha! I see a bunch of them crazy commie hippie-types on the silo crew! Probably gonna fill it up with that mare-a-jew-wanna! Better go fetch the shotgun, Martha!"

JUST MISSED THE SIXTIES

Then Steve was drawn to the action at a nearby foosball table. Foosball is the Americanized version of Fussball, which means foot and ball in German. The inventor of the first foosball table was a Frenchman named Lucien Rosengart, an employee of the Citroen automobile factory. Most people don't know this, but he also invented the first seatbelt restraining system. The foosball game looks like a tiny soccer field on a tabletop. In Point, we called it "foos."

"Hey, Joe, you ever played any foos?"

"Oh, yeah. Last year, Casey, Don, and I used to fool around on a table in the basement of the old dorm. I learned a few tricks."

"Oh, yeah? Well, I think we can beat these guys at the table now. What do you say, Joe?"

"Okay, let's do it!"

Steve got up and put a quarter on the end of the table, which meant that we would play the winners of the game that was now in progress.

"You want to be goalie or forward?"

I told him I'd take goalie. Last year, I mastered the trick of getting maximum goal coverage using all three goalkeepers. Steve was happy to play forward.

Soon, it was our turn. We took our positions at the foosball table.

Steve yelled, "Foos the ball!"

The opposing forward dropped the ball through a hole on his side of the table, and the game began. Like riding a bicycle, my foosball skills returned. With intense focus, I tracked the ball's course and kept our goal defended. On the other hand, Steve played without restraint. He was a lunatic. Screaming and cursing, long hair flying everywhere, he lunged his men back and forth across the table, sometimes spinning the bars. The opponents were totally distracted. We handily beat them. Now the table was ours and, until some other team beat us, all the games were free.

Steve announced to the bar, "Attention, ladies and gentlemen! Put your quarters down! See if you can beat the two crazy hippies at the foosball table! Yee Haw!"

JUST MISSED THE SIXTIES

Instantly, three new quarters appeared on the table.

Steve said, "First up! Let's roll!"

And the battles began. The first two matches were a breeze. The combination of my solid goal-keeping with Steve's frenetic forwarding was too much for most to handle until it was the Foos Brothers' turn to play.

They looked like twins. As they took their places at the table, I noticed their matching ball-caps with "Foos Brothers" stitched on the front. Their matching shirts had a picture of a foos-man, and underneath the picture, it read:

FIRST PLACE WINNER
1973 SUMMER FOOSBALL TOURNAMENT
STEVENS POINT, WISCONSIN

Steve said, "Hey, look, Joe. These guys won a tournament last summer. I wonder if there were any other teams in the contest!"

Their goalie said, with a heavy Austrian accent, "Excuse me. Please refer to us as the Foos Brothers; there were over 200 teams in the competition."

Steve said, "And the winning team gave you their shirts! Wow! That was awfully nice of them."

"Excuse me, again, you are awfully wrong. We won. And you play awfully, too, Mr. Forward Man. I see you being all crazy and stuff. That trick will not work against our superior technique. Now, let us begin. We have a lesson to be teaching you."

These Foos-Brother guys were good, damn good. Both had the entire repertoire of shots at their disposal: push shots, pull shots, pass shots, and angle shots. Their ball control was phenomenal. They could deftly pass from one foos-man to the next, from goalie to forward, catching and controlling the ball and quickly kicking into the goal.

We were stunned. Steve played quietly, his flamboyance gone. Every goal we scored seemed like a significant achievement. We knew we were doomed because they were outscoring us at a rate of three to one. When the game was over, we slunk back into our booth. Steve pointed a finger back at the table.

"We'll get you next time, Foos Brothers! Then, you'll see who has a lesson to be teaching!"

I said, "Steve, those guys look older than us, like seniors. We can get the table back next year after they graduate."

"No way, dude! I'm not waiting for next year! We're gonna get that table back the next time we visit!"

Al said, "Well, it's so nice to have you boys back in the booth with me. I felt like I was drinking alone for a while there."

Steve said, "Al, I hate the Foos Brothers. Next time, we've got to figure out how to beat them!"

Al said, "I know! I could cut their fingers off!" Then he reached into his pocket and pulled out a brand new Swiss Army Knife.

Steve said, "Well, isn't that cute! Al has a new little toy! Look! It's even got a little tiny tweezers and toothpick too!"

Al said, "Don't knock it, Steve. The blades on this thing are razor-sharp! And guess what I learned from reading this pamphlet here while you guys were busy kicking your little balls around. They actually hand these out to the dudes in the Swiss Army!"

Steve said, "Well, who would a *thunk* it, Al? Why would they call it a Swiss Army Knife if they didn't give it to the Swiss Army?"

Al looked at his knife and said, "Oh yeah."

I'm not sure I like this combination of Al and sharp knives.

JUST MISSED THE SIXTIES

From Table to Raid

Two weeks later, there was another pounding and yelling at the front door of my apartment, which meant that Al and Steve had returned. They were excited, as usual.

"Hey, Joe! Come on down and get into Al's car! We're going to the silo company to get a job!"

I grabbed my coat and hopped into the back seat of Al's rusting, green, '65 Ford LTD. Fifteen minutes later, we were pulling into the gravel parking lot of the silo company. On the left was a barn surrounded by stacks of concrete blocks. On the right was a double-wide trailer with a sign above the front door:

RIB-ROCK SILOS
MAIN OFFICE

We bounded up the steps and burst into the front office. To our right, a middle-aged man was sitting at his desk. He looked up and grinned, a big, friendly smile on his round, clean-shaven face. He spoke with a Hungarian accent.

"Gentlemen! Welcome to Rib-Rock Silo! My name is Pat. How can I be of help to you?"

Al said, "Hello, sir, uh, Pat, we'd like to apply for a job. We heard you're putting together some new silo construction crews."

Pat spoke with great enthusiasm and pointed at his desk.

"Look at my desk - it's covered with orders for silos! I'm sitting here, wondering - how am I going to build all these silos this summer? But then, next thing you know, you guys come walking in the front door... almost a complete silo crew! Thank you, Mother Mary!"

JUST MISSED THE SIXTIES

"Does this mean we have jobs?"

"You not scared of heights, are you?"

I said, "No, not me, Pat. I live off-campus and sleep on the top of a triple-level bunk bed!"

Pat looked us over one more time and said, "Yes! This will be good for you boys! We'll put a little muscle on your bones! Oh yes! We'll get you into good shape, right?"

What am I getting into?

Then he asked us when we could start. I told him I could start the first week of May, and Al and Steve could begin in a month once they found a place to live. We filled out some paperwork, shook hands, and were done. Climbing back into Al's car, Steve was ready to celebrate.

"Yee-haw! Now we're a bunch of blue-collar hippies! Hey, let's go back to the Yacht Club and have a brew. I'm mighty thirsty after all this job-hunting! Maybe we could play a little foos too!"

I said, "What if the Foos Brothers are there?"

"Don't worry, Joe! Al got us something to help us beat those guys!"

"What... his Swiss Army Knife?"

Steve said, "No, no, Joe. Looky here!"

Steve held up a bottle of little white pills.

I said, "Those are White Cross! The same ones Jay gave me to help with final exams!"

Steve said, "Oh yeah, White Cross! Here's what we got to do. We'll take one now – so we'll be ready by the time we get there. No, better yet, let's take two. Our powers will be limitless!"

Great idea! Let's take a double dose of a non-prescribed stimulant.

He handed me two of the little white pills, and I gulped them down with my saliva.

Al parked in front of the Yacht Club, and we grabbed a booth by the foosball table. I went for beers while Steve put a quarter on the table. No Foos Brothers were in sight yet. This was a good time to warm up, just in case they did show up. When it was our turn to play, we easily beat some newbies and captured the table. Steve made his usual announcement to the entire bar, proclaiming that the Crazy Hippies now own the foosball table and daring anybody to try and take it away from us. A line of quarters quickly appeared on the tabletop. I was looking at the foosball table when the third quarter was being set into place, and then I looked right into the eyes of a Foos Brother. He was giving me a stare-down.

Steve said, "Sit down, Fool Brother, and wait your turn."

"We will be watching you, Crazy Hippie players! Don't screw yourselves up!"

Steve said, "Hey, Fool! I'm too jacked-up on speed to be scared of you!"

The Foos Brother turned from Steve to me. Once again, he looked into my eyes and said, "Crazy Joe, you better watch your speed!"

He knows my name!

We quickly dispensed of the two teams before the Foos Brothers. I was a little worried because I didn't think I was feeling any effects of the White Cross.

I hope I haven't developed a tolerance for the stuff!

It was time for our replay with the Foos Brothers. I grabbed the goalies. Steve put the ball in play, and the match began. Their midfielder got the ball and passed through Steve to the forward. They made a shot on goal. I blocked it. They got the ball back. I blocked the next shot.

Steve said, "Thanks, Joe!"

I yelled, "Get the ball, Steve!"

"I'm trying, man!"

The ball came my way once again, and I trapped it. I worked it back and forth, looking for a clean shot up the field. Suddenly, the ball looked like it was rolling in slow motion.

The White Cross is working!

I noticed that The Foos Brothers also seemed to move slowly. I pushed the ball left past the Foos Brother forward. He couldn't keep up with me. I snapped my wrist and kicked the ball. It traversed, untouched, the entire length of the field and clattered into the goal.

Steve yelled, "Boo-yah!"

I said, "We scored first!"

Good shot, Joe! Say, why don't you take forward for a while?"

I said rapidly, "Okay, Steve. That sounds good to me. Let's switch."

Then, the game started going back and forth. Goals were scored by whichever team's forward could get control of the ball. I'd make a goal, and then Foos Brother forward would make a goal, etc. A crowd began to form around the table. People were standing on barstools to get a better look. Everyone wanted to see the Foos Brothers go down. The score was tied 10 to 10. The next goal would be to win the game.

Steve said, "Hey, Joe, I'm tired of watching them score on me. Could we switch back again?"

"No problem, Steve. I'll take goalie again. Let's switch."

And so, the battle for the last goal began. Steve got his frenetic style going once again. I was calmly blocking everything that came my way. The crowd increased even further in size and intensity.

When it seemed like the game would last forever, Steve tried something different. He purposefully kicked the ball back to me.

"Look out, Joe, it's coming your way!"

The move froze the Foos Brothers. I trapped the ball. The Foos Brother forward anticipated my push shot. Instead, I pulled and kicked. The snap of my wrist sent the ball, once again, the length of the field, untouched and into the goal.

The crowd erupted. Steve was hugging me and screaming, "We did it! We beat the Foos Brothers!"

The Foos Brothers stood calmly, shaking their heads.

One of the Brothers said, "Tonight, a lesson has been learned to us. Do not play foosball with crazy hippies jacked up on speed."

Steve said, "We love you, Foos Brothers, thank you! You can keep the table. I've gotta go finish my beer!"

"Please do not hug us, thank you!"

JUST MISSED THE SIXTIES

I slid back into the booth with Al. I was incredibly jacked up from the amphetamines and the euphoria. Al was drunk and ranting.

"Man, I miss those days of Second East. Those were great times. You remember those days, right, Joe?"

"Yes. Yes, I do, Al."

"Well, you know who screwed it up for us, don't you?"

"Um, we did because we flunked out or got kicked out?"

"No, stupid! It was that Kaiser bitch! You know? I think she was out to get us right from the start! Remember that meeting in her little apartment? Remember all those stupid rules, like no sex and having no privacy? Why those people could walk into your room with their pass keys anytime they felt like it!"

"Yeah, that really sucked."

"She's just on a power trip, man! I want to bring her down a notch or two. We should go to the dorm and see what we can do."

"Okay, but the only problem is - I'm not allowed in the dorm anymore."

"Well, we can do something in the parking lot! We could do something to her car!"

Steve said, "You could put sugar in her gas tank! That would fuck-up her engine!"

I said, "Great idea! I'll run to my apartment, grab some sugar, and meet you in the parking lot!"

I sprinted from the Yacht Club to my apartment. Vaulting up two steps at a time, I bounced into the living room. Roger was there watching TV.

"Hey, Joe! Where are you going in such a hurry?"

I was speaking rapidly again. "Hi, Roger! You wouldn't believe it! We just beat the Foos Brothers at the Yacht Club! They were last summer's tournament champions, you know! Anyway, we're going to put some sugar in my old dorm director's gas tank because she's a bitch, and that's what caused all our problems. Anyway, I'm going to the kitchen now. I'm going to get some sugar. Bye!"

"Far out, man!"

JUST MISSED THE SIXTIES

Stealthily approaching the Hyer Hall parking lot, I felt a sense of foreboding. The night was dark and misty. Warm air was blowing in gently from the south. A fog was vaporizing off the snow banks like smoke. You could almost see the water molecules jumping into the air, atom by atom.

Hunching over, I walked between the cars. I heard a whisper.

"Psst, Joe! Over here!"

I found Al crouched by Gertrude's car. Three of her tires were flat. Al held up his new Swiss Army Knife.

He said, "Hey, Joe, I saved a tire for you!"

Gosh, what a pal, saving a little tire-slashing for his buddy!

Without thinking, I grabbed the high-quality knife with its 12 functions, including tiny tweezers and an even tinier toothpick. I was amazed at how easily the blade pierced through the sidewall of Gertrude's steel-belted radial. I handed Al the bag of sugar. He tried to put some into the gas tank but mostly succeeded in dumping it onto the gravel below the car.

Al said, "Man, getting sugar into a gas pipe is hard. Oh fuck, who cares."

Oh, she'll never notice that pile of sugar on the ground.

Then Al said, "Let's go!" and we returned to The Square.

It took about 2 hours and six beers to calm down from the speed and the adrenaline. Then, I returned to my apartment and slept through most of Sunday morning. My new apartment mates were pretty excited about the previous night's activities. They wanted to join in the fun.

One Fish, Two Fish

After groggily making my way up to the kitchen, I found Roger and Kevin. They were eating lunch.

"Well, it looks like our little anarchist has arisen! Good morning, Joe! Or should I say, good afternoon!"

"Morning."

"So, tell us, Joe, how did your little sugar caper go? Was it sweet revenge?"

Roger and Kevin laughed.

"Oh my God, guys, I'm a little fuzzy right now, but I think we did a little more than putting sugar in her gas tank!"

"Uh oh! What did you do, Joseph?"

I wasn't sure how they would react, but I told them about the tire slashing. I was relieved when they laughed. I was shocked when they started brainstorming more ways for me to get revenge on the Kaiser. Roger had an idea.

"Hey, Joe, next week I'm going to Sheboygan to do some smelt fishing. After I clean up my catch, I'll save the slop. Maybe we can mail it to Gertrude! Imagine her surprise when she opens a package to find a bunch of fish guts and heads looking up at her!"

I liked the idea. Roger taught me a few facts about smelt fishing. Smelt, or as they say in Wisconsin, *"schmelt"*, live in the Great Lakes and look like little tiny salmon. They grow to about eight inches - tops. Smelt-dipping is a popular springtime activity in the state. It's not uncommon to see entire families out on the piers, flashlights in hand, using dip nets to scoop up the wriggling smelt from the ice-cold waters of Lake Michigan. The fish are prepared for eating by chopping off their heads, cutting open their bellies, and scraping out the guts.

JUST MISSED THE SIXTIES

The remainder of the fish, including fins, tail, and scale, are deep-fried until crunchy.

Kevin said, "That sounds like a great idea, Roger. If you let me help you eat the fish, I'll help you clean them!"

Roger said, "It's a deal. Hey, guys, I've got a joint. Are you interested in having a toke?"

Oh yeah! It's cool to be off-campus because we don't have to worry about broken fans and Wing Directors.

I said, "Yes! And I've got this hilarious record we can listen to while we smoke!"

So, we toked in the living room, and I played the *Child's Garden of Grass* LP. I told them how I'd used the record to win a Stoned Music Competition in the dorm.

"Can you believe it? I even beat Pink Floyd!"

"That's far out, man!"

"Oh yeah, and that's just one of the hundreds of crazy things we did back in Second East!"

"No shit, what else did you do?"

And so, I told them everything I could remember. I told them of the window fans, the Hut, the Clearing, and the campfire stories. I told them the games, including Charge, Stoned-Night Frisbee, Atom, chess, Risk, and the Stoned Music Competition. I told them the crazy stuff about the firecrackers, the poison ivy, and Second East Live. I told them about the S.D.S. and my troubles with Gertrude and Mr. Phillips. I described the colorful characters of the wing, including QP, Chuck, Casey, Al (and Steve), Jay, William, Tim, Spitz, Don, Lewis, and the Professor.

The only person I neglected to mention was Rachel. I didn't want them to see me choke up.

Roger said, "Oh, man! That sounds like the best wing ever!"

Kevin said, "I wish we could have been there."

"I wish you guys could have been there too."

JUST MISSED THE SIXTIES

The following Sunday, Roger, true to his word, returned from Sheboygan with a cooler full of freshly caught smelt. When I entered the kitchen, Roger and Kevin were busy cleaning and frying them.

"Wow, it sure smells good in here!"

"There's your heads and guts, Joe. You know, I was thinking. Maybe a box of stinky fish guts wouldn't get through the regular mail. Maybe we should deliver it personally to ensure it gets to Hyer Hall."

"Okay, but you know I can't enter the dorm anymore."

Roger said, "No problem, Joe. I'll walk inside and hand it to the person behind the desk. They won't know who the hell I am."

We put the pile of entrails into the refrigerator for the night.

We scrounged up an old shoebox on Monday morning and poured in the fish heads and guts. We wrapped the box in brown grocery bag paper and addressed it to Gertrude Kaiser, Hyer Hall.

I accompanied Roger on the walk to the dorm. It was bright and sunny, another day of above-freezing temperatures. The only remaining snow was in the largest mounds by the parking lots. Spring was coming to northern Wisconsin.

I stopped fifty feet from the dorm.

"Roger, I've got to stop here. This is as close as I'm allowed to get."

"Don't worry, Joe, I've got it from here."

I watched as he walked past Gertrude's flat to the front door, then up the stairs and into the lobby. Seconds later, he was briskly descending the stairs. Just seconds after that, a curtain flew open in a window of Gertrude's flat. And there she was, Gertrude, holding the package and looking at me. I stared back, frozen, like a deer in the headlights of an oncoming snowmobile.

Oblivious to the scene at the window, Roger put his hand on my shoulder and spun me around.

"Mission accomplished, little buddy! Let's split!"

His momentum pulled me along for a few steps until I could move my legs again.

JUST MISSED THE SIXTIES

What a fry! She saw me! How long will it take her to add one and one together?

I had my answer three days later when a cop knocked on the front door.

JUST MISSED THE SIXTIES

The Dormitory Strikes Back

The first time a cop knocked on the front door, I was getting dressed for the day. Roger stuck his head in my bedroom door.

"Hey, Joe, there's a cop down there asking for you. What should I tell him?"

"Tell him I'm at class. Thanks!"

"No problem, dude."

Then, I did what any decent, law-abiding citizen would do. I slipped out the back window and onto the roof of the back porch. After crawling backward down the roof, I hung from the gutter and dropped to my feet. Kevin, busy locking his bicycle to a tree in the backyard, witnessed my descent.

"Hey, Joe, are you practicing a fire drill?"

"Yeah, something like that – I'm running from the heat!"

Working through the backyards, I found a way to campus that avoided the busiest streets. All the way, I was mentally kicking myself. *Why did I stand there like an idiot and let Gertrude see me?*

The second time a cop knocked on the front door was Saturday morning, and everyone was gone from the apartment except me. I was sleeping in. The knocking was relentless. Half asleep, I figured that someone must have accidentally locked themselves outside. Wearily, I shuffled down the stairs and opened the door. A cop was standing there in uniform. He had a big smile on his face.

"Can I help you, officer?"

"Excuse me. I'm looking for a Joseph Roman. Would that be you, by chance?"

How does he know what I look like?
"Yes, sir, that's me."
"Hello, Mr. Roman. I'm Officer Dave. Would you have time to come to the station to answer a few questions? It shouldn't take too long."
"Uh, okay. I'll throw on some clothes and come right back."
"I'll be here."
I yanked on some jeans and a sweatshirt. Looking at the back window, I was strongly tempted to flee but resisted the urge.
*That would **really** make me look guilty!*
So, I returned to the front entryway.
"Mr. Roman, I'll give you a ride in the squad car. You can sit up front."
Okay, at least I'm not in the cage in the back – that's a good sign.
We parked in front of the police station. Officer Dave escorted me through the station to his desk. The other officers ignored us.
"Sit right here, Mr. Roman. Can I get you a cup of coffee or something?"
"No, thank you, sir. I hope this doesn't take too long."
"Oh, this shouldn't take too long. I'm going to ask you a few questions about the night of March 26th. Try to answer the best you can remember, okay?
"Okay."
"Do you remember what you were doing that night? It was just the Saturday before last Saturday."
"Um, let me see if I can remember. Yes, I was at the Square like most weekend nights."
"When you say, 'we,' who are you referring to?"
Damn!
"Al and Steve."
"Did you go anywhere else besides the Square that night?"
"I went back to my apartment when we were done."
"Mr. Roman, there's something you need to know. On the night of Saturday, March 26th, a campus security guard said he saw

someone in the Hyer Hall parking lot. That's the same night that the Dormitory Director Gertrude Kaiser's car was vandalized. All four tires were slashed, and sugar was poured into the gas tank. The security guard identified one of the vandals from student identification photographs. He looked like this."

Officer Dave held up a copy of a student ID picture. It was mine.

"I'm toast!"

"So, let me ask you once again, were you in the Hyer Hall parking lot on the night of March 26th?"

"Yes... I was... I think I remember now."

"Joseph, would you mind if I record the next few questions?"

"No."

What choice do I have?

He swiftly pulled a little recorder from a desk drawer and set up an attached microphone, pointing it at me. I noticed it was a cassette recorder, like the Professors, except with tiny cassettes.

I wonder if it has Dolby? I wonder what he'd say if I played a duck call?

"First, I'm going to read you your Miranda Rights. You have the right to remain silent. Anything you say can and will be used against you in a court of law. You have the right to speak to an attorney. If you cannot afford an attorney, one will be appointed to you. Do you understand these rights as they have been read to you?"

"Yes."

"Having these rights in mind, do you wish to talk to me now?"

"Yes."

With that response, I waived my Miranda Rights. I didn't know anything about waiving Miranda Rights. All I knew was that I was about to spill my guts, squeal like a pig, sing like a canary, and tweet like a stool pigeon.

"Joseph Roman, could you please tell me what happened in the Hyer Hall parking lot on the night of March 26th?"

I said, "Al and I met at the parking lot after drinking at the Square. We wanted to play a practical joke on our old dorm director,

Gertrude Kaiser. I poured some sugar on the ground next to her car to look like we put it into the gas tank."

"And what was your accomplice, Al, doing while you were pouring sugar on the ground?"

"I don't know, he was... uh... always on the other side of the car from me."

"When you left the Hyer Hall parking lot, were the tires slashed on Miss Kaiser's car?"

"Maybe, but it was hard to see anything because it was so foggy."

Wait a minute, it was foggy! How did that guard see me?

"Thank you, Mr. Roman. I've got all I need. You can leave now."

What? No ride home in the squad car?

Walking away from the station, I had two revelations: I was starving, and the police would be looking for Al because of my testimony. I remember the last time we talked about snitches; Al said something about cutting off their balls! With that memory, I felt a massive surge of adrenalin kick-start my heart and stoke my anxiety. I quickly changed course for the Yacht Club to get a hamburger and a beer, something to vanquish each of the revelations, respectively.

At the Yacht Club, I sat on a barstool and placed my order. Looking left, I recognized a familiar face. It was Grizzled Old Dude #1 from the very first meeting of the UWSP SDS.

"Hey, dude! It's me, Joe! Remember - from the SDS?"

"Oh yeah! Hey, Joe! How are you doing?"

"Okay, I guess. Say, whatever happened to you guys? You got us started, and then we never saw you again! We did some good stuff, man!"

"Oh yeah, right. I'm sorry we couldn't be there for you guys, but right after that first meeting, my partner started having some heavy flashbacks. I had to take him back to a clinic in San Francisco for special treatment."

"Oh no! I hope he's okay."

"Don't worry. He'll be fine. He's a survivor. Anyway, I heard you guys did all right for yourselves! You made a couple of petitions, and you got the campus to reverse its long-standing rule on mandatory housing for freshmen and sophomores! Right on, brother!"

We shared the traditional hippie handshake.

I said, "Yeah, that turned out surprisingly well. Too bad I just screwed things up today with the cops."

"The cops? Oh no! Tell me what went down, man."

I told him about my little vandalism adventure with Al in the Hyer Hall parking lot and today's interview at the police station.

Grizzled Old Dude laughed and said, "Oh, man, he bluffed you good!"

"What? Bluffed?"

"Oh yeah! The cops can say anything they want to get you to talk. Guess what, Joe? There was no campus security guard in the parking lot that night! Officer Dave was fishing, and you took the bait! Too bad you didn't talk to me first, man. I could have told you about their little tricks."

"Oh shit, Al's gonna kill me!"

"You better tell him first before some cop hauls his ass down to the station. Say, that wouldn't be your friends walking in right now?"

Swiveling to the right, I spotted Al and Steve entering the bar. I swiveled back.

"How did you know...?"

But the Grizzled Old Dude was gone. I began to sweat like a pig.

Go Ask Alan

Al saw me and said, "Hey! Joe! It's good to see you! We were gonna go to your place after we grabbed some lunch. We've got some great news!"

Good thing. They're too excited to notice my distress.

Steve said, "We just found ourselves a bitchin' little pad to rent for the summer!"

Al said, "Yeah! We were driving down the street and saw a *For Rent* sign in front of a house, so we called the number on the sign. Next thing you know, we're at the landlord's place signing papers!"

Steve said, "It's a whole house, man! And it's furnished too! It's got three bedrooms, so we each get our own private fucking room! Can you believe it? Now we got our own little hippie love shack!"

It sure beats the submarine bedroom.

Al said, "Here is a key and a lease for you to sign. The address is on the lease - if you want to check it out sometime, it's only a few blocks away. Just sign the lease and take it to the landlord in the next week or two."

Jamming the keys and lease into my pocket, I tried to talk. I could barely mumble.

"Um. Wow, guys. That's super cool. Yeah, cool."

When am I going to tell Al about the cops?

Al said, "Hey, Joe, you look pale today. Are you okay?"

Steve said, "Yeah, you do. What's the matter, Joe?"

"Um... School. Yeah, it's school. There's lots of homework and reports to do. It's got me freaked out."

Al said, "What a downer, man. I never let that crap bother me. It's such a downer."

JUST MISSED THE SIXTIES

Downer! That's what I need!

"Say, Al, speaking of downers. You wouldn't happen to have any more of those blue pills you gave me for the Wishbone Ash concert?"

"Sure! Why didn't you say so? I got some here in my right jacket pocket. Now, if you would have wanted an upper, I keep those in my left jacket pocket."

Steve laughed, "Al, you're a fucking, walking pharmacy!"

Al whispered, "Well I have a friend behind the pharmacy counter, if you know what I mean. Now hush, this ain't exactly legal, you know!"

I swallowed a downer with some beer, sat back, and waited for that nice, relaxing buzz. Steve bought the next round, and the toasting began soon after. After we had one for the new house and two for the new job - I was starting to feel just fine.

Steve said, "Boys, now that we got jobs and a place to live, we're just a bunch of solid citizens, right?"

"Right!"

"We may be stoned-out hippie freaks, but now we're making money and paying our taxes to good old Uncle Sam and doing all that respectable shit!"

I raised my glass and yelled, "Here's to good citizens! Al, may I have another downer, please!"

"Shhhh, Joe! Keep it down, would ya? Are you trying to get me in trouble?"

"No, Al, I'd never do anything to get you in trouble, again, never! Please remember that, okay? Let me rephrase that. I'll never do anything to get you in trouble from now on. No, I mean from ever on."

"Huh? Okay, Joe, here - have another pill."

After taking the second downer, I noticed the bar was filled with pretty, attractive co-eds. Suddenly, any inhibitions I ever had completely melted away.

JUST MISSED THE SIXTIES

Tonight, I'll do what no man has ever had the guts to do!

I stood up on my barstool and faced the crowd. Extending my arms, I made my pitch.

"Attention! Attention, all females! May I have your attention, please? I'm here at this bar today for one reason, one reason only. I think you all know what I mean! If anyone here wants to help me, please see me now."

I sat down and turned to Steve.

"Do you think it will work?"

He pointed behind me and said, "Hey, Joe, you have a taker!"

As I turned to see her, the jukebox was playing "Honky-Tonk Woman." She looked all right: long black hair, tight blue jeans, a little cleavage, and a lot of makeup.

*I think I found **my** Honky-Tonk Woman.*

She smiled and said, "Maybe *I* can help you out tonight. Do you know someplace we can go?"

Yes, my new apartment! Thank you, Al and Steve!

Yanking the new lease from my pocket, I said, "Sure do! Let's go!" I waved goodbye to the boys. Al gave me a thumbs-up. Steve saluted.

Walking briskly to the apartment, we exchanged names. I immediately forgot her name.

Then she said, "Um, we have this little club up in Wausau. It's a sex club. If you're interested, maybe you should check it out sometime."

I think I have to start visiting Wausau.

Upon arriving at my new summer home, my libido was suddenly replaced by a strong urge to check out my new pad. It was a modest, two-story brick structure in the middle of a block of similar houses. In the front yard was a crab apple tree loaded with buds just about to burst. We walked up a couple of stairs to the front stoop, which was on the left side of the front of the house. I fished the key from my pocket. It worked, and I said, "Yeah!" as we entered the living room.

Straight ahead, the room connected to a small dining room and the kitchen. To the far right, a narrow wooden stairway led to the second floor.

The house was furnished, just as Al had said. The living room had a dark green couch, a loveseat, and an easy chair—early American. Also, there was a coffee table and some side tables. I had an epiphany.

"That's it!"

"What? What's it?" she said.

"I know exactly where I will put my sound system!"

"Oh, screw that! Let's go upstairs and, you know, do what we came here to do!"

"Okay, let's go check out the bedrooms."

We went upstairs and found four doors leading off a short hallway at the top of the stairs: a bathroom and three bedrooms.

I said, "Well, let's see. This could be Al's room, and this could be Steve's room, and this could be my room."

"I don't care! Pick one. Let's go!"

"Okay, let's say this is my room. Oh, look! There's a bed, a nightstand, and a dresser!"

Suddenly, she grabbed me. Breathing heavily, she began kissing me all over my face.

"Oh, look! There's even a walk-in closet!"

"Fuck the closet! Fuck me!"

I returned her embrace and tried to feel some passion. She reached down and patted my crotch.

"Joe? Are you okay?"

"Um. Sorry, I think there may be another reason those pills are called downers. I'm sorry about this. Oh well. Maybe someday, someone will invent a pill that makes things go up! Wouldn't that be cool? Anyway, wanna go back to The Square?"

"Sure, maybe you could introduce me to one of your friends."

"Okay, Rachel."

"My name's Rebecca, not Rachel."

"Right. Sorry about that."

JUST MISSED THE SIXTIES

As we approached The Square, I heard so much bedlam I thought there must be a riot. Turning a corner, I beheld a scene I'll remember for the rest of my life. People were pouring out of every bar and celebrating. They were hugging, screaming, and dancing in the street. It was mass delirium.

I yelled at the first person I could find who wasn't going completely bonkers, "What is going on here?"

"Haven't you heard? The President just resigned!"

"Nixon?"

"Who else? He didn't want to be impeached, of course! Bye!"

He jumped off the sidewalk to join a conga line gyrating down the street. Everyone was raising their beer bottles to the sky.

Oh my God! The other petition! It worked!

"Hey, Joe! Congratulations!"

Looking across the street to find the source of the voice, I spied Grizzled Old Dude #1. He flashed a peace sign. I thought I saw Rachel standing beside him, waving at me. But then my view was blocked by a swirling, screaming mass of drunken students. I started climbing a nearby light pole to see over the mob. The crowd noticed and began cheering me on.

"Higher! Higher! Higher!"

Sitting at the top, I calmly surveyed the scene. It was just too chaotic to spot the Grizzled Old Dude or Rachel.

I slid down the pole and returned to my old apartment with its submarine bedroom. It was time to sleep off the night's dose of booze and barbiturates.

The next day, I woke up feeling okay. Somehow, I wasn't bothered by the events of the previous day: the talk with Officer Dave, my worries about Al, or my lack of performance with the Honky-Tonk Woman from the Wausau Sex Club. It had been just another crazy day, and I was glad it was over. I took it easy, hanging around the apartment and doing schoolwork.

JUST MISSED THE SIXTIES

Unfortunately, Monday morning started with getting awakened, once again, by a loud and persistent knocking on the front door. Like before, I shuffled down to open the door and was greeted by a cop asking for Joseph Roman. This time, it wasn't Officer Dave, and he didn't want to take me to the station. Instead, his mission was to hand me an envelope. Inside the envelope was a summons. It said the City of Stevens Point wanted to see my ass in court this Friday.

Jailhouse Rock

The following week of school passed much too quickly. I went to classes, did homework, shopped, ate, cleaned, and watched a little TV – all the usual activities. I even wrote a two-page book report on John Quincy Adams. But before I knew it, it was Friday morning, and I had to appear in court. I dressed in my best slacks, button-down shirt, and V-neck sweater.

It was a quick walk to the courthouse next door to the police station.

I arrived at the exact time indicated on my summons. At the entrance to Courtroom #2, I handed the summons to an officer at the door. He pointed and said, "Sit on the defendant's bench, over there, and wait until they call your name."

I took a seat. There were thirty to forty other defendants of various ages, male and female, casually dressed and looking grim. I sat as far from them as possible.

Oh my God, I don't want to look at these people; they all look so... guilty!

Instead, I looked around the room. It was a typical small-town courtroom. There were rows of wooden benches resembling pews. The Judge sat behind an elevated, cherry-finished wooden desk. To his right, a flagpole hung the American flag, and to his left hung the Wisconsin state flag. A bailiff and a court reporter were seated below. A couple of cops loitered against the wall.

Oh my God! There's Officer Dave!

The Judge pounded his gavel, and another day of the court began—the cases before mine passed in a blur. Names were called, defendants approached the bench, charges were read, and pleas were requested. The folks who pled guilty were sentenced, and those with a not-guilty plea were told to schedule a follow-up court date with the clerk in the back of the room. It was quick and efficient, an assembly line of justice. My mind was racing.

What a fry! How did I get into this mess? Did Officer Dave lie to me? What are they going to do to me? What if my folks find out? What if Al finds out? He'll kill me for sure! He can never find out! If I'm lucky, the cops won't catch him. Maybe I can think of something clever to say to the Judge.

"Joseph Roman, please rise and approach the bench." I walked to the bench.

The bailiff asked, "Are you Joseph Roman?"

"Yes, I am, sir."

"Joseph Roman, you are charged by the city of Stevens Point, Wisconsin with the willful destruction of private property on March 26th, 1974. How do you plead?"

"I plead not guilty for two reasons, your honor. First off, it wasn't willful. You see, we'd just beaten the Foos Brothers at the Foosball table in the Yacht Club. Do you know who the Foos Brothers are? Well, they happen to have won last summer's Steven's Point Foosball Tournament, and anyway, we were excited, and then someone said, 'Hey, let's put some sugar on the ground by the cars in the Hyer Hall parking lot, so people will think that someone put it in their gas tanks. So that's my second point. It was just a spur-of-the-moment practical joke, you see?"

There was complete silence in the courtroom. No one had ever said so much to the judge before, ever.

The Judge said, "Officer Dave, could you come here for a second?" Officer Dave walked over to the Judge. They whispered together briefly. Officer Dave walked back to the wall. The Judge whacked his gavel. BANG!

"Three days or ninety dollars!" He banged his gavel again. "Next!"

The bailiff took my arm and led me to the cashier's station on the side of the courtroom.

JUST MISSED THE SIXTIES

The cashier, a stern-looking middle-aged woman, asked if I would pay the ninety dollars or serve the three days. I looked in my wallet and counted two dollar bills.

I said, "When can I do the three days?"

She said, "You don't leave this building without paying the ninety dollars or doing the three days."

I said, "Oh. You can't just send me a bill?"

"No."

I looked at the policeman standing nearby. He was folding his arms and eyeing me suspiciously. I considered my options.

Well, three days would only be like a long weekend. I'd save ninety bucks. What do I have to lose?

Like a contestant at a game show, I said, "Gimme three days!"

The officer exchanged a look with the cashier before leading me through a door to the back room - where the new guests are processed.

There were two tables. A young woman in uniform met me at the first.

"Welcome to the Steven's Point Hilton. Please empty your pockets on the table."

I took out my wallet, keys, cigarettes, lighter, and loose change. She grabbed the wallet, keys, and loose change and shoved them into a manila envelope. She let me keep the cigarettes.

Good thing – that's like cash in the slammer.

"Please step to the next table so I can get your prints."

She pulled out an ink pad and some official-looking documents. After stamping my inked digits on the paper, she slid me a box of tissues.

"Here, clean off the ink with these. Officer Frank! We're ready!"

Officer Frank popped out of an adjacent room filled with TV monitors. One was tuned into a show on bass fishing. Officer Frank, who looked like he might be a couple of weeks from retirement age, ambled over with a little hitch in his step.

JUST MISSED THE SIXTIES

"Officer Frank, meet Joseph Roman. He's going to be our guest for the next three days. Please take him back to, um... let's say, room number 2. Okay?"

"Sure thing, Peggy. Buzz us in, please."

Peggy pressed a hidden button, and we buzzed into the cell block. Frank closed the door behind me. CLANG! I stood looking down a hallway with ten cells, five on each side. All the cells were empty.

I said, "Oh my God! It's the little rooms with bars!"

Officer Frank said, "What did you expect, son, a hotel suite with a whirlpool and a balcony?"

Frank showed me to room number two. I sat on one of the cots and wished it was three days later. Suddenly, that song, the one my ex-room-mate loved, came to mind.

"Thirty days in the hole"! No! No! I've got to think about something else!

So, once again, I thought of Napoleon. After escaping exile on Elba, he secretly re-entered France and wooed the French Army back to his side. With the army behind him, he returned to Paris and easily reassumed his role as Emperor. The English and the Prussians promptly sent armies to defeat him again. Napoleon marched his troops out to meet them and lost the fight at Waterloo. The Coalition had to decide again what to do with Napoleon. This time, they exiled him to an island much farther away, St. Helena, about 2,000 kilometers west of the coast of Africa in the middle of the South Atlantic Ocean. Napoleon never left the island alive. He spent his remaining lifetime writing his memoirs. Six years later, he died.

Unfortunately, unlike Napoleon, I had neither paper nor pencil to write my memoirs, so I lay on the cot and tried to relax.

Ten minutes later, I heard the buzz of the hallway door. Looking over, I saw Frank escorting another guest.

Please don't put him in with me!

Frank put him in with me. Now I had a cell-mate, a prison buddy. He ambled over to the other cot and sat down. He was about my height, with long, dirty brown hair - a drifter. His clothes were stained, and so was his face. He wore torn blue jeans and a sweatshirt, proudly announcing, "I Visited the House on the Rock."

Yeah, like he knows anything about architecture.

He spoke first, "Hey, man! What you in for?"

Oh no! He wants to have jail talk.

"Destruction of private property, you know - vandalism."

"Cool! You wouldn't believe what I'm in for. Fucking littering man! It's a joke. These cops are out to get me! Do you know how I know that? Because every time I come into town, I see a police car! I don't think that's a coincidence, you know? Anyway, I'm driving along minding my own business, and this cop was behind me, you see, and I threw a can out my window, and the fucker pulled me over! Can you believe it? Can you?"

Oh no, he wants me to answer!

"Uh... no way, man."

"You know what? These cops are out to get me! Do you know how I know that? Because every time I come into town, I see a police car! I don't think that's a coincidence, you know?"

Oh no! He's a repeat offender who repeats the same thing repeatedly until you want to scream! I don't know if I can take it! I've got to get out of here!

And then he said, "Say, dude, you wouldn't happen to have a coffin nail?"

"Pardon me?"

"You know... a smoke?"

"Oh. Yeah... yeah. Here you go."

"Thanks, dude. Fucking littering man! Can you believe it? These cops are..."

"I know! They're out to get you!"

"Shit! How did you know I was going to say that?"

I walked to the cell door and yelled, "Officer Frank! I have a question!"

Moments later, there was a BUZZ, and Officer Frank strolled down the hallway.

"Yes?"

JUST MISSED THE SIXTIES

"Can I pay my fine and leave?"

"Sure, you can. Anytime you want to."

"Do you take checks?"

"Yes, we do."

"Can I make a phone call? I have to call someone to bring me my checkbook."

Frank took me back to the processing room and pointed to a phone on the wall beside his TV room.

"Do I just get one call?"

"No, that's only on TV shows. Here, you can have the phone for 15 minutes, okay?"

"Okay."

I tried to remember a phone number, any phone number. The only number that came to mind was Casey's home number back in Wauwatosa (867-5309). I thought Casey's Mom could tell me Casey's new phone number, so I called. I was relieved when she answered the phone.

"Hello, who is this?"

"Hello. This is Joe, Joe Roman. How are you doing, Mrs. Stockton? I hope I'm not interrupting you."

"Oh, hello, Joseph. I'm just fine. I was keeping myself busy cleaning Casey's coin collection. You know he saves all those silver quarters and dimes from before 1964. He also saves those old pennies he calls 'Wheaties'. Anyway, I always tell him, 'Casey, you better watch out. You never know where that money's been!' But he ignores me. So here I am, cleaning off all his coins with Lysol. You know that Casey loves to collect things!"

You can't imagine all the pussy he's been collecting lately, Mrs. Stockton.

"So, Joe, it's good to hear from you. I haven't seen you since I picked you boys up at the bus terminal. You were so tired you hardly spoke! If you ever come home again, you should stop by and say 'hello'. Anyway, what can I do for you? How's school going this semester?

"It's going well, Mrs. Stockton, and that's what I'm calling about. I'm hoping you can help me. I'm trying to contact Casey to see if he wants to study together for finals, but I lost his phone number. Would you have it handy? If it isn't inconvenient for you, that is…"

"Oh sure, Joe, you're in luck. I was just talking to Casey at his new dormitory. He should still be there now. Here's the number…"

She gave me the number, and we said goodbye. I quickly dialed Casey's dorm and was very happy when Casey answered immediately.

"Casey, is that you? This is Joe."

"Whoa, that's weird; I was just talking to Mom. I thought she was calling me back with *one* more question."

"That's funny! I just got your number *from* your Mom. Anyway, Casey, I can't talk too long because I'm in some deep shit here, and I need you to do me a big, big favor."

"Okay, Joe, what the hell did you do this time?"

And then I told him where I was and where to find my checkbook.

Jail Break

Twenty minutes later, the cellblock door buzzed, Officer Frank appeared, and I was freed from incarceration.

"Well, Mr. Roman, your buddy is here. I guess your little stay with us is about to end. I hope you were comfortable."

"Yes, I was, Officer Frank." I turned to my cell-mate (The Repeat Offender) and said, "Goodbye and good luck! Watch your back!"

"Thanks, man! Watch your back, too, man! You know they're out to get me! See you around sometime!"

I certainly hope not.

Casey was waiting for me in the processing room. He handed me the checkbook.

"How much is this going to cost you?"

"Ninety dollars and one cigarette."

"One cigarette?"

"For my cell-mate - that's a small price to pay for safety in the joint."

Opening the checkbook, I asked Peggy, "Can the fine be reduced for the 45 minutes I already served?"

"Mr. Roman, thank you for giving me the first laugh I've had this week. The answer is no - ninety dollars, please."

I wrote the check and gave it to Peggy. She gave me back my stuff.

Walking away from the courthouse, Casey was quick to lecture me. "Okay, Joe, what kind of shit did you do this time? I bet that Al was involved, too, right? Am I right?"

I nodded.

"I thought so. I told you that Al was no good. What happened?"

"Uh... did you hear about Gertrude's car?"

"No shit! That was you? Jesus, Joseph and Mary, Joe! Stay away from Al, okay?"

"I will. Right after this summer is over."

"What? This summer? What are you talking about?"

"Um... I'm renting a house with Al and Steve this summer."

"Oh God, Joe, no! Those psychos? Are you out of your mind?"

"Don't worry. I can handle it, Casey. We'll be busy building silos all week. I've learned my lesson. I'll be fine. I can only hope that the cops never catch Al because then he'll find out that I squealed on him. And then I'll be toast."

"What?"

"Don't worry, they'll never find him. He's like one of those guys living in society's cracks. Anyway, how's Don doing?"

"Okay, I guess. The last time I saw him, he said he had been promoted to Driver. You know, one of those brown UPS trucks?"

"Cool. How's Kathy?"

"We broke up."

"What? Sorry to hear that. May I ask what happened?"

"No problem. She caught me screwing her best friend, Terry. You remember Terry from Crandon?"

What? Hoover Dam?

"No shit!" I said, "She seemed like such a... a nice girl."

And a complete prude, too.

"Crazy, huh? Turns out she had the hots for me all along. The first time we were alone, she was all over me! Did you know she has little freckles on her left butt-cheek that form a smiley face?"

"No, I didn't know that. So, are you with Terry now?"

"No, we broke up when she caught me with Brenda."

"Brenda – you don't mean B-52, do you?"

"Yeah! Yeah! That's the one. She's the one that got you in trouble for screwing in your room!"

Yeah, right, I can only wish.

Funny thing is… I picked her up at a concert, just like you did. We got stoned and made out in the ladies' bathroom. It was too bad that I was at the concert with Terry then, and Terry came into the bathroom and caught us. Man, B-52's breasts are amazing! Isn't that funny how her left nipple is about twice the size of her right one?"

"Uh…right. Yeah. I was just about to say that. So, is Brenda your girlfriend now?"

"Nah! Not since I met this chick from the Wausau Sex Club. Can you believe there's a Wausau Sex Club?"

Oh my God! He had the Honky-Tonk Woman too!

"Gosh, Casey, I might have heard about them. Did you actually go up to Wausau to see the club?"

"I did, I did! Rebecca invited me to Wausau to check out the club, and I went. It's at this huge house. It's a mansion looking out at Rib Mountain, simply gorgeous. When I arrived, Rebecca greeted me and told me about this 'initiation' they have for newcomers. It's really, fucking far-out! I had to wear a blindfold and take off all my clothes. Then, one of the women in the club had sex with me. I'm telling you Joe, it was the best sex I've ever had in my life! Okay, so here's the best part. When it was over, I got to take off the blindfold and see my partner. And it blew my mind! You'll never guess who it was!"

"Gertrude Kaiser?"

"No, asshole. It was Cricket! Good old Cricket, and now we're together for good!"

"That's it now? Just Cricket for you?"

"Right! Just Cricket! And, of course, group sex as long as Cricket is part of the group."

"Well, congratulations. That sounds really… uh… romantic, Casey."

"It does, doesn't it? Well, do you want to know something funny? Now that I'm doing it almost anytime I feel like it, even with lots of people, and it's okay, well, sex isn't quite as fun as it used to be."

"I'm sorry to hear that, Casey, but you know what? Life can't be just one constant orgasm."

"It can't? Why not?"

"It's because you need to recharge. Your body has to rebuild its desire. You have to let the current build-up, and when your desire is so strong you can't think of anything else, the sparks will fly, and it's magic once again! Just take a week off, at least."

"I guess it's worth a try. Say, when did you get so smart?"

"Well, when you're doing hard time in the slammer, you got plenty of time to do nothing else but think."

"Joe, you were in there for only 45 minutes!"

"And for those 45 minutes, when I was locked in the can, I thought about everything I was missing: the feel of the sun's warmth on my face, the sound of birds singing and children at play. You know, it's all those things you folks on the outside take for granted, like rainbows and puppy dogs. You can't understand it till you've been there, my friend."

"Joe, here's your apartment. I'll see you around. And don't do anything stupid this summer!"

The Summer of Stave

I hadn't thought much of the impending summer as of yet because, once again, it was finals week. I took the tests without the shelter of my little white-cross helpers since it was only three classes. And then I got my grades, two Bs and one C, so I'd gotten through the semester without too much damage to the old GPA.

Al and Steve came by the apartment the weekend after finals and helped me load my stuff into the back of Al's Ford. I said goodbye to Roger and Kevin, and we all hoped to run into each other some random day, perhaps at The Square.

Taking my clothes upstairs at the rental house, it was interesting to see that Al and Steve had chosen precisely the rooms I had picked for them on my night with the Honky-Tonk Woman, Rachel.

No, not Rachel; I mean Rebecca.

When I returned to the living room, Al said, "Hey, Joe, we left a spot for your sound system on this table."

Wow, and that's just where I was planning to put it!

Steve said, "Hey, guys, we got to let the neighborhood know that some crazy hippie long hairs have just moved in!"

Al said, "Okay, Steve, how do you plan on doing that?"

Steve said, "Joe, put your speakers in the window. Al, help me take the couch out to the front yard. Joe, bring out some beers!"

Soon, we were relaxing in the front yard, drinking beer, smoking cigarettes, and listening to tunes. Steve entertained us with his red-neck character.

"Would you look at that, Harold? Some of them long-haired hippie-types done moved into the neighborhood! Listen, they're playing some of that devil music! I tell you, this place is going to hell in a hand-basket!"

Switching back to regular Steve, he said, "Hey, Joe, why don't you put on your ZZ Top album? I want to hear some 'Tush'!"

I complied, and soon he was singing along, "I said, Lord, take me downtown; I'm just looking for some tush!"

I said, "Steve, look over there! I think downtown is coming to you with some tush."

I pointed up the street at a group of about a dozen young men and women running toward us, wearing ski masks and nothing else.

"Oh my God, Joe, it's a bunch of naked (neck-id) people running up the road! My prayers have been answered! Al, Al, look at that!"

Al said, "Those are streakers, Steve!"

"What? What the hell is a streaker?"

"I saw it on TV a couple of days ago. It's this new fad. All over the country, people are running naked through public places. They're doing it at ball games and concerts and stuff. It's fucked man! You'll never catch me doing that shit!"

The streakers passed by at a brisk jog. Suddenly, Steve was overcome.

"Wait, you streakers! Wait for me! I want to be a streaker, too!" He jumped up and pushed down his pants. Then, running across the front lawn in his underwear, he pulled his t-shirt over his head. For a moment, he was blinded. BOOM! He smacked into the neighbor's tree and tumbled to the ground beside it.

"Ow! God damn it! That really hurt!" He finished yanking the shirt off his head. He moaned, "Alan, I missed the streakers!"

Al scolded, "Steve, get your clothes back on right now! Come over here and sit on this couch!"

"Do I have to?"

"Yes! You do! You're grounded. Be a good boy, drink your beer, and light this joint."

"Okay, Al."

JUST MISSED THE SIXTIES

A couple of beers later, I said, "So, guys, how's the new job going at the silo company?"

Steve said, "Oh yeah! I'm a blue-collar man, all right!"

Al said, "It's okay, we're not on a silo crew yet. Pat's got us on the stave team for now. Staves - that's what they call the cement blocks that make up the walls of a silo. We load stave forms into a cement-pouring machine in the afternoons. They are filled with cement, and we stack them to dry overnight. The next morning, we crack the finished staves out of the forms. Anyway, we'll see what Pat wants us to do tomorrow, silo crew or stave-team. Well, dudes, I'm bushed. I'm hitting the sack."

The following day, we walked into the office of Rib-Rock Silos, looking for Pat. He was happy to see us.

"Hey there, Joe, welcome to the company! Steve and Al, you boys can go to the stave team again. Joe, follow me to the barn. I'll get you working on doors."

"Silos have doors?"

"Oh sure, they got doors! How do you think the farmer gets the feed out for the cows? They got lots of doors; you don't see 'em 'cause they're hidden inside the chute, you know. There's a door every three feet in the chute 'cause that's how tall the staves are. They're made of wood inside a concrete frame. We make the wood double-thick (tick). The doors got to be strong so the feed don't break on through to the other side."

We walked past the stave room. I spotted Al and Steve flipping concrete staves out of metal forms and arguing.

"Al, tomorrow night, we're going streaking!"

"No! No, we're not, Steve!"

A couple of table saws and a pile of boards were in the next room.

"This is where you and John will cut and nail the doorboards together. Where is that John? He must be in the rebar room. John is a veteran, you know, just got back from Vietnam. He doesn't like to talk about it too much, though. Let's go look in the next room."

Inside the rebar room, I saw a pile of steel rebar rods lying next to a rebar bender and cutter. A welding station with a gas cylinder, gun, and face mask was in the corner.

"Here's where you and John will make the rebar squares that go into the door frames. The stave team will let you know when they're making door staves so you can bring 'em the rebar squares. Oh, here comes John now."

John had been out back, having a smoke. He walked into a back entrance, crushing out a cigarette butt in the dirt with a twist of his boot. He was dressed "whole-army": khaki boots, pants and jacket. He was a troubled dude. He shuffled towards us, slumped over, and looking at the ground. Long, scraggly brown hair covered the sides of his face. A bushy mustache covered his top lip. His cheeks were sunken, and his jacket hung loosely from his shoulders.

"John, this is Joe. He's going to work on making doors with you. You show him what to do, okay?"

"Far out, I got me a little helper now."

"Yes, John, it is far out. Next week, we'll get you boys on a crew, okay?"

"Promises, promises."

Pat left. John and I walked back to the door-cutting room. John started ranting.

"Shit! Pat keeps telling me he's gonna put me on a crew so I can make some real money, but where am I? I'm still back in the God-damned barn making God-damned doors - getting paid shit by the God-damned hour."

"Oh."

Then he looked up at me, "Sorry, kid. I'm sorry you had to hear all that. Sometimes, it seems like I was born under a bad sign – nothing good happens to me. But hey, I got you to help me now. We'll pound out all the doors we need in no time! You ever worked a table saw before?"

"No."

"Ever bent and cut rebar?"

"No."

"Ever welded? Let me guess, no?"

"Sorry, no."

"Well, what kind of good-for-nothing dumb-asses is Pat hiring nowadays?" I looked down. "Don't worry, kid, I'll teach you everything you need to know. Hell, it ain't hard."

And so, John showed me how to cut the boards. It was easy - it was clearly marked on the table saw. We zipped out enough boards for 100 silos.

"Now we got to nail 'em together." He placed the cut boards into a metal frame, two layers deep - the second layer perpendicular to the first. He grabbed the nail gun and fastened the boards together.

"Zip, zip! Easy as pie! Now you can make some while I have a smoke. Got a cigarette?"

He went out to smoke. I put together ten doors, then decided to go out and join him.

"Hey, Joe, I'm glad you came out. Do you have another smoke? I swear I'll bring some tomorrow."

I gave him another. Despite what Pat had said, I had to ask about Vietnam.

"You know, John, I've heard so much about Vietnam on TV and in the news, but you're the first person I ever met who was actually there. What was it really like?"

His entire body tensed up, and he said, "I am so sick of people asking me about Vietnam. It's making me crazy! Everyone wants to know, 'Did you burn down villages and kill innocent women and children?' For God's sake, what the hell is wrong with this world? Listen, Joe, here's all you need to know. The only thing I ever did was sit on my ass, all day and all night, on some barstool in Saigon, drinking Mai Tais! That's it. Got it? Can you dig that, man?"

"Oh. Yeah! Sure - whatever you say!"

Then, his left cheek twitched. "And I don't know nothing about no Agent Orange neither!"

He stalked away. I went after him.

JUST MISSED THE SIXTIES

"John, are you okay? Can I get you a soda or something?"

"Follow me? Don't follow me. I'm just fine. I got my Orange Crush."

I tried one more question.

"Did they have big mosquitos over there?"

He turned and laughed, "Oh yeah! If they landed on you, they'd knock you on your fucking ass!" He mimicked being knocked over. He was in a good mood once again.

The next day, we worked in the rebar room. John showed me how to cut, bend, and weld the rebar rods into perfect squares. I bent more rods when he went out for his usual two-cigarette break. I noticed some short waste pieces lying on the ground. Feeling creative, I tried writing my name with pieces of rebar. With a bit of practice, I got handy at forming letters. I welded a J, O, and E side-by-side and linked them together on a straight piece of rebar as a base.

This will look cool on the wall!

I made an Al and a Steve, and then a rebar Rachel. That night, I put the names on the walls. Joe, Al, and Steve were in a grouping above the couch, and Rachel was on the wall above the sound system.

A week later, Pat called everyone to the office. He was putting together two more silo crews.

Please don't put me with Al!

My wish came true. I wasn't teamed with Al. I was assigned to a crew with John, Steve, and a foreman named Brad. Al was on a crew with three other guys from the stave team.

Steve, John, and I got into our crew truck and waited for Brad to arrive. Soon, a jeep pulled into the lot and parked next to us. We watched as the Incredible Hulk stepped from the vehicle. He was so buff he could have been on the cover of a muscle magazine. Besides his brawny body, he was clean-shaven, severely crew-cut, and sporting mirrored aviator glasses.

Steve softly sang, "From the halls of Montezuma..."

John yelled, "Howdy, Brad!"

JUST MISSED THE SIXTIES

"Good morning, John. Is this my crew?"

"Yes, sir, Brad, sir. This is Steve, and this is Joe."

"Welcome, boys." Looking us over, he said, "Well, well, we're gonna get these boys into shape, right, John?"

"Damn straight, sir!"

"Okay. Here's the deal. I'm the first man. John is the second man. You two are what we affectionately call 'Grunts'. You'll find out soon enough why you're called Grunts. Now, let's get to our first job."

Brad got behind the wheel, and John rode shotgun. Steve and I were in the back. In the pick-up bed behind us were all the tools and gear necessary for building a silo. The silo parts, including staves, doors, ladder, and roof, were waiting for us at the job site. The Truckers had already delivered them.

Steve said, "Brad, were you in the army like John?"

Brad didn't like that. "Don't you ever, ever call my squad 'army'. We were Special Ops, a highly trained, super-fit, and efficient group of fighting men. We were a special team."

John turned and winked, "Yeah, they were 'special' all right. Those were the idiots that actually volunteered to be there!"

Brad said, "Hey, John, while you drafted slackers were sitting around the base, we were out in the bush, engaging the enemy!"

"That's right, and every time you special boys got into a jam, we had to go out and save your special little asses!"

"Hey, somebody had to remind you pot-smoking, long hairs, there was a war going on!"

"Hey, Brad, long-hair, short-hair, it don't make no difference once the head's blown off."

Brad sighed, "Very true, John, very true."

Steve said, "Hey, can't we all just get along?"

Brad said, "John, give me the directions to the job site; let's go."

About an hour later, Steve asked, "Daddy, are we there yet?"

Brad said, "Hey, no complaining back there, or I'm pulling over right now!"

JUST MISSED THE SIXTIES

Then he pulled out a cassette tape, popped it in, and cranked up the volume. Steve and I stared at each other in wide-eyed wonder when we heard Olivia Newton-John's sweet, sweet voice singing "Let Me Be There." We thought it was hilarious.

I said, "Ha! You? You're an Olivia Newton-John fan?"

Steve said, "I can't believe it, a tough guy like you!"

That's when he did it – he pulled over to the side of the road. He rammed the gear into the park, twisted in his seat to look back at us, and scowled.

"Listen to me, boys. I'd gladly crawl, naked, over a mile of broken beer bottles just to smell her shit. Can you understand that?"

I said, "I understand, Brad; I feel the same way about Joni Mitchell."

Steve looked at me and said, "Joni Mitchell? You mean Rachel, don't you, Joe?"

"Oh… yeah. I guess I do."

Soon, we were at the job site. Brad drove up the farmer's long, gravel driveway and parked by the barn. About 20 feet away was a 10-foot square concrete pad. Brad pointed to the pad.

"That's where we're building the silo."

I said, "Brad, where's all the stuff? You know, where's the staves, doors, roof, and hoops – the stuff we're making into a silo?"

Brad smiled, pointed across a field to a tiny shed, and said, "Everything's over there by that shed."

"And just how is it going to get from over there to here?"

John said, "That's what Grunts are for! Ha!"

Steve said, "Why the hell did the truckers put the stuff over there instead of over here?"

Brad winked at John and said, "Because I told 'em to. Pat said to get you boys into shape!"

"Oh, man! Thanks, Pat!"

"You'll thank him later. Now, get going, Grunts! Bring me some staves! We got a silo to build!"

JUST MISSED THE SIXTIES

Steve and I began the first of at least 500 trips, back and forth, from the shed to the pad. Brad and John interlocked the staves into a circle, the side of one stave neatly fitting into a groove, also called the rib, on the adjacent stave.

When the circle was finished, Brad told us to fetch four hoops, the slightly curved metal rods that would hold the circle of staves together. Then the four of us, located at 90-degree intervals around the silo, each joined two of the hoop ends together with giant metal couplers and lug nuts. Turning large ratchet wrenches, we tightened the lug nuts - securing the hoops snugly around the circle of staves. Then, it was time to form the next circle on top of the first.

The work became rhythmic: Haul some staves, haul some hoops, and tighten them in place. Brad and John, working inside the silo, pieced together a temporary wooden floor to be hydraulically raised as the silo arose. Staves, at first transferred by hand, were now being hauled to the top using motors, ropes, and hooks.

For hours, back and forth, back and forth, we walked. Steve began entertaining me with his redneck character.

"Look, Martha, our silo's being built by a bunch of them long-haired hippie freaks! We better keep an eye on them, gotta make sure they ain't smoking that whacky tobaccy. Lord knows what kind a silo they gonna build if they be all doped-up!"

Then he was singing "The Streak", but with his own unique lyrics:

JUST MISSED THE SIXTIES

The Grunt
By Steve
(Apologies to Ray Stevens)

"Hello, everybody. This is your action news reporter with all the news that is news across the nation, on the scene at the job-site.
There seems to have been some disturbance here.
Pardon me, sir, did you see what happened?"
"Yeah, I did.
I's standing over there by the shed, and I see him come streakin' around the stave pile!
He warn't wearing nothing but his steel-toed boots and a hard hat!
I hollered, 'Look out, Martha!'
But it was too late.
She'd been lug-nutted!"
Oh yeah, they call him the Grunt!
Look at that, look at that!
Well, he's as dumb as a…

From the top of the silo, Brad yelled, "Okay, Steve, we've all heard enough!"

"Oh, come on, Brad, I got a lot more ideas!"

"May I remind you, Steve, we are on the customer's property?"

"Oh yeah, good point."

And just then, the farmer stepped out from behind the shed and said, "Wee, doggies! That Ray Stevens is a gas, ain't he? Hey, boys, I got a special treat for you. Follow me over here."

"Can we, Brad? Can we?"

"Okay. Okay. You can take five."

We followed the farmer into the milking barn. Rows of cows stood before us, lined up in their stalls with automated milking bags covering their udders. The beasts lowed as the pumps rhythmically churned. Flexible tubing ran from each cow up to the ceiling, connecting to a network of PVC pipes that ultimately drained the fresh milk into a large, gleaming, stainless-steel vat in the corner.

JUST MISSED THE SIXTIES

"Come over here, boys, have a taste of this."

He picked up a ladle, slid open a door on the top of the vat, ladled milk into little paper cups, and handed them to us. The milk was delicious.

"Ain't nothing like it, right boys? Just the way mother nature meant it to be."

Steve said, "Farm out, man!"

By 6:30 PM, Steve and I were exhausted, arms aching, hands numb.

I said, "Brad, can we quit now? I don't think I can pick up another stave!"

"Hell no, Grunt! We work till sundown. Remember, we don't get paid 'til the silo's done!"

Why must we work on the longest days of the year?

Finally, the sun settled deeply enough into the western horizon for Brad to call it quits.

"It's too dark to work now, boys. Let's go grab a bite."

Steve said weakly, "Yeah. I think I earned that steak today."

Brad said, "Steak? Sorry, Grunt, we're getting burgers. Let's go."

We grabbed a quick burger at the local diner and drove to our motel. Steve and I collapsed on the twin beds in our room.

I said, "Oh my God! I hurt in places I never knew I had places."

"No shit. I can't move a muscle."

"I'm just going to lie here for a minute before I get ready for bed."

Knock, Knock, Knock. "It's time to get up, boys! Let's go! Silo's not gonna build itself!"

"Oh my God – we just laid down!"

"Well, at least we don't have to get dressed."

We dragged our protesting bodies onto the truck. Brad drove us to the diner for breakfast.

JUST MISSED THE SIXTIES

After everyone had ordered their coffee and eggs from the waitress, Steve said, "I haven't slept like that in years! Man! I was out like a light."

John said, "Lucky you! I had to listen to Brad snore all night! Well, not all night; he did stop for a little while. And then, when I thought to myself, 'Thank God, this is my chance to fall asleep,' he starts shouting in his sleep - crazy shit like, 'Stay the course!' and 'They hate our freedoms!' Jesus, Brad, what's going on?"

"Sorry about that, John. Let's say I have a few war-related issues that need to be worked out."

After breakfast, it was back to the site for another day of working from dawn to dusk. Midway through the afternoon, we topped out the silo—no more staves to carry. With a whoop and a holler, Steve and I danced a little victory jig. Steve was called to the top to help Brad and John build the roof. My job was to bolt together the ladder that would run from the ground to the top of the silo. The stainless-steel ladder came in 8-foot sections. After it was assembled on the ground, it would be pulled up to hang from the top of the silo. I laid out the sections in the field and fastened them together in about a half hour. Then John let down a hook, which I connected to the top of the ladder. As he hauled it to the top, I had to keep a firm grip on to the ladder bottom so it wouldn't smash into the side of the silo. Once the ladder was hanging correctly, my next job was to bolt the ladder to the hoops. Working my way up the silo, I reached the top in about twenty minutes. After finishing the roof, Steve, Brad, and John began climbing down.

Brad said, "We're going down for a break. Come on down after you finish those last couple of bolts. Oh, and take a second to enjoy the view."

I tightened the last bolt, and, looking up, something caught my eye—a single, red-tailed hawk circling just below the clouds.

He must be eight miles high!

JUST MISSED THE SIXTIES

I clambered over the top and stood on the temporary wooden flooring. Around me was a 360-degree, panoramic view of the bucolic Wisconsin countryside. For a moment, I felt like I was sitting on top of the world, but then I thought of Rachel, and suddenly I was overwhelmed by a deep feeling of emptiness.

Just like Napoleon, with that bird, I share this lonely view.

Two days later, we were popping the wooden doors into place inside the chute, which meant we were done. The farmer signed some paperwork. We thanked him again for the milk, hopped into our truck, and drove away – our first silo under our belts.

Brad said, "Hey, boys, I got this new cassette you might enjoy! This group calls themselves the Bachman-Turner Overdrive."

Soon, we were singing along.

Taking care of business, it's all mine! Taking care of business - working overtime! Work out!

I'd survived a week of silo construction. Now, all I had to do was survive the weekends with Al.

I wonder if it's time to tell Al about the cops. I'll have to think about that.

Wheels of Fire

The first three weekends, between building silos, were strictly recovery times - which meant sleeping late, eating large meals, taking long hot baths, and mostly relaxing. After that came the weekends of shopping: buying clothes, records, and a ten-speed bicycle. We were getting paid good money for our hard work, so let's enjoy it!

One weekend, I leisurely explored the countryside on my new bicycle while Al and Steve traveled to Tomah to visit with old friends and do more shopping.

When they returned, Al was eager to show off his latest acquisitions.

"Check out this record, man. I've meant to get this for a long time - Ten Years After!"

"Oh yeah, they're cool. They were at Woodstock. Put it on."

Listening to the lyrics, I couldn't believe my ears when I heard,

> *"I'd love to change the world,*
> *But I don't know what to do,*
> *So, I'll leave it up to you."*

"Al! Al! Do you know what this means?"

"No, I just like the song."

"It means they've given up! They've lost the passion, the desire, the fire!"

"Who gives a fuck. Shut up and listen."

Once again, I couldn't believe my ears when I heard,

JUST MISSED THE SIXTIES

*"Tax the rich,
Feed the poor,
Till there are no
Rich no more."*

"Al! Al! Do you know what this means?"

"Yeah, it means if we tax the rich too much, then everyone will be poor. We got to cut taxes, man!"

"Cut taxes! Now that you have a job, you want to cut taxes?"

"Yeah, there are too many taxes! Have you looked at your check stub?"

"Al, we can't stop helping the poor! When did we stop worrying about poor people and start worrying about the rich?"

"Joe, it's just a song! You're overthinking it! Hey, I have something else to show you: a new toy. Maybe you'll think this is cool. Check out this baby!"

I remember his Swiss Army Knife, Al's last 'toy' that got me into a bunch of trouble!

Al reached into his duffle bag and pulled out a rifle. Steve and I exchanged wide-eyed looks of shock.

Oh my God! I've got to get rid of that thing!

Al set the rifle on the coffee table and said, "I'll tell you more about this puppy as soon as I get a beer. I'm dying of thirst."

When he left for the kitchen, I took the opportunity to grab the rifle and flee.

I've got to hide this thing!

I started for the stairs but wasn't fast enough.

"Hey, Joe! Where are you going with that gun in your hand?"

"Uh… I was seeing how much it weighs. Pretty light, eh?"

"Yeah, pretty cool, huh? It's called a thirty-thirty rifle. It's really popular with the hunters because it's light and has a small recoil."

I said, "I didn't know you were a hunter."

"I'm not. Look! Here's a box of shells I bought too! You can't have a gun without the ammo!"

JUST MISSED THE SIXTIES

Steve said, "Al, put that thing away before someone gets hurt. Let's go lock it in your car."

They walked out the front door to Al's car just as the neighborhood was filled with the roar of motorcycles. Three bikers parked their rides on the street behind Al's car.

Steve yelled, "Look, Al, it's my old gang, the Tomah Terrors!"

I looked out the window to see the gang. The motorcyclists were wearing matching jackets with *TOMAH TERRORS* stitched on their backs. The O in Tomah was a wheel on fire, and the O in Terrors was a skull and cross-bones.

Beneath the stitched Tomah Terrors was stitched their "nom de bike." On one jacket, it read "Born to be Wild," another dude had "Born to Run," and the third said, "Born on a Bayou."

I'm not sure that the third guy has the concept.

Of course, the motorcycles were Harley-Davidsons, aka Hogs, another pride and joy of the city of Milwaukee. Wisconsinites William Harley and Arthur Davidson designed the first hogs in 1906 with the help of outboard motor pioneer Ole Evinrude. Their bikes are popular for customizing into the "chopper" look, made famous by the movie *Easy Rider*. The three bikes out front were fully customized choppers.

The gang was eager to hit the town. Steve said, "Let's go to The Square, boys!"

Steve, Al, and I each joined one of the bikers, riding double. I was with Born on a Bayou. Then we took off, looking for adventure in whatever comes our way. *Yee-haw!*

The Shit Hits the Fan

And then, one weekend, it happened; the shit hit the fan. It started like a typical weekend – with Brad dropping the crew off Friday in the Rib-Rock Silo parking lot. Brad noticed there was a police car sitting in the lot.

He said, "It looks like he's waiting for someone."

I looked at the cop car and instantly recognized the driver.

Oh my God! It's Officer Dave!

And then Steve said, "Joe, you can catch a ride back to town with John. I'm gonna wait here for Al's crew to get back – Al and I got some stuff to pick up."

I said, "I can wait for Al, too."

To warn him!

"No, Joe, you better get back to the house."

I took the ride with John, and when he pulled up to the house, I spotted an unusually large number of cars and motorcycles parked in front of it and up and down the street.

I said, "Looks like someone's having a party," and hopped out.

John said, "Ha! That's funny. I'll see you in a couple of hours," and drove away.

What did that mean?

When I opened the front door, I didn't know what to expect, although it was nice to receive a cheer.

"Yea! Joe's here! Now the party can start, right, Joe?"

I scanned the scene. People were sitting everywhere. The Tomah Terrors were at the dining room table.

I said, "Hi, guys! Boogey on!"

JUST MISSED THE SIXTIES

Jay, Spitz, and the Professor were on the couch.

I said, "Jay, Spitz, and Professor! What a surprise! It's great to see you guys again!"

Then I saw two gorgeous, topless, blonde twins sitting on the loveseat.

"Hi, ladies! How ya doin'."

One of the Tomah Terrors started to yank on the tone arm of my precious record player roughly.

"Hey! Please be careful with that turn-table!"

What? Did I see topless women?

Spinning back, I said, "Well, well. Hello, ladies. Where are you from, my dreams?"

Oh my God, they're identical twins!

Topless Twin #1 said, "We're from Tomah. We're here for Al and Steve's big party. Do you know where they are?"

Now, I don't know much about Tomah, Wisconsin, except, of course, they have a motorcycle gang called the Tomah Terrors, and Al and Steve come from there. And now I also knew that these lovely ladies called it their home. I also knew that if you've ever driven by Tomah, you may have seen a sign on the edge of town that reads, "Where the I's Divide." I find that interesting. Some towns are proud of their geographical gifts, like a mountain vista or a beautiful beach. Other towns proclaim their spirit of friendliness or goodwill. But that's not so for Tomah, Wisconsin. Their claim to fame is that, here in this location, in this great country, two interstate highways (I-90 and I-94) that had been temporarily sharing the same road once again split apart to travel their separate ways. It's a lot to be proud of, to be sure, but if I were mayor, I would immediately tear down that sign and replace it with a new one proclaiming, "Home of the Tomah Twins."

I said, "Steve and Al should be here soon. They're picking up some stuff."

Turning back to the couch, I tried again to obtain eye contact with my former Second-Easters. But they couldn't keep their eyes off the Tomah Twins. I could almost see the drool dribbling down their chins.

"Guys? Welcome to the house for our party! I sure wish I would have known about it. I'm going upstairs to clean up. Could you, uh, keep an eye on things for me?"

They nodded, "Yes".

Yeah, I bet they'll keep their eye on things.

After bathing and dressing, I returned to the living room and the party. Even more guests had arrived. I spotted Steve in the kitchen, tapping a beer keg. Party supplies, such as munchies and cups, were on the counter.

I said, "Hey, Steve, I see we're having a party! What a surprise!"

Steve looked up from the keg with a big grin on his face. "See, Joe! I told you we could have a big house party with all your old college buddies! I invited my pals from Tomah too! It should be a great night. Yee-haw! Now help me pass out these beers, okay?"

"Where's Al? I thought you were waiting for him?"

"I was, Joe, but then something weird happened. I'll tell you about it later."

Oh no! Officer Dave!

I did as he instructed, and with the help of the Topless Tomah-Twins, we quickly distributed frothy cups of brew to everybody in the house.

When Steve entered the living room, I said, "What do you mean something weird?"

Steve ignored me and held up his cup, "Everyone raise your beer and toast to the craziest fucking party that the town of Stevens Point will ever see! Yee-haw!"

Someone yelled, "Chug your beers, everyone!"

"Chug! Chug! Chug!"

"Steve, what happened to Al?"

"Come on, Joe, we gotta get more beers for this crowd!"

We passed out another round.

"Steve, you're not answering my question. Where's Al?"

"Later, Joe, I have an important announcement."

"What could be so…"

"Listen, everybody. Everyone raise your glass in toast again – this time to Joe! It's his birthday!"

Oh my God! That's right! I forgot my birthday! I'm not 19 anymore!

"Chug! Chug! Chug!"

After several more chugged glasses, Jay passed some joints around, and Steve pulled out a leather wine flask.

He said, "Who wants a drink from the magic wine flask? One sip is all you'll need!"

When the flask reached me, I took a giant slug. It was sweet and fruity, not bad. I took another pull.

"Joe! You might not want to drink too much of that stuff!"

"Why not? It's pretty good!"

"Because! I loaded it with all the leftover chemicals from my stash back in Tomah. It's got some mescaline..."

Jay said, "Oooo! From the sacred peyote cactus!"

"And it's got some psilocybin..."

Jay said, "Oooo! From the magic mushroom!"

"And a little acid."

The Professor said, "Ah, yes, lysergic acid diethylamide, also known as LSD or by the street name 'acid'. It was first synthesized in 1938 by the Swiss chemist Albert Hofmann."

"And I threw in a couple of amphetamines, just for kicks."

I said, "No shit!" and took another long slug. I don't know why I did it. Blame it on the beer or perhaps nerves.

What was happening to Al? Did Officer Dave nab him?

Passing the flask, I asked again, "Steve, where's Al?"

He said, "Oh yeah. It's really weird. Right after you left, Al's crew got back. Then, when Al got out of the truck, the cop in the parking lot jumped out of his car, walked over to Al, and started talking to him. The next thing I know, Al's getting into the squad car, and they're driving away!"

And that's when Steve's drugs kicked in.

JUST MISSED THE SIXTIES

At first, the drugs affected my "Observer". Some scientists refer to our consciousness with the concept of the Observer. The Observer is the part of your brain that perceives the sensory input from all over your body, sorts it out, and builds a picture of the world to help you determine your actions. As the potion from the magic flask took effect, my Observer started taking little breaks, randomly turning itself off and on again. I experienced a series of disconnected events, similar to the graveyard scene in the movie *Easy Rider*.

Suddenly, I was sitting at the kitchen table, a cigarette in my hand, looking across at Tim, QP, and Chuck's smiling faces.

"Tim, QP, Chuck! When did you guys get here?"

"Ha! Welcome back, Joe! We've been talking to you for about an hour."

The next thing I knew, I was dancing like a crazy Cossack in a circle with Steve and the Tomah Terrors in the dining room. "Green Grass and High Tides" was blasting on the stereo.

Next, I was sitting on the easy chair in the living room. "Frampton Comes Alive" was playing on the stereo. Rachel was there. She was talking to me. *Rachel!* I focused as hard as I possibly could.

"Rachel, is that really you? Are you here talking to me? How did you find me?"

It was like a movie from the fifties. My peripheral vision was a blur. Rachel's face, a little out of focus, filled the frame, and it was beautiful.

"Yes, Joe, it's really me, Rachel. Everyone from Hyer Hall was talking about going to your party here."

"No shit! I wish I was here to enjoy it."

"Oh my! That's so funny. Happy birthday, Joe! Oh, and you know, I never got to thank you for what you did."

"What did I do?"

"We won! The petition! Now freshmen and sophomores can live off-campus! Remember?"

"Oh yeah, that! Wow. Too bad I had to get kicked out of the dorm when I won."

"Yes, that's true, but now anyone can move out. And that brings me to my big news - I live off-campus! I've got this great little one-bedroom flat for next semester. I'm living there right now - just me and my pet cat. You should stop by sometime!"

"Sure, but what happened to that poet guy, you know, Michael, with the pipe, the Kama Sutra, the back massages, the dental meditation, and all that stuff?"

"Oh, him? He dumped me a while ago. He met some chick at a poetry conference, and when he found out her father owned a publishing company, he put the moves on her. I bet he's using her to get some of his work published. He was a creep anyway. I should have seen it coming. Even before he dumped me, he became sarcastic all the time - especially when he found out I was saving your Lucky Underwear story!"

I said, "Hang on to that story! It's going to be a classic someday. Who knows, maybe it will get published in a collection of short stories!"

Rachel said, "Anyway, Joe, here's the address of my new apartment. Stop by and see me sometime!"

I said, "I will! I will!"

She handed me a slip of paper, and I shoved it deep into my pants pocket.

Wow, I've got a second chance with Rachel!

But then, one of the Topless Tomah Twins spotted us and decided to play a little joke.

As I was saying to Rachel, "I can't tell you enough how good it is to see you again, Rachel; I think about you all the..."

A Topless Twin walked over and said, "Hello, Joe. Is this seat taken?" and sat in my lap. "Hey, Joe, I haven't given you your birthday present yet."

Now, any guy who's ever had a beautiful, topless woman sit in their lap at the same time they're talking to the woman they just realized is truly the love of their life will know exactly how I felt at that moment. Mixed emotions don't even begin to describe it. At first, it felt like winning two lotteries simultaneously, but realizing I could only keep the winnings from one. Despite my condition, I also realized the Tomah Twin was probably playing a prank. I hoped Rachel realized that, too.

But Rachel quickly stood, said, "I think I better go now," and walked briskly towards the door.

I stood up, picking up the Tomah Twin like a sack of potatoes, and followed Rachel across the room.

"Rachel, it's not what it looks like!"

But she was gone, and once again, so was I.

The next time I was cognizant, I was lying on the living room couch. The room was dark. I could hear conversations in the dining room, the kitchen, and upstairs. I vaguely saw other people in the living room—dark shapes sprawled out on different pieces of furniture. I saw the hulking shape of a brown UPS truck parked on the front lawn through the front window.

Don!

One of the dark shapes on the floor arose, shuffled towards a corner, and stopped directly in front of the left speaker. I heard his fly unzip and watched him assume the pee position.

I leaped from the couch, "Noooo! Go outside and do that, man!"

He said, "No, I can't go out there, man! They're watching for me! The cops are out to get me!"

I grabbed his shoulders and spun him around. It was the Repeat Offender from the City Jail.

"I can't go out there, man. They'll see me! They're out to get me, you know! Hey, you got a coffin nail I can borrow?"

"Sure, go get it!" And I threw the cigarette out the door and onto the front lawn. He scrambled out to fetch it.

"Hey, man, I hope they don't see me out here!"

"Better run!"

I slammed the door and locked it. I had to find Steve to tell him about the riffraff getting into the house and joining the party. I bounded up the stairs. On the landing, I saw Steve's bedroom door was shut. Two Tomah Terrors (Born to be Wild and Born to Run) sat on the hallway floor.

"What are you guys doing here?"

"We're guarding Steve's door."

"Well, you guys should guard the front and back doors so the neighborhood bums don't wander into the party!"

They looked at each other, and I walked right by them and into Steve's room.

Apparently, motorcycle gangs aren't very good at guarding much of anything.

I shut the door behind me. Steve's room was dark except for a beam of moonlight shining through a slit in a curtain. My vision followed the light beam to a second moon on Steve's bed. This second moon wasn't keeping still; it was in rapid motion, clenching and unclenching, pumping back and forth. Lying beneath Steve's lucky ass was a Topless Tomah Twin. I quickly left the room.

Looks like Steve got my birthday present.

Back in the hallway, I noticed the Tomah Terrors were gone.

Maybe they went downstairs to guard the doors like I told them to!

Suddenly, there was a blur of motion followed by a painful blow to my midsection. I was being shoved backward into Al's bedroom. My stomach ached from the hard object being rammed into my gut.

Falling backward, I saw the object. It was Al's brand new thirty-thirty rifle. Standing there, clutching the weapon with two hands, was Al. Al raised the rifle, took a shooter's stance, and aimed at my head.

"Joe! You asshole! You ratted me out to the cops! I thought you were my friend! You're going to have to pay for this!"

I was raising my hands defensively when I spotted the silhouette of a cowboy hat and a baseball bat in the hallway light.

"Al, I'd like to introduce you to my Louisville Slugger!"

Al started to turn, but it was too late. I heard a CRACK, and Al crumpled to the floor. William knelt on Al's chest, pulled some rope from his belt, and began hog-tying him like a baby steer.

JUST MISSED THE SIXTIES

Gosh, it is handy to have a cowboy around.

William looked up and said, "Hi, Joe! Good to see you again! Don't you worry about Al – we got him." Then, a group of ex-Second Easters picked up Al and hauled him down the stairs. Steve was with me, helping me down the stairs. He set me down on the living room couch.

"Here you go, Joe. Now, this time, stay on the couch, okay? Sit back and enjoy the ride. Here, I'll even play your favorite song."

I closed my eyes. He put on "Incense and Peppermints".

My favorite song!

Soon, a few more "trippers" joined me on the couch. They were puffing cigarettes. The smoke started stinging my eyes, and then the hallucinations began.

At first, I was standing in the middle of a huge anti-Vietnam War demonstration. Chanting hippies were everywhere. The cops were throwing tear gas canisters.

Ouch! The gas is burning my eyes!

The crowd began to chant, "The whole world's watching! The whole world's watching!"

Oh my God! It's the 1968 Democratic Convention. That's when Mayor Daley's thugs beat the shit out of the hippies! I've got to warn them!

I yelled, "Run away! Run away!" I tried throwing back the canisters, but there were too many. Soon, I was overcome by the gas. I sat and put my head between my knees. The chanting faded away.

A minute later, I raised my head and saw I wasn't at the protest anymore.

Where am I?

I was sitting at the end of a long hallway. It looked like a dormitory

It's Second East! Oh no! I'm not supposed to be here!

Walking down the hallway, I opened every door as I passed. The rooms were empty.

Where is everybody? Did everyone move off-campus?

JUST MISSED THE SIXTIES

In one room, the desk was charred black.

It must be the Professor's old room!

Finally, at the end of the hall, I found my old door with the bumper sticker TEENAGE WASTELAND.

It's my second-semester room!

Suddenly, I heard a commotion coming from the end of the hallway. Looking back, I saw Kerry, Jim, Gertrude, and Mr. Phillips walking side-by-side briskly toward me.

Kerry said, "I got my passkey, Joe. I'm going into your room!"

Jim said, "Not on my watch, you're not getting away with those shenanigans!"

Gertrude said, "Joseph, you have three strikes! You are not welcome (velcome) here anymore!"

Mr. Phillips said, "Mr. Roman, this dormitory is off-limits to you, as well as all the dormitories on Jupiter, Mars, and Neptune."

I turned, quickly opened the door, and stepped inside to... where?

It's not my room! It's the Clearing! They must have made a few adjustments to the door!

Looking across the field, I saw a pocket watch sitting in the grass. It was just like the one from the episode of The Twilight Zone that QP had told us about at the campfire. The only difference, and it was a big one, was that this watch was about four feet tall and had legs!

Maybe this is the watch that controls time! Perhaps I need to press the button to return to real-time and escape this crazy dream!

I started walking towards the watch. Then the watch did the craziest thing – it ran away.

I have to catch that damn watch!

I chased after it, running through the field. I began passing familiar figures. First, I passed my parents.

Mother said, "Stay away from that marion and herijuana, Joseph!"

JUST MISSED THE SIXTIES

Father said, "Be careful who you choose for friends, Joseph. They can get you into trouble!"

I passed Napoleon, standing in his classic pose, one hand tucked under his coat.

Napoleon said, "I told you, Joseph, never invade Russia!"

I said, "Hey, Bonaparte, what you got under your coat?"

He pulled out his hand and flashed a Swiss Army Knife.

Holy shit!

I started running harder after the watch. The watch ducked into The Hut, and I followed.

Ha! I got it now! It's trapped!

I stepped inside the entrance to the Hut. I couldn't see at first because it was too dark. But after my eyes adjusted, I saw Casey, Cricket, Steve, and the Tomah Twins inside a sleeping bag and having an orgy.

I said, "Oh, sorry, guys. Did anyone happen to see a giant pocket watch with legs run through here?"

They continued their orgy, oblivious to my presence.

Suddenly, Casey stopped, turned, looked at me, and said, "I told you that Al was going to be trouble!"

I stepped back, out of the Hut – right into City Courtroom #2.

I didn't know the Hut connected to the Courthouse!

I was standing in the back, by the defendant's benches. I looked to the front of the courtroom and saw Officer Dave. He held up the giant pocket watch, and the Judge looked down at them. The watch was futilely churning its little legs in the air.

Oh no! They're having a time trial!

Peggy and Officer Frank were standing by the processing room. They looked eager to lock time into a cell. In slow motion, the judge lifted his gavel.

He's about to sentence the watch! I have to do something!

Walking up the aisle, intent on freeing the pocket watch, I passed Grizzled Old Dude #1 sitting on a bench.

He said, "I told you that cop was bluffing!" Looking further down the bench, I saw Tim, Jay, William, QP, Chuck, Casey, Don, Spitz, and the Professor. They all nodded at me. I was about to ask them to give me a hand when the judge slammed down the gavel.

He proclaimed, "Three days or ninety dollars!"

I yelled at the judge, "Three days! I can't wait three whole days! I'll pay! I'll pay for me, and I'll pay for Al, too! Please put me back in real time!"

Suddenly, there was a roar of engines. Everyone looked to the back of the courtroom. Steve and Al were sitting on a pair of Harley-Davidson chopper motorcycles. Al held up his new rifle and yelled, "All of you, put your hands in the air!"

After everyone complied, Steve drove to the front, grabbed the giant watch, and drove towards an exit on one side.

Steve paused at the door and yelled, "Joe, I told you not to drink too much from the flask!" Then he sped out the door.

I followed. I ran up the aisle and out the exit. But when I stepped through the door, I didn't find myself on the streets of Stevens Point. Instead, I was on the playing field of a giant foosball table.

Either I'm tiny, or this table is huge!

The field was perfectly straight, with white lines at regular intervals. There was a loud WHOOSH past my right ear. I looked over and realized I'd just missed being kicked by a giant foos-man. Looking downfield, I spotted the watch running in a zigzag fashion to avoid other kicking foos-men. A voice boomed to my right. It was a Foos-Brother.

"Hello, Joe! We have a lesson to be teaching you!"

"You got to help me, Foos Brothers! I'm trying to catch time – but it's too fast for me!"

The other Foos-Brother boomed to my left, "Crazy Joe, you better watch your speed!

Running frantically ahead, ducking and darting from the kicking foos-men, I was inches away from catching the watch. It was almost within my grasp when I said, "Ouch!" A kick in my rear sent me tumbling into the goal. Like Alice in the rabbit hole, I fell for a long time.

JUST MISSED THE SIXTIES

When I finally landed, seated on my butt, I heard the familiar sound of sitar music. Looking up, I saw the same ancient Buddhist temple I'd dreamed of many months before. Parting the beads that hung in the door-frame, I spotted the Far East Man seated in a lotus position on a grass mat, surrounded by lotus flowers, burning candles, and smoking incense.

"Welcome back, Joseph! As before, are you here for knowledge and enlightenment or simply to get your rocks off?"

"Greetings, Far East Man. Today, I am here for the first two things you say."

"Good. Well, my son, what is it you wish to know?"

"Two things: First, when will I get back to reality, you know, real-time and real people?"

"Relax, my son. Reality will once again regain control. It always does. This will happen as soon as your body metabolizes the large number of hallucinogenic materials you have ingested."

"Thank you, Far East Man, and the second..."

He cut me off, "I know what the second thing is. It is about Rachel. When reality returns to you again, you must go to her quickly before she is lost from you forever."

"Yes! Thank you, Far East Man! Thank you, Far East Man! Thank you, Far East Man..."

And then I awoke in my room, in my bed. It was morning, and sunlight came softly through my window today.

The Morning After

I jumped out of bed and washed up. I leaned on the sink, looked in the mirror, and recited my *new* morning mantra.

"I'm twenty, I've always been twenty, and I'll always be twenty."

I descended the stairs, wondering what surprises awaited me. Halfway down the steps, I was paralyzed by a frightening sight. I spied Al's shining bald spot over the back of the easy chair.

My first thought was to turn, run up the stairs, enter my room, and lock the door, but then I heard William yell, "Come on down, Joe, it's safe!"

Tentatively, I took a few more steps and saw the smiling faces of all my old wingmates from Second East seated around the living room.

William said, "Come on down, Joe! Look! Al's tied up!"

I looked and saw it was true. Al was tied to the easy chair.

Al said, "Joe, please tell these chuckleheads to let me go! And tell them to get me some more ice for my head - I've got a splitting headache! And get me some more aspirin, too."

William said, "Don't worry, Joe, we're not going to untie Al until you say it's okay."

"Really? What's going on?"

William spoke first, "Well, Joe, I'll go first. I drove to Point for the Second East Reunion and your birthday party. I'd heard about it from Jay. Anyway, I was parking down the street from your house, and what did I see? I see good-ole Al come outside, grab a *RIFLE* from his car, and walk back into the house."

Steve interjected, "Yeah, the cops had grabbed Al at the silo plant, taken him to the station, and accused him of vandalism, based on your statement! Al was really pissed."

Al chimed in, "Yeah, I was pissed, all right."

I said, "I'm sorry I ratted on you, Al, but the officer told me the campus security guard had seen us!"

Al said, "Joe, you're an idiot for letting the cop mind-fuck you like that. Another thing that pissed me off was that I had to walk home from the police station. Fortunately, or perhaps unfortunately, the walk home took me by the Square - so I comforted myself with a few too many shots of Jack Daniels. That's when I got this great idea, or maybe a stupid idea, that I would scare you just a little to teach you a lesson. And that's when your cowboy buddy must have come to the rescue. The next thing I know is – I'm sitting here in this chair all fucking tied up! Oh yeah... and with a God-damned splitting headache! Holy shit, it hurts!"

William continued, "Right. When I saw Al with the gun, I grabbed my bat and followed him inside and up the steps, just in case there was trouble. Then, I saw him shove you down and aim his rifle at you. Oh man, I thought, 'I gotta save Joe!' So, I tapped him on the noggin with the bat!"

Al said, "That fucking hurt, man!"

William said, "I hardly hit you! I think you passed out drunk!"

"Maybe you're right; oh man, my tongue feels like the entire Russian army marched over it with muddy boots!"

Steve laughed and said, "Hey, there were never any worries, men. I hid Al's bullets the first day he brought that damn rifle home. It wasn't loaded. He wasn't gonna hurt nobody!"

I said, "Well, it kind of hurt when he jammed it in my gut!"

Al said, "Well, you hurt me when you ratted on me, man!"

I said, "Al, he told me they knew we did it - someone saw us!"

"Joe, if they had known you did it, they would have charged you immediately. He was fishing!"

"Okay. I know I was an idiot, but I was scared. Say, Al, I'll pay your fine. It should be ninety bucks, just like mine."

JUST MISSED THE SIXTIES

Jay said, "Yes, Joe, we have already determined that you will pay Al's fine if there is one. We had a 'house trial' last night."

"A house trial?"

"Yeah! After Al passed out, we brought him to the living room, put him in the easy chair, and tied him up. Steve sat you down on the couch over there. A couple of hours later, Al woke up, and we had a trial."

Grizzled Old Dude #1 said, "And I was the judge."

"Oh yeah! I saw you there in my dream! I saw all you guys!"

Jay said, "Anyway, we had a pretend trial to figure out what happened."

Tim said, "It was cool; it felt like a real courtroom!"

Jay continued, "We had everyone tell their side of the story, even you! In the end, you offered to pay Al's fine. At least, we think you said that; you were also talking about saving time from going to jail, but we didn't pay too much attention to that stuff. Then Al said he was okay with that if we gave him some aspirin. We took you upstairs and put you to bed when it was over."

"Holy shit! That's great! But, Al, you've been tied up here all this time?"

Suddenly, Al threw off the ropes. "No, we just put them there this morning - so you'd feel safe."

"Ah! No shit! What a fry!

Then the Grizzled Old Dude #1 said, "Al, remember there are a few other rulings we made in our little courtroom."

"Oh. Yeah. I promised not to point my gun at anyone. Right, William? I think it's some 'Code of the West.'"

William said, "Al, it's just never, ever, a safe thing to do! Oh, and that Code of the West crack reminds me of your other promise last night. Remember?"

"Oh yeah, that one. I promised to stop making cowboy jokes."

Casey said, "Or short people jokes."

Al said, "Yeah, I was getting to that...shortly."

Chuck laughed and said, "I think you promised, in general, not to be such a prick anymore."

"Fine. Fine. I promise not to be a prick anymore. You guys must thank Steve and me for the wonderful party!"

After everyone said, "Thanks," Steve said, "Does this mean we're all getting along? Yee-haw! Hey, Joe, I told you I'd get all your college buddies together for a party, and on top of that, everyone will be friends again!"

I said, "Wow! This is great. What a relief. I was so worried about what would happen when the cops found you, Al. So, anyway, what did you tell the police?"

"I did what any decent, law-abiding citizen would have done; I told 'em *you* did it."

I laughed and gasped. Shoving my hands in my pants pocket, I felt a slip of paper, and then I remembered someplace I needed to go as soon as possible.

"Guys, it's been so great to see you again. I wish I would have been mentally here this weekend to enjoy it completely! But I have to go – there's someone I need to see."

Casey said, "We understand, Joe - love calls!"

As I left, Steve cued up "Glad" by Traffic on the sound system.

> *Sing Sing Sing*
> *Country Joe and the Fish*
>
> *Open my mind, I've been dreaming,*
> *Open my mind, I've been dreaming,*
> *After all this time, it seems so strange;*
> *I woke up today and changed my way of living.*
> *Sing, sing, sing!*
> *Sing, sing, sing!*
> *Sing me a love song!*

Open My Mind

I stopped at a gift shop on my way to Rachel's apartment. I wasn't sure what to get—a card or a gift. Then I saw Flo, the lady from the Housing Office.

"Flo! What a surprise! What are you doing here?"

"Well, if it isn't Joseph Roman, Mr. Trifecta! How are you? How did that apartment work out for you? Oh, to answer your question, I own this place. I work that other job just for the insurance benefits."

"I see. Well, the apartment was fine. I finished the semester. Now I'm in a different place with some guys I work with."

"Well, that's just peachy, Joe! So, what are you looking for today? Can I help you find something?"

"Well, maybe. I'm looking for something – for someone. But I have no idea what to give her."

"Oh! It's a 'her', is it? Why don't you tell me a little something about this lucky lady? Is she your girlfriend?"

"I hope so! I don't know. She reminds me of Joni Mitchell, in a way. The funny thing is our favorite song together was 'Chelsea Morning.'"

"'Chelsea Morning'! Well, I know just the thing!"

She led me down an aisle of candles and candleholders and pointed at a collection of incense owls.

"In the song, she offers to bring incense-owls to her lover!"

"Perfect! I'll take them."

Standing before Rachel's door, I paused to gather my thoughts. Finally, I knocked.

The door opened, and there she was, dressed in bib overalls, holding a mug of hot chocolate, complete with mini marshmallows swirling about in a circle. Behind her, on the kitchen table, I spotted a partially completed crossword puzzle beside a bowl of oranges.

"Hi, Rachel! I'm so glad I caught you at home! I'm sorry. I was really out of it this weekend when you came by. And I'm really, really sorry that I was such a shithead back in the dorm. I miss you - a lot. Can I see you again sometime?"

I thought I saw a tiny little smile.

"What about that girl at the party? Did she give you a nice birthday present?"

"That's Steve's girlfriend. That was her idea of a joke. It was stupid. Please believe me, Rachel. I've thought of no one else but you since that day when I was a complete asshole. Hey, look! I've got something for you! Incense owls! So, what do you say? Would you like to see me again sometime?"

This time, there was no mistaking her smile.

"Joe, you can see me anytime. You know, when I went to your party to tell you how proud I was that the petition had succeeded and how happy I was in my new apartment, I saw you there and thought, 'Wow, he looks pretty good, like he's been working out or something.' But what really got me was when I saw my name on your wall, made out of little steel bars and displayed right above your sound system! I know how important music is to you, Joe, so for you to put my name up there – well... you had me right then!"

I pulled her into my arms. We kissed once.

"I've got a question for you, Joe. What ARE the four things that life is made of?"

"Hmm... let me think about it. Well, you and me, and then there's love and music, and we must include chocolate!"

"Joe, that's five things.

"You're right; the *five* things in life are you, me, love, music, chocolate, and kittens."

"Joe, that's six things!"

"Hah! What is this - the Spanish Inquisition? Come on, Rachel, let's get back to the kissing."

Suddenly, there was a loud HONK in the road. Looking out the window, I saw a big, brown UPS delivery truck. Don emerged from the front door.

"We've got a special delivery for Joe and Rachel!"

He pulled open the sliding door on the side of the truck. A crowd of people emerged, jumping onto the grass. Everyone was there! It was the gang from Second East and then some! Casey was accompanied by Cricket. Spitz took Sally, and Tim took Sue. Chuck, QP, Professor, Al, Jay, William, and Steve jumped out, and next, I was surprised to see Rubberhead and Gary, but then I was amazed to see Lewis, Lynette, Lundees, John, Brad, and the Grizzled Old Dude #1 pop out. The Tomah Terrors and the Tomah Twins were there, too. Everyone was wearing a Second East t-shirt, even the Tomah Twins.

Oh my God! I wonder if Gertrude's coming? Nah...

Steve said, "Hey, Joe! We couldn't let you get away like that!"

Al said, "We're going to finish the party right here at Rachel's! You don't mind, do you, Rachel? After all, you're an honorary Second Easter, too!" And he threw her a shirt. "Today, every one of you is an honorary Second Easter! Forever!"

Everyone cheered.

"Let's get in the living room! Bring the boxes and the keg!"

Everything, including cups and more munchies, was carried inside. Don brought in a large shipping box from the truck.

QP stood to announce, "I'd like to thank Al and Steve for organizing the first, of hopefully many, Second East Hyer Hall reunions. Yeah, Al and Steve!"

Tim spoke next, "I say, once a Second Easter, always a Second Easter! I'd also like to welcome all the friends of Second East who are here with us today. You are all honorary Second Easters, today and forever!"

Al said, "Let's not forget to say happy birthday to Joe. Joe? Where is Joe? Where's Rachel?"

Cricket said, "Look!" and pointed to the bedroom door.

Casey said, "Oh, it's the drawing of a necktie. You know what that means. We have to give them their privacy."

QP said, "Don, open that box and pass out the instruments!"

Don opened the box and started passing out kazoos, duck calls, and crow calls.

"Let's play!"

And in the End

    I moved into Rachel's little apartment for the fall semester. I called my folks to tell them my new address, and this time, I felt pretty good about it.

    I never walked into a UWSP campus dormitory again.

    A Chinese proverb states, "The miracle is not to fly in the air or to walk on the water, but to walk on the earth".

    I think "to walk on the earth" means accepting life for exactly what it is. I finally accepted that the Sixties were over and they were never coming back. I'd accepted that Hyer Hall was Gertrude's place and that it was time for me to grow up. I didn't need to party to be happy. Most importantly, I accepted my feelings of love for Rachel. And that's all I needed.

THE END

JUST MISSED THE SIXTIES

Where Are They Now?

Joe and Rachel shared Rachel's new apartment for the rest of their undergraduate days. They married, a pharmaceutical company hired Joe, and Rachel became a school teacher.

Casey and Cricket married and started a porn-video business. Best sellers include *The Wausau Sex Club, Cowboys, Whipped Cream,* and *I'll Listen to Your Flute If You Play My Piccolo.*

Tim is a high school biology teacher and guidance counselor.

Al is a pharmacist's assistant.

Jay and Don started an international package delivery business with frequent stops in Tijuana, Acapulco, and Panama.

William opened a western-themed bar in Milwaukee, complete with a mechanical bull ride.

QP hosts a radio show called *The Last DJ* at an underground station in Mexico.

Chuck inherited and sold the farm in Wisconsin to buy a farm in Rocky Mountain High, Colorado.

Spitz married Sally, became a high school swim instructor, and fathered five children: Ayden, Brayden, Cayden, Hayden, and Jayden.

Steve married Topless Twin #1 (or was it #2). Currently, he tours the country as a stand-up comedian, telling redneck jokes.

Gertrude works at the Waupun State Correctional Institute.

The Tomah Terrors and The Repeat Offender reside at the Waupun State Correctional Institute.

www.ingramcontent.com/pod-product-compliance
Lightning Source LLC
Chambersburg PA
CBHW060821050426
42453CB00008B/524